LOOKING GOOD ONLINE

LOOKING GOOD ONLINE

The Ultimate Resource for
Creating Effective Web Designs

Steve Bain with Daniel Gray

VENTANA

Looking Good Online: The Ultimate Resource for Creating Effective Web Designs
Copyright ©1996 by Steve Bain

Library of Congress Cataloging-in-Publication Data
  Bain, Steve.
    Looking Good Online: The Ultimate Resource for Creating Effective Web Designs / Steve Bain.
      p. cm.
    Includes index.
    ISBN 1-56604-469-3
    1. World Wide Web servers. I. Title.
  TK5105.88.B35 1996
  070.5'79—dc20   96-9752
                                              CIP

First Edition 9 8 7 6 5 4 3 2 1

Printed in the United States of America

Ventana Communications Group, Inc.
P.O. Box 13964
Research Triangle Park, NC 27709-3964
919.544.9404
FAX 919.544.9472
http://www.vmedia.com

Limits of Liability & Disclaimer of Warranty
The author and publisher of this book have used their best efforts in preparing the book and the programs contained in it. These efforts include the development, research, and testing of the theories and programs to determine their effectiveness. The author and publisher make no warranty of any kind, expressed or implied, with regard to these programs or the documentation contained in this book.

  The author and publisher shall not be liable in the event of incidental or consequential damages in connection with, or arising out of, the furnishing, performance or use of the programs, associated instructions and/or claims of productivity gains.

Trademarks
Trademarked names appear throughout this book, and on the accompanying compact disk. Rather than list the names and entities that own the trademarks or insert a trademark symbol with each mention of the trademarked name, the publisher states that it is using the names only for editorial purposes and to the benefit of the trademark owner with no intention of infringing upon that trademark.

Macromedia End User License Agreement
By opening the CD-ROM packaging, the end user agrees to the terms of the Macromedia End User License Agreement at the back of this book.

Chief Executive Officer
Josef Woodman

**Vice President of
Content Development**
Karen A. Bluestein

Managing Editor
Lois J. Principe

Production Manager
John Cotterman

**Technology Operations
Manager**
Kerry L. B. Foster

**Product Marketing
Manager**
Jamie Jaeger Fiocco

Creative Services Manager
Diane Lennox

Art Director
Marcia Webb

Acquisitions Editor
Neweleen A. Trebnik

Developmental Editor
Michelle Corbin Nichols

Project Editor
Jennifer Rowe

Copy Editor
Marie Dobson

Assistant Editor
Patrick Bragg

Technical Director
Dan Brown

Technical Reviewer
Walter Arnold

Desktop Publisher
William Hartman

Proofreader
Tom Collins

Indexer
Ann Norcross

Cover Illustrator
Laura Stalzer

About the Authors

Steve Bain is a graphic designer, illustrator, and writer in Vancouver, Canada. He has been involved in the progression of digital publishing since before its vast popularity began, and was an early adopter of interactive multimedia development and Internet communications. Steve is pursuing a career in digital publishing, concentrating on digital design, Web site consulting, and design management in commercial and corporate communications.

Steve contributes columns and articles for numerous magazines and computer-related publications dealing in print, interactivity, and online communications. Steve is the author of Special Edition, *Using CorelDRAW! 6*. His columns and articles can be seen each month in the German, Spanish, and English language versions of *Corel Magazine*. He is also a contributing editor to publications dealing with digital communications and design, including *Online Design Magazine*.

Daniel Gray manages the editorial content of *PrePRESS Main Street*, and writes for a number of graphics and Web-related publications. The books he has written about the computer and graphic arts fields include the bestselling *Inside CorelDRAW!* and *Web Publishing with Adobe PageMill*.

Acknowledgments

Looking Good Online is the kind of book that is the combined effort of people who spend much of their time trying to keep themselves up-to-date on changing trends in computer technology (if that's even humanly possible)—the World Wide Web being just one of them. This includes the professional designers who created the examples in this book, to the behind-the-scenes talents such as the staff at Ventana, whose task it is to create the highest quality publications possible for readers like you.

I would like to gratefully acknowledge the cooperation of Web site pioneers James Hering of Temerlin McClain Advertising, Jeff Dionese of the *USA Today* site, David Lytel of the White House site, Lynn Brock of OnlineFocus, and Michael Nanfito of FreeRange Media for providing insight into their experiences in designing some of the world's current top Web sites. Their insight and vision will help guide many new and aspiring designers in the endless creative opportunities provided by the World Wide Web.

I'd also like to thank my technical editor Walter Arnold, transcribing expert Christine Weibe, and contributor Dan Gray, whose contribution came at the perfect time. I'd also be out of my mind not to thank my wife, Wendy, for her patience and encouragement throughout these book-writing adventures. And I'd like to thank our two-year-old, David, for his inspiration, and as always to whom this book is dedicated.

Contents

Section III Professional Web Site Design

Introduction

Looking Good Online is written for both experienced and inexperienced Web site designers, project managers, and Internet dabblers. For these people we provide a clear focus, solid design guidelines, and tips for creating effective, comprehensive, and usable Web sites—whether the sites consist of one or a thousand pages. You may already have within you, certain skills that will make you a great Web designer. If you're a writer, you'll knock out the text portion of your site in no time; if you're an artist, you'll be superb in the creative construction of your Web site design. Your presentation skills may come naturally, or they may have been acquired from your personal experience in any of the occupations listed below. In any case, this book will surely bridge the gap between what you already know and what you need to know—to look good online.

+ Artist

+ Illustrator

+ Information technology professional

+ Storyteller

+ Database manager

+ Multimedia developer

+ Writer

+ Desktop publisher

✦ Computer systems professional

✦ Designer

✦ Photographer

✦ Multimedia artist

Communication: Before & After

Communication, at least in the traditional sense, is constantly changing. Smoke signals replaced beating drums, which were in turn replaced by messengers. Today's messengers include: the postal system, newspapers, radio, television, cellular telephones, and e-mail, to name a few. Each of these methods of communication seemed as revolutionary at their introduction as the Internet seems today. Are we experiencing a communication revolution—or merely the next logical step in our technological progression? If you find out the answer, let me know.

The pace at which people communicate today is rapidly transforming the world into a global community. The Internet has opened doors that allow people to easily access national and worldwide news, weather, and business information such as up-to-date stock reports. They are able to access financial services and perform daily conveniences, such as, online banking, material purchasing, stock trading, and so on.

The World Wide Web is becoming the greatest stage on Earth. The Web's audience may be small in number, but they are empowered with the capacity for interaction. Web users can choose where to stop, where to look, and where to listen. More importantly, Web users can even make their *own* presence known—across the globe, if others are so inclined to stop at their site. Many Web page authors are staking out the Web as a stage to showcase (and often sell) their thoughts and ideas. This they do, regardless of whether their ideas are good or bad, moral or immoral, legitimate or otherwise. The Web is *already* a center stage and an open marketplace for all—in the truest sense of the word.

There exists no shortage of willing and eager participants in the World Wide Web. In its early beginnings, the Web consisted of only a few thousand users and remained that way for years. These were mostly technical and computer professionals—many of them were thought of as elite—perhaps adding to much of today's allure of being on the Web. For many today, becoming connected to the Web seems a natural part of doing business. It's a club anyone—with the correct resources—can join.

For those who realize the potential of this communication medium, the very nature of the World Wide Web brings to light a multitude of communication issues. Language, the most obstructive of barriers to overcome, is one such issue. Navigation, visual esthetics, style, theme, mood—all play an important part in the design of a site. Other human-oriented concerns such as culture and religion also play a small part. Let's not forget though, an enormous portion of the world's population still has no idea what the World Wide Web is. And many people have just begun to learn how to access the Web—which itself presents another important design consideration.

Building Design Skills

The sweeping popularity of desktop publishing has played no small part in Web site development. Many of the same skill sets and resources used in desktop publishing are transferable to the Web. In fact, with little or no additional hardware or software, you can begin a rewarding experience via the Web. Desktop publishing has graduated from being simply a software tool set used by graphic designers and layout artists to make publishing readable, to an occupation unto itself.

In your explorations of the Web, you've likely discovered only a small percentage of really good quality sites to visit on the Web. Although it takes only technical skill and a little knowledge to compose pages for the Web, it takes thought, consideration, planning, and experience to create pages that viewers will enjoy. It's called good design. While design is an important consideration in print, it is one of the most critical factors in creating Web pages.

A well-designed Web site can have immense business benefits for a company using the Web for the exchange of information. With good design, small businesses can appear every bit as competitive as large ones, and can participate on a level playing field. By providing the correct tools for personal interactions and business transactions, the Web can help small businesses become large ones.

As a Web page creator, you're not simply publishing information on an electronic billboard, but creating an environment in which to exchange information interactively with your audience on a one-on-one basis. The World Wide Web is a medium much more powerful than publishing passively used books or magazines, because the best Web sites make the reader a participant, rather than a spectator.

Patience Is a Virtue Most People Lack

For most professional people time is money, and wasted time is undoubtedly lost income. For Web page visitors, there's nothing more irritating than being forced to wait while an image-happy Web site slowly materializes on their computer screen—especially when users know it's costing them. Waiting is just something most people hate—even when what they're waiting for is important.

Imagine, for example, that you're not feeling well and you go to see a doctor. But, when you go to this doctor, you end up waiting an hour or more in the waiting room. Moreover, while you sit and read magazines from last year, you swear to yourself that you're going to change doctors—and given enough motivation that's exactly what you'll end up doing. Most people share your reaction—even if the doctor is well qualified and fulfills all their health needs. The same goes for the World Wide Web. Visitors to sites that take forever to load—because the design wasn't given careful consideration—will eventually find other sites to fulfill their needs. And after all, why shouldn't they?

Catering to the average person's patience limit is a constant concern, but there are other important factors to consider such as functionality. While good design can be colorful, attractive, and pleasing to the eye, it should be well-planned so that if users must wait for any elements, it will be worth their time. A well-designed Web site is visited by users, simply for information exchange, transactions, or entertainment, and the design is something that often becomes transparent, seamlessly guiding the user. Or good Web site design is something that provides the user with an actual memorable experience, and may even invoke a strong emotional response.

There are all kinds of design styles on the Web. Some sites can be easily categorized as fluffy or artsy— not the type of material most users would sit and wait for. Or, on the other hand, there are grim-looking Web sites that contain pages featuring reams of text for you to read and nothing else to make the site enjoyable. Good design is the key to making your Web site one worth visiting.

How to Use This Book

This book is divided into three sections:

✦ **Section One**: "Contemplating a Web Site" discusses the purpose, audience, and rationale of establishing a Web site. This section helps you make decisions about design considerations, editorial latitude, and sources for information and content.

✦ **Section Two:** "Designing a Web Site" identifies common design elements, navigation, and typographic considerations. This section contains information about effectively preparing photographs and graphics for use on the Web, as well as a discussion of advanced design techniques. It also includes a chapter on how to troubleshoot existing pages to improve their effectiveness.

✦ **Section Three**: "Professional Web Site Design" takes a case study look at some of the most sophisticated and high-profile sites currently on the Web. It discusses design strategies, approaches, techniques and planning of these significant sites with the professionals who actually created them.

Nothing Stays the Same

As we all know, the Internet is constantly changing—sites that were there one day may be gone the next. Plus, Web sites change addresses almost as frequently as people do. At the time this book went to press, all of the addresses were correct, but in the intervening time, a site may have moved or simply been shut down. If a site has moved, you may still be able to get to it through a link at the old address. If it has been shut down, well, it's probably just gone. In that case, just move on—you'll probably find something even better!

Who Should Read *Looking Good Online*

Looking Good Online is geared toward understanding, creating, and improving basic design aspects of online Web sites. This book is for the novice who has a desire to be effective in these design aspects. It is written with the understanding that not everyone is a technical wizard when it comes to computers. The following is a list of people who should read this book:

- ✦ Desktop publishing professionals migrating their current skills and talents to the Web.

- ✦ Communication professionals who write, edit, illustrate, or design any type of digital publishing material seen by others.

- ✦ Small business owners creating their own Web site.

- ✦ Entrepreneurs looking to promote, market, or provide information about any product on a worldwide scale.

- ✦ Corporate communication managers who need a clear focus and understanding of good and bad Web site characteristics.

How Technically Minded Must You Be?

While producing and viewing Web pages is always done using a computer, it is not necessary to be a technical wizard to either view or produce Internet Web sites. Often, much of the reference material surrounding the Web can be highly technical. Design however is not a technical subject, but has more to do with a mix of common-sense esthetics blended with creativity.

Looking Good Online will be a valuable resource to you—no matter what your technical skill level. This is a generic-style design guide, independent of any particular hardware or software. Whether you use a Macintosh computer or a PC, or dedicated page-creation software such as PageMill, FrontPage, or Backstage Designer to produce your Web pages, using good design sense will improve the effectiveness of any page. The skills in producing well-designed Web sites are not features of the software you are using, but originate in your own understanding of design.

> The skills in producing well-designed Web sites are not a feature of the software you are using, but originate in your own understanding of design.

Weaving Your Own Web

Every day it seems, there's another set of professional skills that the digital worker has to know to survive in the business world. Producing even a few well-designed Web pages is a task that can easily be done by one person; however, many steps need to be taken to achieve that task. *Looking Good Online* fleshes out those steps in a logical, easy-to-follow fashion. Let's face it, you may be an absolute expert in a certain area, or very good at several different things, but when it comes to Web site design, it's highly unlikely your previous expertise will encompass all the necessary skills.

Web design is an exciting new area for creativity. Regardless of whether you are a lone individual, creating a Web site for or by yourself, or whether you are part of a Web site design team, *Looking Good Online* will serve as a valuable source of focus and inspiration.

Steve Bain

Section I

Contemplating a Web Site

Defining Your Web Site

If you've just opened this book and turned immediately to the first chapter, congratulations are in order. You've correctly chosen to start your Web site design process at the very beginning. Understanding the basic concepts involved in planning and designing a Web site will give you a solid foundation on which to build. This first chapter will help you determine the purpose and objective of your site and begin developing a strategy for producing and managing it. Whether you are designing a personal information page or a huge corporate site, you'll ultimately need to sit down and ask yourself a few questions—and, hopefully, come up with more than a few answers.

Let's assume you already have your own computer, it's properly configured to browse the Web, and you've had the opportunity to view at least a handful of sites. In doing so, you've probably had some of the good and bad experiences I'll be referring to in this chapter. If you haven't the first clue what's good and what's bad in terms of site design, let your own instincts guide you. After all, you *are* the audience.

Unfortunately, many first-time Web site developers race to register a domain name for themselves. Instead of taking the time to plan out their sites, these developers start by putting up any image or graphic they can think of just to reserve a spot for themselves on the World Wide Web.

The bad news is that instead of enticing their users with little teasers of what might be found at the site in the future, the exact opposite often happens—they end up *discouraging* more viewers than they *encourage*. Contrary to popular belief, the Internet audience is not an easily fooled crowd, dazzled by pretty pictures. In reality, the exact opposite is true. For example, in the early days of Web site construction (and even today) it was quite common to encounter sites featuring clever graphic arrangements and illustrations implying that the site was "Under Construction"(see Figure 1-1).

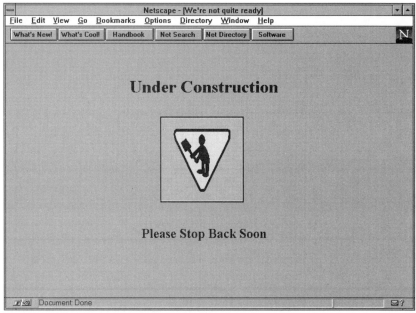

Figure 1-1: Sites featuring this kind of development tactic do themselves no favors and encourage their visitors to go somewhere else. This tactic is neither interesting nor inviting, and borders on apology.

Of course, even to have an under construction message appear on a user's monitor forces him to sit and wait, which is something most people view as a waste of time. Placing this or similar messages in a site, instead of posting something useful, will be viewed by users as poor planning or laziness. It's much better to leave a site off the Web than to put up one of these pages.

This tactic is an all-too-common example of insensitivity to the expectations of the user, and ignores the basic principles of the Web itself. The Internet is all about choice. No one is being forced to sit and use it. Avoid disappointing your audience at all costs.

Avoid disappointing your audience at all costs.

Being in its early stages still, design on the Internet has few if any rules. The sky is the limit. How your site design turns out is something that will separate the successes from the failures. When a site has been designed by a technical guru whose programming skills allow him to include incredibly clever features in the site, but whose lack of creativity has made the site dull-looking, its users are not going to appreciate those clever features. Users will find the interface either boring or too complex to deal with.

It doesn't end there, though. Some sites on the Internet today are repurposed documents that are nothing more than electronic slide shows or expensive page turners. These sites quickly lose visitors, who realize they could be thumbing through a good magazine and getting the same (or much more) enjoyment, faster and cheaper. There's no benefit from having this type of material on a Web site if the computer can't do something with the data. If the information isn't what your audience needs, and they can't interact with it, they simply won't stick around.

Determine the Purpose of Your Site

One day, someone is going to tell you their big idea for a new Web site. They'll be excited, enthusiastic, and barely able to sit still—which is just the sort of person you *want* to have planning a Web site. While you listen to their concept, however, you will gradually realize that their enthusiasm may be a bit out of place and that their plans just won't work financially or logically. As you listen to their proposal, consider their ideas objectively— something they may be unable to do. Thinking objectively is key to planning a Web site.

Every day, Web sites go up on the Internet that don't really belong there. It's not that they don't fit in, but that they offer nothing of real value. Take the "vanity" site for example. This is a Web site usually owned by a company (or someone with money to burn) who decides that they need to have a presence on the Web. Unfortunately, a *presence* is all they really get out of their investment. Vanity sites usually feature little more than company or corporate "puffery."

Being able to think of the Web site in an objective way is difficult—especially if it's your own idea. However, it's an exercise you simply have to go through to design a successful site.

Is a Web Site Really What You Need?

Think of a Web site in the same way you would a business plan. With so many Web designers missing the mark, you need to consider whether a Web site is an appropriate communication vehicle for your message. You have to know what your objectives are before beginning the project. Ask yourself these questions:

- ✦ What will be the main purpose of this Web site?

- ✦ Is the Web the right medium for this purpose?

- ✦ Can a Web site compete with traditional alternatives?

- ✦ Who will the audience be?

- ✦ What type of language (dialect, as well as tone) will appeal to that audience?

- ✦ Will the site be capable of any special functions?

- ✦ Is this part of a larger site?

- ✦ Is it possible that this site will expand in the future? If so, how far?

Whether you come up with any concrete answers to these questions or not, simply asking them marks the beginning of your design process. The key is to ask the question, "Why is this Web site going up?" If your primary reason is because you feel you need to match what your competition is doing, you might want to do a bit more soul searching. Simply having a presence on the Web will not attract traffic to your site, and your site will enjoy no return on investment.

Of all the answers you come up with, perhaps the most important is whether or not a Web site is the best possible solution in the first place. A Web site can be very useful in distributing information to a random number of locations spread over a wide area and throughout various time zones. It may not, however, be the perfect solution if this information is highly confidential, overly abundant, or if the locations you would like to target are incapable of accessing it.

A Web site is a perfect solution in cases where information needs to be distributed to audiences spread over great distances. For example, stock market trading takes place in specific locations, but the information generated as a result of those transactions is of interest to a very large audience spread around the globe. A Web site that provides such information in a timely way will achieve a fair share of traffic, due to its broad appeal.

Another example of a useful and innovative Web site is a merchandise mail-order site. The site is geared toward advertising, but may involve less overhead than producing printed catalogs. It's an appropriate medium because it caters to a broad range of people over a large area who are willing to buy. It can feature special search functions to make locating a product more convenient for the buyer, and in the near future it will be capable of automated purchases, credit approvals, order confirmations, and delivery confirmations. This type of site could even be capable of performing customer service functions like follow-up and personalized "thank you for your patronage" letters.

If communication with the audience you want to reach is hindered by such things as language, age, physical or mental impairment, availability of computer resources, time, and so on, you may not need a Web site, depending on the nature of the information you're presenting. For example, suppose you want to deliver long-distance education to remote areas. Would this be a practical application for a medium such as the Internet? From the outset it sounds like a great idea and one that could greatly benefit areas where access to schooling is limited and illiteracy is

> A Web site can be the perfect solution in many instances where information needs to be distributed randomly over a wide area and throughout various time zones.

a serious problem. But unfortunately most Internet connections are made via digital telephone lines—which aren't likely to be available in many remote areas of the world. It might work someday—just not quite yet.

Technical Design Considerations

The data that makes up any Web page has a little journey to make each time someone accesses the page. Highly simplified, this journey is a four-step process, as follows:

✦ **Step 1:** Data representing the elements on the Web page travels from a server to a modem connected to a phone or cable line.

✦ **Step 2:** Data is converted by the modem for travel through the phone or cable line and sent onward through the line.

✦ **Step 3:** Data travels through the phone or cable line to the receiving modem and is converted back to a language that the computer can understand.

✦ **Step 4:** Web page information is sent through your computer, interpreted by your browser application, and displayed on your screen.

Along the way there are a number of technical considerations that designers need to be aware of prior to implementing certain designs that can slow down or interfere with the traveling data.

Server Limitations

First, there may already be a limit to the number of users who can access your Web site at any given time. The origin of the Web site is a server hooked up to the Internet. Some Web servers (usually maintained by your Internet service provider) limit the number of users who can access the data on the server. This limitation is because of *bandwidth*. Bandwidth can be thought of as the amount of data that a server's connection to the Internet can handle at any one moment. Bandwidth is usually measured in megabytes per second. Make sure that your Internet service provider can handle the size and demand of the audience you are trying to attract.

Bandwidth can be thought of as the amount of data that a server's connection to the Internet can handle at any one moment.

For example, if you are designing a site that makes available downloadable resources such as files or programs that many in your audience will want or need, you need an extremely fast and efficient server (or several servers) with plenty of accessibility for your site visitors. This is usually an issue that is left up to server systems experts, but as the site designer you'll want to be on top of any restrictions before they become a problem. It may be prudent to discuss your needs with the person in charge of the server where your site data is going to be stored.

User Limitations

As far as your users go, their primary limitation is the speed of their Internet connection. This is a great concern for any designer working with the Web. Over the past decade or so, telecommunications technology has become highly advanced. In the beginning, only telephone-line modems were commonly available, but recently cable modems have become a hot feature with their promise of ultra-high-speed data transfer rates.

In the great arena of Internet connectivity, it's important to consider where your users sit; either it's in the cheap seats of conventional modems, in the big corporate sky box of T1 and T3 lines, or somewhere in between. Telephone modem speeds vary depending on the model and when the modem was purchased (that is, whether it is an older or later model). A modem's speed is measured as *baud rate*, namely the number of bits per second the modem may transmit or receive. It wasn't long ago that 2,400 baud modems were state of the art, and users were limited to very small files in order to transfer them within a reasonable amount of time. Now, 28,800 baud modems are quite common and allow for high-speed Internet access and fast computer fax transmission. All digital ISDN connections, which require special phone lines and hardware, offer speeds of up to 128,000 kilobytes per second. And users sitting on a networked corporate T1 line can expect to easily move a megabyte-a-minute over the wire.

Cable modems are relatively new, but the promise for lightning-fast data transfer rates is intriguing. Instead of using the usual telephone line connection and connecting only when in use, cable modems connect to your television cable line outlet and

A modem's speed is measured as baud rate, namely the number of bits per second the modem may transmit or receive.

remain perpetually online just as any cable television service does. Cable companies are also offering cheap monthly connection rates with unlimited access time. Cable modems connect to specialized communications interface boards. Connect time through cable modems is constant and unlimited, and because they operate through cable lines instead of phone lines, the service boasts an errorless and uninterrupted connection, free of dial tones and busy signals.

For the most part, technically-savvy Internet users have been salivating over the approach of cable modems because of their multimedia potential, availability, and relatively low cost. Cable modems can operate at speeds ranging from 500 kilobytes to 10 megabytes per second. Compare that to a 14,400 baud modem and the cable modem measures roughly 40 times faster. To make the prospect of using cable modems even more attractive, hardware companies are developing models that run literally thousands of times faster than 14,400 baud telephone modems.

Identify Your Audience

When it comes to identifying a Web site audience there is no such thing as an average user. Sometimes who you *think* your audience is and who it *actually is* can be quite different. As a site designer, you'll want to do a bit of homework on the subject before you go too far into your process. Knowing your audience's wants and needs, and finding ways to effectively fulfill them will nurture a loyalty that will keep your Web site users returning time and time again.

Demographics Will Help You

The demographics of your Internet audience are extremely important to the success of your Web site, and identifying your audience should be considered an integral part of your design. Make a list of the characteristics you think make up your audience. These characteristics can be defined a number of ways.

The following list merely skims the surface of profiling an audience, but it may help in your thinking process:

✦ Income level

✦ Age

✦ Gender

✦ Race

✦ Religion

✦ Nationality

✦ Technical level

✦ Health and lifestyle

✦ Country of origin

✦ Language

✦ Marital status

✦ Sexual orientation

✦ Attitudes

Sometimes, the very nature of your site will partly determine who your audience is. For example, a Web site providing information about the best game fishing resorts in North America will most likely be aimed at attracting the sport fishing enthusiast. But, what kind of people are generally sport fishing enthusiasts? Could they be business executives, technical professionals, stock brokers, or doctors? If your Web site is set up for business commerce, this will be a critical part of the planning of your site.

Here's How Demographics Help

You might feel that your particular Web site is too small and not worthy of the chore of identifying a market, and you may be right. But in Web site design identifying your audience goes further than choosing the right information. The visual style, the look and feel, and even the structure of the site come into play. The following are only two examples, but hopefully you will see the importance of identifying your audience clearly and how demographics can help you do just that.

Attracting Advertisers

Identifying your audience is a critical exercise if you're considering offering advertising space or sponsorship on your site. It'll be among the very first questions you'll be asked by potential advertisers: "Who is your audience? How big is this audience? How many times will they see my ad in a day, a week, a month? What are their spending patterns? Are they likely to buy my product?" It's identical to the reader profile information available from any magazine or newspaper advertising executive.

On the Internet, the tools exist for collecting exact and specific information about the audience visiting a site. Magazines and newspapers at best can only estimate who their market audience is, whereas a savvy Web site developer may implement features into his Web site for collecting this information from the audience. Sometimes it's through the direct approach of asking questions in a survey or site contest application form. Or, it can be as undetectable as tracking software, built into the site, that records where, when, who, and how the site was hit. In fact, this is exactly what many of the business-oriented Web sites do. By offering incentives for completing visitor or information forms, a Web site can build a database on exactly who its audience is. Identifying who these visitors are is critical to the success of a Web site. This information can then be used to steer the content of the site and to fulfill the audience's needs.

> By offering incentives for completing visitor information forms, a Web site can automatically build a database on exactly who its audience is.

Directing Your Tone & Visual Style

"It's not what you say, but how you say it," someone once said. And this couldn't be more true than on the Internet. It's all in the spin. Your mandate as a Web developer is to find the right editorial tone and visual style to attract (and hold) the attention of your audience.

Suppose you've been commissioned to create the world's greatest Web site on snowboarding. Through (hypothetical, of course) market research you've identified your audience as being between the ages of 16 and 24, mostly male, nearly all high school or college students, and from middle-income families. To maintain credibility, you've got to "walk the walk and talk the talk" of a savvy snowboarder. Visual appeal is essential to this audience, since much of the allure of this sport is fashion trends, risk-taking, and fitness. Your studies have also shown that your audience has an abundance of free time and disposable income. All told, you should consider featuring a more elaborate interface and lots of cool graphics to deliver the information (and of course, marketing drivel). Burlwood, brass, and understated elegance won't do it for *this* market.

Structuring Content

Deciding on the actual structure of your Web site can be creative and challenging at the same time. This is where the fun begins. It is also the most critical stage of the design of your Web site.

Planning a Web site is not unlike planning the structure of a magazine or a book. It may be independent of any graphics or text, and will merely consist of areas or categories of interest. Simple Web sites have a pyramid structure, with the entry point and main access to the site being the top, then fanning out toward the internal structure.

Figure 1-2 shows the first step in planning the structure of your Web site. Simply get the various elements down on paper so you can begin thinking about how they relate to each other and then start contemplating your navigation. Navigation between each of the areas is rarely linear. Navigation through a complex Web site typically involves a spider's web of links between areas.

Concentrate on breaking the information into manageable "chunks," ideally one page but no more than two pages in length. *Chunking* is a term used in hypertext theory that describes dividing information into smaller units, and providing links to the units so that the user may choose his own paths. Chunking decreases the amount of time it takes for individual pages to be transmitted, because each page should be relatively small in size.

Figure 1-2: Quick pen-and-ink sketches on paper are perhaps the quickest way to brainstorm the structure of your site.

To help determine what types of links are necessary, you must decide on an order for your information. Information may be ordered sequentially, chronologically, spatially, or from general to specific. Try to follow a consistent progression. Your users probably didn't sit down and immediately find your site. More likely, they were staring pink-eyed into their monitors for hours before they happened onto your particular site. It's imperative to grab their attention immediately, while providing the means for them to find the information they are looking for in an expedient manner.

For more design guidelines on structuring your content, see the "Keep It Simple" rule discussed in Chapter 2, "Creating Web Content."

Always Communicate Your Message

With all the different ways and methods of getting the message of your Web site across, which one do you use? The answer is quite simple: all of them. The mood and image you create in your design must be communicated in each and every element. From the language of your words, the substance of your backgrounds, to the quality and subtle message of your graphic and photographic images. As in the design of anything, whether it's architectural, mechanical, or artistic, all the elements must combine to establish the overall style and mood of a site.

Integrating Style

Style is a characteristic of your content, but before we get too far into a discussion about style we'd better first figure out what content is. The term *content* is used loosely to refer to any information on the Web site. But, if some of the information you feature is visual, then it logically becomes *visual content*. Content may also extend to any database information that can be accessed as a feature of the Web site.

Launching and maintaining a successful Web site is like managing a radio or television station in many ways. Some experts say that the World Wide Web will give those traditional media some stiff competition for things like audience and advertising revenue. People have normally turned to those traditional media for current information, entertainment, and outside contact. In the same way that television audiences expect a certain style from National Geographic or W5, visitors to your site will expect a certain style to be reflected in the subject matter they read and the images they see, and to some degree they'll expect it to be as timely. As the site designer, you will have control over "programming" and advertising style. This is perhaps the biggest challenge for the designer.

It's not too soon to begin thinking about the quality and credibility of the content you have on your site. Whatever your content is, it has to be accurate. Internet users are really turned off by broken links, incorrect e-mail addresses, or just incorrect data. This includes even simple things, such as telephone numbers, fax numbers, addresses, e-mail addresses, feedback forms, Webmaster contacts, and so on.

Deciding on Textual Style

The text your site users read may be the first, and in some cases the *only*, information they get to see. Users who turn off their image options may rely solely on your text for information, making text a critical part of your site. It's vital that your tone makes your audience comfortable, and speaks to them in terms they can relate to.

Your text must reflect the mood and style of your Web site. In the case of communicating to a younger crowd, the author of the text (which can often be the designer) may choose to use a casual or informal tone rather than a formal one. Take the snowboarding site, shown in Figure 1-3, for example.

On the other hand, if you're trying to appeal to a crowd of business executives, you'll definitely want to use a higher caliber, more formal style of language (see Figure 1-4). Parts of a corporate site featuring an investment portfolio—with information on stock divestitures or capital cost assets—might catch the eye of an investment executive, but would not attract a snowboarder.

It's vital that your tone makes your audience comfortable, and speaks to them in terms they can relate to.

Figure 1-3: This snowboarding Web page communicates visually and graphically with a specific audience.

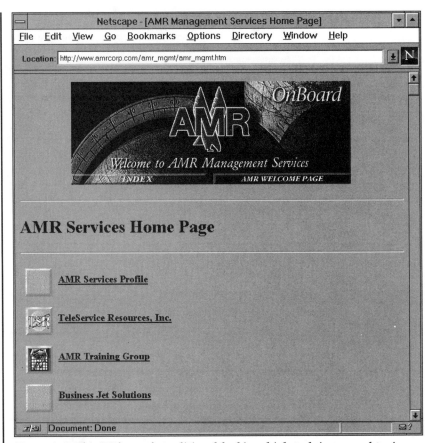

Figure 1-4: This Web page's traditional-looking, high-tech image and topic lineup will appeal to business executives looking to develop serious business relationships.

Now, these examples may be gross exaggerations, but the point is clear. To achieve a successful site—one that remains interesting and speaks to users in their own terms—you must pay close attention to the style of the language you are using to communicate with your users.

Connecting Ideas Through Linking

Unless the Web site you're designing has only a single page (don't laugh, some do), you're going to have to plan which pages link to which *other* pages. Links can either be external or internal, and can be set to react by clicking anything from text to images, logos, image maps, and so on.

External links take the user to other sites containing information that the site designer or firm responsible for the site thinks the user may be interested in. For example, if you're designing a site about child safety, you might want to implement links to sites such as the American Child Safety Association, or the Child Safety Standards Association (if they have a site). You can link directly to such home pages, and let your users hunt and pick for the information they want. Or you can send them to a specific location at a site to find current information on a particular subject. The latter choice will be more appreciated by your users.

Internal links are the more important links because they allow your users to navigate the pages of your site. The links themselves are not important, but what you *link to* and how you make those links is. In other words, if your internal links don't work properly, or are too complex or confusing to follow quickly, users will leave the site and you'll be sunk before you start.

There are several types of internal links, including target anchors, image maps, object links, and text links. In fact, you can make nearly anything into a link, and propel your user to any area of any page.

Using Target Links Within Your Site Pages

The main advantage of target links is that they help your users wade through unreasonably long text documents. If certain pages in your Web site are formatted into unavoidably long textual documents, you can place target links at the beginning of the document that link directly to specific text targets. Experts recommend using target links throughout documents that exceed two pages in length.

The Web page shown in Figure 1-5 is part of the American Airlines Web site. It features an 11-page reference document containing information on international airport codes. Alphabetic target links have been set up to link to the alphabetized list, making it easier for the users to navigate this overwhelming amount of information. (For more information, see Chapter 10, "Design Case Study: American Airlines, AA On Board.")

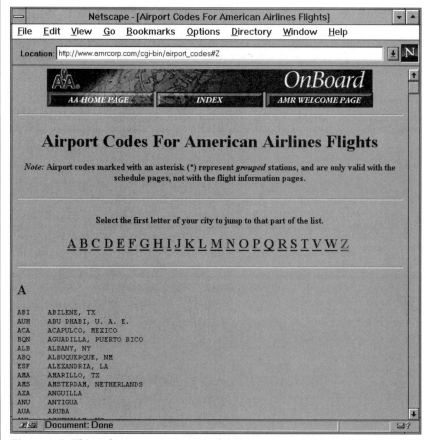

Figure 1-5: This reference page is part of the American Airlines Web site, and features an 11-page reference document containing information on international airport codes.

One potential problem often overlooked when designing target links is how the user can navigate back to the top of the document he is viewing. A solution to this might be adding additional target links periodically that will take the user back to the beginning of the document.

Using External Links to Other Sites

External links connect the users of your site to a completely different Web site. From a business standpoint this may not always be desirable. Sending your users off to another site may mean that they never come back. If the intent of your site is to attract your audience and keep them at your site for as long as possible, you may want to minimize the number of external links you implement. You may also consider burying them deeply in your Web site structure.

You should also pay close attention to the number of external links you create in terms of site maintenance. In fact, once your site is launched, checking the external links periodically should take some priority over checking internal links. As is the nature of the Web, things can change, and what was once a healthy, thriving link to send your users to for reference or more information may have disappeared. Both internal and external linking integrity should be checked regularly, either manually or by using link-management software.

Critical Links for Site Necessities

For a Web site to develop a following of regular visitors, its design needs to include what you might call "creature comforts," or essentially conveniences for the users. They may sound like luxuries or special additional features, but such conveniences are quickly being *expected* by visitors to most sites. In fact, some newer users will remember their first encounter with surfing the World Wide Web as seeing one enormous site with no division between the individual sites they visited. What they will remember most, however, is that they couldn't search an area of information or contact the Webmaster there to give feedback or answer a question.

Some of the standard features people surfing the Web have come to expect from sites include things like news areas, search functions, and automated features to contact the people maintaining the site. Don't omit any of these critical features from your design.

What's New Page

A "What's New" link will appeal to the repeat visitors to your site, and will tell the first-time visitors there's a spot where they can go to get a fast and complete summary of anything they don't see on their first visit, or subjects they might want to stay abreast of as they relate to the topic of your site. It's a critical area to implement from the start of your design, even if your site has just been launched (in which case *everything* will be "new"). On the "What's New" page, include a note about *when* the area was last updated, so your users have a frame of reference about the material's "newness." If your site is small, consider keeping a tight little "What's New" listing right on your front page.

Search Page

If your site is relatively tiny, say, only a few pages, a Search feature may not be practical. On the other hand, if your site is fully loaded with information and more than just a few pages, giving users a device to "screen through" your site's content will be extremely appealing. In terms of design, a Search feature will say to your users, "I realize your time is valuable. Use this handy tool to get exactly what you need so you can get on with your life." Your server's administrator should be able to tell you whether it's feasible to implement a search engine on your site, and how much you will have to shell out to have one installed (and maintained).

In lieu of (or in addition to) the Search feature, you should always provide a text-only, hierarchical index of all the Web pages that make up your site. An index saves your users one of the most prized possessions on the Internet today: time. You will be offering them, at a glance, quick access to your content, and you'll be lessening the amount of "drilling down" they need to do to get where they want to be. Or an index may simply tell your users that your site doesn't offer them anything they need and they'll leave. Either way, your users will come away with the feeling that your site has been well organized and well structured.

Feedback Page

A Feedback feature can be anything including a simple address link to the Webmaster of the site, or a full page of links offering the names of specific people responsible for various areas of the organization or host of the site. Ideally, it will contain e-mail addresses first, and you may consider offering postal addresses, telephone numbers, affiliate links, and so on (see Figure 1-6).

Figure 1-6: The ACNielsen site features links directly from their home page to information about key people at the company.

From the user's perspective, nothing is more frustrating than to visit a site and find out there's no way of contacting the hosts of the site with questions or comments. From a business perspective, not providing a feedback mechanism for the user simply says, "Sorry, this site is a one-way conversation," which could possibly mean lost opportunities or lost revenue. Once you have implemented a feature for feedback, such as a direct-response address, be sure to check the integrity of this particular internal link from someone else's site.

The second most frustrating thing for a user trying to give you feedback is to discover a dead end (see Figure 1-7). Ultimately, this only happens after they have gone to the effort of writing a long, thoughtful note and clicking the Send button.

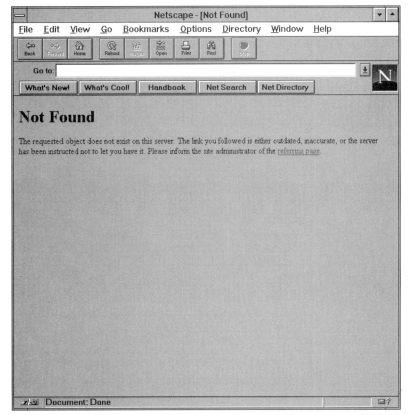

Figure 1-7: Running into this often-seen automatically generated page is the result of links that are not regularly kept up to date.

Navigational Aids

In order for users to maneuver through your site, you'll need to offer them some form of navigation. This can be done a number of ways, the most common of which is through text links in a toolbar. There's a simple reason for this. Internet users often disable their browser's image-loading function. They may be missing all the nifty images you've gone to great pains to design, but as the designer you simply have to plan for it. In fact, in many respects, addressing these more impatient users should take priority over other design aspects of your site. A typical text toolbar may look something like this:

<u>What's New</u> | <u>Home</u> | <u>Search</u> | <u>Feedback</u>

If you're taking advantage of visuals and planning to implement an image-based toolbar or navigation buttons on your site, you should make sure that these features are relatively close to the corresponding text links. Your navigation buttons might look something like Figure 1-8.

What's   Home   Search   Mail Us
New

Figure 1-8: Basic navigation buttons in the form of graphic images should be easily recognizable and should usually be accompanied by a label explaining exactly where the button is going to take the user.

Or an image mapped navigation toolbar might look something like Figure 1-9. *Image mapping* is the process by which you assign a series of vertical and horizontal coordinates to an image file, essentially mapping out areas that, when contacted by a click, will initiate an assigned link. Image mapping can be done with shareware application software such as Hot Spot.

What's New | Home | Search | Mail

Figure 1-9: A simple, flat image map toolbar might look something like this brief toolbar.

There's a good deal to consider when creating an effective Web site navigational system, regardless of whether it's text- or graphic-driven. Chapter 3, "Designing Web Pages," goes into depth on the subject.

Making Your Site Graphically Attractive

Making a site visually appealing usually involves integrating colorful, interesting, and stylish graphics in the forms of toolbars, separators, and clever icons. Done well, graphics can enhance the appeal of a Web site immeasurably. Done poorly, though, you would have been better off leaving the site bland and text-heavy.

Keep the following pointers in mind as you develop your Web site's visual style:

◆ Follow a design theme.

◆ Give your graphic images a sense of dimension.

◆ Keep your graphics colorful without making them distracting.

◆ Spread your graphic images throughout your site.

◆ Make the images lean and efficient.

Develop a Visual Style

It's obvious from cruising random Web sites that most designers try to take advantage of the visual aspects of Web site design, and add images such as photographs and graphically designed interface controls. These visual tools are important for quickly conveying the mood and style of the site, and offer a way for users to begin relating to your site.

To the users, visual images should be worth waiting for, because more often than not that's exactly what they'll be forced to do—*sit and wait*. As a designer, it's your job to minimize the wait time and maximize the quality of the images.

Create a Theme

There are an infinite number of design styles you can implement at your site, limited only by your imagination. Mostly, the challenge will be nailing down a theme. Design elements should have a sense of continuity and commonality. For example, if you choose to use image files to represent navigation buttons, toolbars, bullets, and so on, there should be a degree of commonality. Ideally, you should choose a theme that matches or at least fits in with your subject matter.

Locating Existing Graphics

The design of your images can come from a number of sources, including clip art packages or digital art galleries. There are several that can be purchased quite inexpensively. If you want to include images to embellish your site or to use as design reference, you might also want to check out the numerous royalty-free digital image collections on the market.

Clip Art Illustrations & Photos

For the professional graphic designer, browsing clip art can be a frustrating experience. Designers and illustrators often find most clip art unsuitable for most applications, and choosing to use clip art often leaves the control of design, color, and style in the hands of the vendor and not the designer. Designers often spend time hunting through page after page of thumbnail clip art looking for the perfect image, when they could have spent less time creating the images themselves.

On the other hand, there are many site designers who don't come from traditional print or graphic design backgrounds, and taking the time to learn a drawing or image-editing application is beyond their scope. For this group, using clip art can be a huge time-saver.

One happy medium between these two extremes is to use the option of a clip art base. In other words, adapt the clip art to suit your own needs. Most clip art is editable, as are digital images. Years ago, the use of clip art dramatically increased when clip art vendors began supplying clip art in native formats, so the designer could alter, chop, or otherwise manipulate images to suit other purposes.

As the demand for Web resources increases, software companies are releasing collections of highly specific kinds of clip art in the form of interface components. Many collections of this sort offer images representing backgrounds, photos, buttons, bullets, dividers, alphabets, drop caps, and so on, all designed along a very specific design theme. Capitalizing on this type of artwork can yield acceptable results. Why start from scratch when the resources are widely available and reasonably priced? Of course, you have to be psychologically prepared for the horror of seeing another site show up on the Web, wearing your party dress.

Moving On

This first chapter touches on the most basic elements and issues of designing a Web site: purpose, audience, content, links, and graphics. It provides a basic foundation from which the Web designer can build. There are, of course, many more topics to discuss, and this chapter has given reference to only some of the areas you will need to explore. To discover more about how digital aspects of communicating on the Web can directly affect your site design, continue on to Chapter 2, "Creating Web Content."

Creating Web Content

If your background is in desktop publishing, traditional print, or print advertising, you've definitely got the upper hand in terms of what you need to succeed in Web site design. Requirements are much the same for print publishing and Web publishing design. You'll often hear analogies between the two communications worlds, and the line between them will often become blurred.

On the other hand, while there are many similarities, the ways in which these media are used by their intended audiences are strikingly different. And, in many cases, the "real life" characteristics of the receiving audience, such as buying power, education level, and literacy rate, are not the same between print and online communications.

The Golden Rule: Keep It Simple & Consistent!

If a Web site doesn't spark the user's interest within the first 30 seconds or so, they're outta there.

It seems people are always in a hurry. They use computers so that they can get their work done faster. Time is money—and with this in mind, most people don't have a lot of time to spend surfing the Web. If a Web site doesn't spark users' interest within the first 30 seconds or so, they're outta there. As the site designer, it's partly your responsibility to keep them interested.

Keeping a site simple, easy to read, and easy to navigate should be paramount. Aim low and assume the person you are designing a site for is the lowest common denominator of your entire audience; the user may know little about your subject matter, your site, the World Wide Web, or even computers.

Make Your Content Colorful & Entertaining

Have you ever begun to navigate a Web site filled with text and been nearly put to sleep? Or suddenly realized there are all sorts of things you'd rather be doing, other than hunching over a keyboard, staring into a boring bunch of words and images? That's exactly the feeling every Web site designer should swear to repel.

Besides the visual images at your site, your text should be robust and lively, and the very first lines should entice users to keep on reading. You can't rely on images alone to carry your site design and grab your audience's attention.

Much of your Web site will probably be text; therefore, how that text is prepared is critical. Poorly composed content can be distracting and cause your users frustration, while spelling mistakes can ultimately ruin the quality of your entire site. Don't forget to use your spell checker. And if you can't write to save your life, hire a writer (and maybe save your job).

Many of the same rules that apply in desktop publishing and traditional layout apply to Web site design as well. Here are a few solutions to the most common mistakes Web designers and editors make when composing text for Web pages:

◆ Use plenty of action-packed verbs in your headings and avoid headlining text with static, lifeless labels (see Figures 2-1 and 2-2).

Many of the same rules that apply in desktop publishing and traditional layout apply to Web site design as well.

✦ Make sure the first few sentences of text on your site make full use of any linking potentials. Figure 2-3 shows how this solution can raise the curiosity of your visitors and encourage them to investigate further.

✦ Unless it's unavoidable, don't use abbreviations in main headings or in your text without first explaining the full meaning.

✦ Don't use all capital letters in headlines. All-cap heads are difficult to read in most cases and make your headlines longer and visually denser than necessary (see Figure 2-4). Figure 2-5 shows how the use of mixed case makes character recognition easier and quicker.

Figure 2-1: The services offered by a financial institution reflect the inherent nature of the business and are good choices as headings.

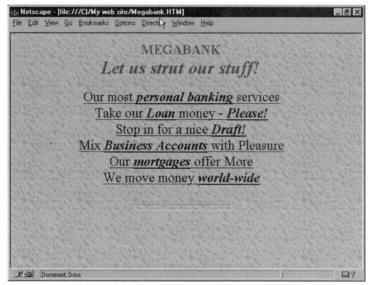

Figure 2-2: Livening up the text using typographic techniques will vastly increase the likelihood that the text will be read by users.

Figure 2-3: Make sure the first few sentences of text on your site make full use of any linking potentials.

Figure 2-4: Many people mistake heavy use of capital letters for emphasis, when in reality using all caps in headlines ultimately works against the readability of the text.

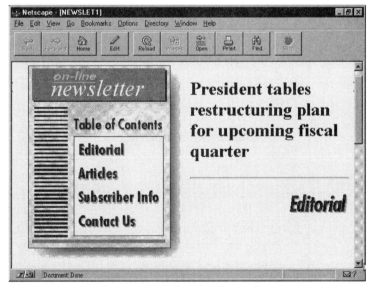

Figure 2-5: Most fonts were designed to be used in uppercase/ lowercase combinations, making character recognition quicker and easier.

Visitors to a site will stay for two main reasons. First, if they know they won't find another site more capable of fulfilling their immediate needs. Second, if they periodically need what your site has to offer, and they perceive your Web site as the best, most up-to-date, and most reliable source. These are the core reasons for visiting and revisiting a site, but there are obviously other reasons. They might include business, curiosity, entertainment, pleasure, challenge, or interaction. Fulfilling these other needs can provide incentives for visitors to linger a while longer.

For example, investors searching for the most recent stock prices will look for a site that gives them the quickest, most reliable information possible. If the investors are reasonably sure the information is correct, they will revisit the site often and may even discover other valuable information, such as methods for predicting future stock prices, and so forth.

Make sure the data or information that you provide at your site is current, reliable, and accurate. If it's not, users are likely to move on to a host of alternatives. There's nothing easier than searching for another source of information on the Web with one of the enormous search engines. Some popular search engines include AltaVista, Yahoo!, Magellan, and Lycos. As a Web designer, you should make it a point to perform a periodic search of the best sources for information similar to that which you are offering. This allows you to stay abreast of your competition, and lets you know which sites your visitors may switch to if you let them down.

> Make sure the data or information that you provide at your site is current, reliable, and accurate.

Spell Checking & Editing

There's no excuse for poor grammar or spelling mistakes. Your visitors will be extremely critical of any errors they find—even if they don't let you know it. Generally, most people don't have any tolerance when it comes to spelling mistakes. Errors of this kind will inevitably give site visitors the impression that your Web site has been hastily or unprofessionally produced.

While spell-checking and grammar utilities are quite effective in finding misspelled words and misused phrases, they can't replace the accuracy of a traditional reading of the text by a

Having an editor read through the text you've written is a critical step in any design or production process.

trained or at least semi-trained editor. Having an editor (or a sequence of editors) read through the text you've written, before and after having worked on your Web site pages, is a critical step in any design or production process. The same tried-and-true editing practices apply to any publication, whether it involves a Web site, a business report, a magazine, or a novel.

Professional publishers know the damage poor editorial practices can cause to a publication's perceived value. That's why they invest a great deal of time and expense to ensure the quality of their editorial content. So, too, should the Web site designer or production team.

Following the "Keep It Simple" Rule

Make the language you are using simple, especially on your home page. Don't use long-winded technical terms most people won't understand. Use short, everyday layman's terms. For example, if your site provides information on how to keep pets looking their best, you might be tempted to use "Canine Coiffures" when you really mean "Dog Grooming"—a term that most people will understand (although it may be disdained by the average French Poodle owner).

Also, use common terms as opposed to "literary" ones. A Web site that focuses on criminal behavior might make a reference to *modus operandi*, when it should simply use M.O., so that most people will recognize it immediately. Or, instead of saying "deoxyribonucleic acid," the site should simply say "DNA," as people know it, and so on.

Avoid using mysterious acronyms in your Web site text. Acronyms can alienate your audience. Using an acronym whose meaning is usually known only to an audience intimately familiar with your site's subject matter will ultimately work against you. Especially if you use such acronyms in headlines or subheads, whose whole purpose is to generate interest and encourage your visitors to read the body text. Text that is full of acronyms is not only confusing but visually distracting as well.

There will be times, however, when you will need to use some acronyms, such as in Web sites whose subject matter is technical, scientific, or political. In these cases, the accepted editorial practice is to fully explain the meaning of the acronym in brackets immediately following the first mention of the term.

Determining Page Size

Determine the sizes of your Web pages by following these simple guidelines:

✦ Make your home page design the most appealing page of all.

✦ Limit your home page to one page.

✦ Limit the subsequent pages to two (ideally only one).

✦ Keep the memory size of your pages to no more than 40,000 bytes, including all text and graphics.

For your visitors, the most critical page of your Web site design will undoubtedly be the "Welcome" or greeting page, commonly referred to as the *home page* of the site. In fact, the visual equivalent in the print world would be a magazine cover or the front page of a newspaper. On the Web, first impressions count. If the first page of your site is obtrusive, offensive, disorganized, bland, or otherwise uninviting, visitors will automatically assume the remaining contents of the site are similar in appearance, usefulness, and functionality.

This first page also must reflect, as much as possible, the intent and purpose of the site. It's very likely your visitors followed a link from a search engine that suggested your site to help them find what they were looking for. Make sure this page clearly identifies your topic and subject matter. Implement as many navigational tools as you can from this entry point, to provide answers to as many of the anticipated user inquiries as possible.

Also, studies have indicated that many people seldom scroll beyond what they first see on their screens. So, ideally, your Web home page must cover as much as possible in a single screen page, including site identification, navigation, critical links, and so on. Try not to go more than two pages. If you find this an impossible task, it's time to rethink your priorities to determine the most important elements. If your site is content-heavy and multiple links become too cumbersome, consider implementing an efficient image map toolbar or a secondary information page.

Setting a Visual Stage Through Design

In addition to quality content, to keep users interested you need to focus on the visual aspects of your site. These visual elements include the tiny colored bullets that draw attention to points in your text and the appearance of navigation toolbars; but they extend even further to the overall visual theme of the site. A theme can be as simple as a marbled pattern in your background, buttons, and toolbars (see Figure 2-6), or as complex as a three-dimensional theme featuring realistic buttons and extruded headlines. A theme can also be simply a certain typeface used in a particular way across the pages of your site, or even a stylized drop cap like the one in Figure 2-7.

- This is my first point
- Secondly, this is next
- Finally, this is last

Figure 2-6: Incorporate design themes such as three-dimensional buttons or random patterns into your pages.

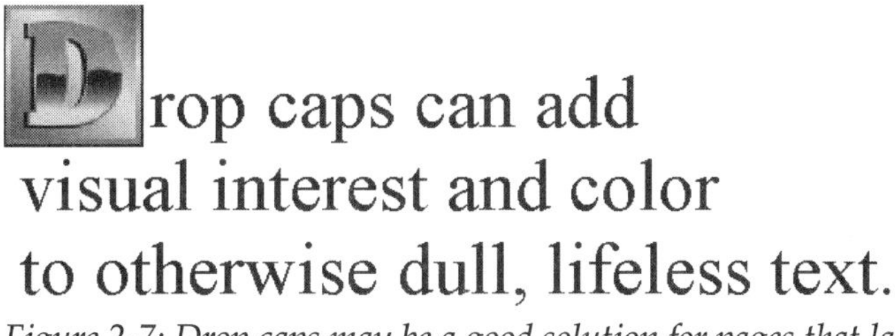

Drop caps can add visual interest and color to otherwise dull, lifeless text.

Figure 2-7: Drop caps may be a good solution for pages that lack any other graphic relief, and to carry out a design theme.

Other elements that impress users enough to make them want to remain at a Web site include the following:

+ The site is colorful and lively, making it attractive to view.

+ The images are interesting and of good quality.

+ The language and tone of the text contain irresistible humor.

+ The text is filled with significant facts, figures, and information, and is easy to follow.

+ The site features a useful search engine.

+ The site offers a service or merchandise that's available nowhere else, free of charge.

Adding Interest to Your Pages

Adding color to text for high-lighting and emphasis can be an effective way of livening up an otherwise color-void page.

Adding color to text for highlighting and emphasis can be an effective way of livening up an otherwise color-void page. Most browsers support color in some form. Beware though—there are some design hazards to watch for when applying colors to text. A text color strategy should be set out when planning the overall design of your site.

Figure 2-8 shows one way to customize your Web page with color using the Document Properties | Appearance | Use Custom Colors check box and options available in Netscape Gold.

Colored text must be easily legible on a textured or colored background. The aim should be for high contrast between the background color and the color of the text. For example, if you plan to have a very dark background, the color of your text should be as light as possible.

Selecting the
same colors for
both hypertext
links and
emphasis will
cause confusion
and frustration
for your users.

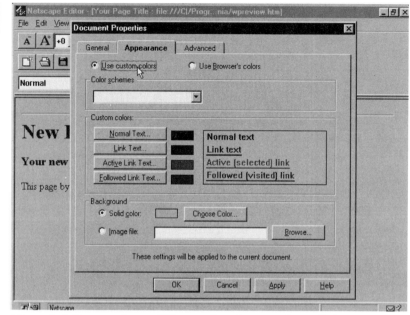

Figure 2-8: You can choose different colors for normal text, link text, active (selected) links, and followed (visited) links using a product such as Netscape Gold.

Color links should also be considered when planning your text colors. If you have set a specific color scheme for your site and links, you will definitely want to avoid selecting those same colors for text. Selecting the same colors for both hypertext links and emphasis will cause confusion and frustration for your users. Consider setting out the colors of your linked text immediately *following* the selection of your background colors and textures. Then go ahead and select the colors you would like to use for highlighting or emphasis. Selecting your text colors *before* you select your linked-text or background colors will be difficult and involve a lot of trial and error.

There are two other features supported by some browsers that should not generally be considered "attractive" features. These are the Blink and Marquee text effect features.

The Blink text feature directs attention by turning on and off the screen display of a particular word or phrase. You can find the Blink effect under Properties, Character, Style in Netscape Gold (see Figure 2-9).

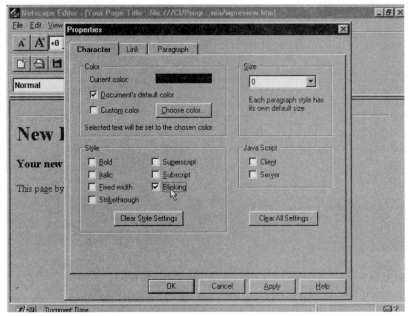

Figure 2-9: Character effects such as Blink are available in many editors, but in most cases these devices are more likely to detract from your text.

The Marquee effect, when implemented through the use of a JavaScript, makes text appear to be riding through the bottom of your browser's frame. The speed of the text varies depending on the speed at which the user's system is operating. This effect is used mostly for messages, such as late-breaking news, special offers, and important notices.

While both the Blink and the Marquee effects are novel, entertaining, and widely used, they mostly work against the interests of serious Web site designers because they tend to draw the user's attention away from the rest of the page. Just because you *can* use them doesn't mean you *should* use them.

Another interesting way to add pizzazz to your pages is to use animation. The simplest way to do this is to use animated GIF89a images. The *Looking Good Online CD-ROM* includes all the software tools you need to create your own GIF89a animations, and Chapter 6, "Advanced Design Techniques," goes into detail on GIF and other animation methods, including Shockwave and Java.

Linking It All Together

Because it's easy for Web users to become distracted, led astray, or lost, navigation around your Web site needs to be simple, logical, and unbelievably obvious. The Keep It Simple rule is paramount when it comes to guiding users through your site. If your site features information users require, or an area you would like them to see, make it available to them in an obvious way. If they're able to reach this area, you've done at least half of your job. As the designer, you'll also need to provide users with a way to return to where they came from, or to move onward in a new direction.

Linear Versus Nonlinear Navigation

Online navigation is typically nonlinear and requires a different design approach than you would use for traditional media. Compare the Web communication medium to what most people are used to, such as reading a book or newspaper, or watching television or a movie. For example, if you're a novelist, you can assume that your readers will absorb the information in your book in a linear way, reading from front to back. If you're producing a movie or television show, you can assume that your audience will simply sit and watch your work from beginning to end, which is, again, strictly linear. But, if you're designing a Web site, this assumption goes out the window.

Persistent navigation toolbars—toolbars that remain with users wherever they go in your site—effectively solve this problem by offering links to the critical areas of your site. While most browsers offer forward and backward navigation through clickable option buttons, some don't. And because good design caters to the widest possible audience, you're obligated to accommodate this group by including keyboard alternatives.

Navigation around your Web site needs to be simple, logical, and unbelievably obvious.

As users navigate from your home page downward, then upward, and sideways, in a sense they're climbing through the catacombs of a pyramid shape, with the home page being the top entry point. Ideally, this pyramid should be as flat as possible, with as many links from the home page to the interior "chambers" as possible, but not more than three links deep. This may only be possible in smaller sites, however. As your site grows, add as few links to your home page as possible.

The Two Click Rule

One rule of thumb to follow is the "Two Click" rule. Link material to your home page so that users should never need more than two clicks to get where they want to be at any given time. In many instances, though, such as in site-searching functions and Help features, the Two Click rule is impossible to adhere to, and exceptions to the rule will be unavoidable.

The Two Click rule also demands that your users have the needed tools to navigate your site in a nonlinear way. They'll need to branch from one part of your site without having to go back to the home page to orient themselves. This means that your toolbar or critical-link list will need to include all parts of your site, without exclusion.

A Sense of Seamlessness

If you're consistent in the structure, visual appearance, and content design of your site, your users will begin to adapt to the unique environment that you have created. As they become more engrossed in the information contained on your site, the design elements such as toolbars, backgrounds, and visual images will become secondary in support of the content they are servicing.

If you achieve this level of user satisfaction, you will have accomplished one of your major goals as the site designer. This can be done through the use of common graphic images, headlines, and toolbars—but most of all backgrounds. Web site visitors identify with backgrounds quickly and easily.

If you've ever encountered a site where the background suddenly changed abruptly, you probably felt as if you had "gone off the edge of the carpet" or mistakenly followed a link to another site. When this happens, instead of feeling comfortable and concentrating on the content, the user will become disoriented and check the Uniform Resource Locator (URL) location to make sure the main site address hasn't changed. This is the very reason why achieving a consistent environment is crucial.

Assigning Links to Text

Writing effective Web site copy is an extremely specific skill requiring imagination, creativity, and technical knowledge. This function is sometimes referred to as interactive writing or online content editing. First, the written text must be completely readable regardless of how many terms incorporate text links. Remember, not all of your users will want to follow all of the links. For your textual content to be valuable to your users, it needs to communicate clearly.

Next, your text needs to expose as much of the underlying Web site content as possible without being too distracting or wordy. Often, the individual doing the copywriting or editing is also the same one providing the HyperText Markup Language (HTML) coded document. Doing both tasks at the same time makes writing for links much easier and more immediate. In fact, it may make the most sense to compose the text directly in an HTML editing software program—assuming, of course, that you employ good writers who already know HTML (or are using state-of-the-art programs, like Adobe PageMill).

Working in reverse, with already existing text, is much faster and easier than originating it yourself—especially if the text involves a specialized subject. Editing existing documents involves simply repurposing the text for the Web. Long text documents must be chunked down into smaller ones, and relevant pieces of the document links need to be buried deeper within the Web site for your users to reference if they need or want to. This only works, of course, if the original text is clear and has already been well organized. If it isn't well organized, it'll be much quicker for you or an editor to perform a basic rewrite, working in the links, rather than trying to preserve the original format.

Finally, avoid using the words "click here" in your Web site messages. There are two ways, the right way and the wrong way, to write interactively without distracting your visitors and maximizing your linking options. To illustrate the wrong way, read this fictitious and exaggerated example of welcome text on a home page:

> Welcome to our Web site; we're glad you could make it here. Our site is called StockLine. If you wish to know more about us, *click here*. This can provide you with important information about the New York Stock Exchange or a quote if you *click here*.
>
> You can also visit our NASDAQ lineup by *clicking here*, and to see the latest top-performing companies, *click here*. Internationally, our site also features the Toronto Stock Exchange, Vancouver Stock Markets, and the Nikkei Stock Exchange. Check them out by *clicking here*.
>
> For a more detailed look at market activities, see our newsletter, LineWatch, by *clicking here*. If you need information on specific companies, check out our company press release archive by *clicking here*.

In the previous example, the text is long and unnecessarily wordy. The most prominent words on the page are "click here" instead of words that describe the actual subject matter. The message itself measures roughly 600 characters and addresses 7 links. The following example demonstrates the futility of repeatedly using the words "click here" by making the same introductory text more concise and interactive:

Welcome to **_StockLine_**. We supply **_market quotes_** from exchanges across the globe, including **_NYSE_**, **_TSE_**, **_VSE_**, **_Nikkei_**, and **_NASDAQ_**.

See our hand-picked list of **_Top Performing Companies_**. Or check out current market trends in our **_LineWatch_** online newsletter. Get company inside information from our **_Press Release Archive_**.

If there's one thing visitors are bound to know, it's how to recognize a link. This example measures 266 characters and addresses 12 links. This fully link-loaded version is more usable as well, because the visitor isn't forced to try to see beyond the words "click here."

Help Your Audience

If your Web site is going to be successful, you'll need to cater to the widest audience possible, including the huge number of Internet beginners migrating to this medium. With the number of users on the Web still growing, a good Web site should offer Help features for newer users who get disoriented, confused, or completely lost.

Well-designed site navigation will likely take care of the majority of problems, but there remains the possibility that some of the features you have designed into your site may not match the capabilities of every browser. Remember, you're designing for the lowest common denominator. One solution to this dilemma might be including a Help feature in the form of a navigation button on the main page, or perhaps in a Feedback section. A Help section could be structured with a list of hyperlinked terms covering items such as troubleshooting site features, and so on (see Figure 2-10).

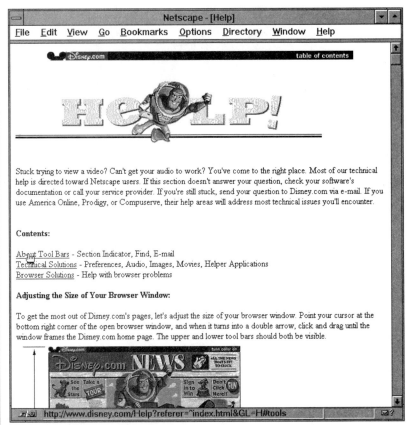

Figure 2-10: The Disney site features one of the most complete Help sections available on the Web, offering solutions for dealing with a wide range of technical bugs over three platforms.

Working Within Limitations

When Harry Callahan said, "A man's got to know his limitations" in *Magnum Force*, back in 1973, perhaps he was foreshadowing what San Francisco's Web designers would be faced with en masse in Multimedia Gulch, two decades later. While it's noble to dream of building a cutting-edge Web site, it's quite another thing to be able to actually implement it. It's safe to say that we are all constrained by the limitations of the medium and tools, as well as our timeframes and budgets. Chief among these unfortunate realities are the constraints and limitations of HTML itself.

Sharing Design Control With the Audience

In many respects, the users have much of the key design control at their fingertips. Users control many facets of how the information displays on their screens. They choose which browsers they use, and then they can set their own preferences for design elements such as font type, font size, font color, link colors, and so on. Users can control the display of graphics by leaving them on or turning them off. Because of these factors, you have to design for the lowest common denominator because you can't guarantee that your user's browser will be capable of handling anything more than the very basics.

In terms of HTML specifications, the site designer has little freedom or flexibility. In contrast to the wave of desktop publishing software applications available that offer unlimited typographic controls in layout and design, the typographic choices in Web design are virtually nonexistent. In fact, there are more controls over the appearance of type in the *user's browser* than are available to the Web site designer. The Web site designer is forced therefore to be innovative and use workarounds to compensate (see Chapter 3, "Designing Web Pages").

Typographic Constraints

Text size is the most dynamic element available in hypertext markup, but even in the case of type size, the designer's tools are severely limited. The size of type in a Web site design is based on a size relative to the default set in the user's browser. Theoretically, the design of a site could look entirely different from one browser to another, depending on the preferences setting chosen. This user setting is called the *Base Font* and may be any font installed on the user's computer and any type size (see Figure 2-11). The setting of this user default size will also affect how the layout of your Web site appears to users. Obviously, the advantage is slanted toward the users.

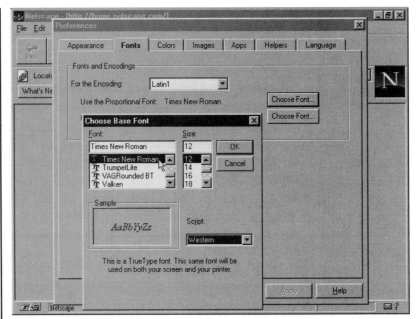

Figure 2-11: Users have complete freedom to control the font and type size of their browser's own Base Font, making type flexibility for the Web designer quite a challenge.

The choices you have available in your Web design are based on the relationship to this user default setting, and involve setting the text to either a larger or smaller size than this default. Basic sizes range between -2 (two incremental sizes *smaller* than the default setting) and +4 (four incremental sizes *larger* than the default).

Typographic controls for the Web designer can be summarized in a short list:

✦ Type size relative to the user's default size (see Figure 2-12).

✦ Text alignment, including left, centered, and right (see Figure 2-13).

✦ Type style (bold, italic, superscript, subscript, strikethrough, and/or fixed width).

✦ Type color (user default setting, or by site specifications).

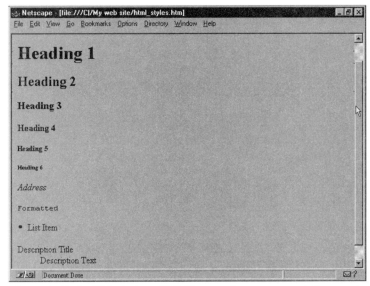

Figure 2-12: In Web design, HTML type sizes are essentially preset featuring these relational sizes.

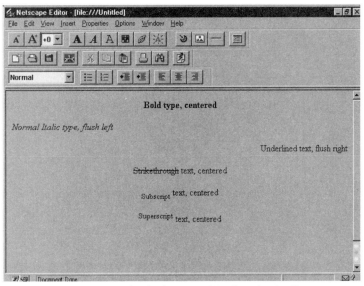

Figure 2-13: Text may also be formatted in these basic alignments and typographic styles.

HTML markup sizes have been preset to specific named styles based on sizes, styles, and indents. At the time of this writing, these styles included headings 1 through 6, address, formatted, list item, description title, and description text.

✦ Normal (based on a default size 0)

✦ Heading 1 (bold, based on a default size 3)

✦ Heading 2 (bold, based on a default size 2)

✦ Heading 3 (bold, based on a default size 1)

✦ Heading 4 (bold, based on a default size 0)

✦ Heading 5 (bold, based on a default size -1)

✦ Heading 6 (based on a default size -2)

The other preset styles remain at a fixed size of 0 (normal), but change according to typographic style (bold and italic) and indent.

✦ Address (normal italic, based on a default size 0)

✦ Formatted (fixed width, based on a default size 0)

✦ List Item (normal bulleted, based on a default size 0)

✦ Description Title (normal, based on a default size 0)

✦ Description Text (normal indented, based on a default size 0)

In the design of Web pages, default text colors may be set to any color within the 256-color system palette, and are based on RGB (red, green, and blue). Colors conforming to RGB standards are measured in terms of color values such as 255, 255, 255, meant to represent white, and 0, 0, 0, meant to represent black. For example, Netscape Gold's HTML editor (see Figure 2-14) offers a standard collection of 48 basic colors based on an ideal uniform color collection. Limiting your color selection to basic uniform colors is perhaps the safest way to go when choosing colors. Again, the reason for this relates to designing for the lowest common denominator—the browsers that only support basic colors.

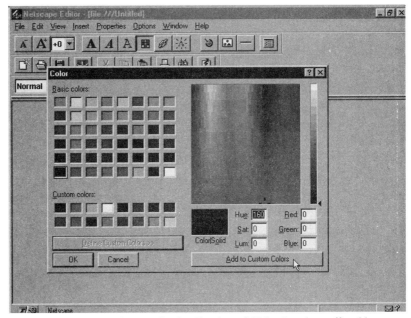

Figure 2-14: Notice the standard collection of 48 basic colors offered by Netscape Gold.

However, the Netscape editor also allows for selecting custom colors, in the full range up to 16.7 million, or enhanced SVGA display. You'll find more information about tweaking color palettes, and the Netscape Palette in Chapter 5, "Creating Digital Content."

Text Formatting Limitations

While there may be plenty of bugs to fend off, the act of formatting HTML text is no picnic. You won't find an overstuffed picnic basket filled with goodies, and you can forget the high level of text control that you've gotten accustomed to in your word processing or desktop publishing program. While HTML text controls have progressed rapidly in just a few short years, they still fall far behind what's possible for the printed page.

Text in paragraph format may be crudely formatted using the Indent commands featured in HTML and supported by many of the current editing software programs and browsers (see Figure 2-15). For example, Netscape Gold 2.0 features commands to either increase or decrease indents equivalent to five spacebar spaces in character sizing for each step. Indenting of the body text below headings as in Figure 2-15 causes the heading to stand out much more than it would if all text were formatted flush-left. This type of spacing causes the body text to take up more space; but remember, this is the World Wide Web, where white space isn't a concern. White space, or the empty space around and between lines of text and images, is essentially free. It doesn't occupy server space or paper space but merely acts as a separator to be used to its maximum potential by the designer.

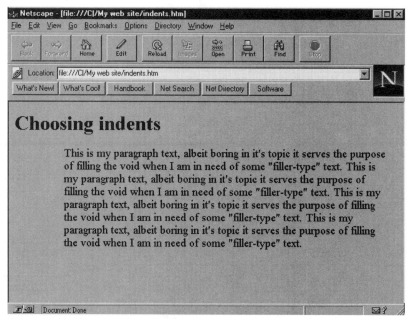

Figure 2-15: Rough indenting of text may be achieved without adding additional keystrokes to Web page documents, offering another method of formatting text for the designer.

Image-wrapping is also a crude form of text formatting from the perspective of adding images to your Web page document. Many HTML browsers currently support image-wrapping. Again, Netscape appears to feature the most user controls, including formatting options to set the image to align with the top, center, bottom, baseline, or descender of the first line of text in the paragraph adjacent to the image being formatted. You may also choose to wrap the text around the left or right edge of the image (see Figure 2-16).

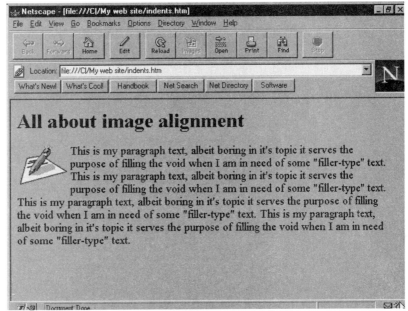

Figure 2-16: Wrapping text around an image is a way of formatting text from the perspective of the image position. Designers often are forced to manually line-break text to accurately organize it.

Netscape Gold offers the added flexibility of forcing changes to the set dimensions of an image, or to set the horizontal and vertical space around the image and assign a border thickness measured in pixels.

HTML's Table commands afford the most formatting control of all. The use of tables allows you to create everything from multicolumn text to intricate spreadsheets. While the raw HTML coding can be hard to master, the latest crop of Web page editing tools makes table creation a breeze, by hiding all the codes. Chapter 6, "Advanced Design Techniques," includes a discussion of table do's and don'ts, as well as insight on the big daddy of HTML page layout features—frames.

Know Your Copyright

With the onslaught of images and content pouring onto the World Wide Web, you'd think copyright laws would become more lenient, but that's not the case. In fact, the exact opposite has happened. Some of the old copyright laws have been revitalized to envelope digital rights, while a few new laws have surfaced. The understanding is that copyright protection has been beefed up to accommodate the increased likelihood of misinterpretation of the law. Loopholes in certain laws have been eliminated, and some of the grayer areas have now been made crystal clear.

Using Other People's Work

For the beginning designer, it would be so much simpler to download and copy images of backgrounds, buttons, and so on, rather than go to the effort of designing new ones each and every time a new design is needed. For the Web site content researcher or writer, it would be even easier to copy content from the Web, or anywhere else, and use it for their own digital publications or whatever use they choose. In reality, these practices are illegal. Copyright penalties are harsh, and punishment for breaking copyright laws is swift. Copyright laws also extend internationally, so even content found across the oceans is protected.

Now, dirty little deeds aside, let's say you weren't aware you were breaking any laws when you scanned a photograph out of a magazine and integrated some or part of it into your Web site design without getting permission. Would you be exempt from the law or immune from punishment? The answer is—not a chance.

Copyright laws encompass all types of original work in digital form or otherwise. This includes many of the multimedia modes now becoming popular at many Internet Web sites, including textual information, digitized photographs, digitally recorded audio, digital musical instrument digital interface (MIDI) formats, and so on. Copyright infringement even includes common artwork such as tile flooring patterns and certain printed cloth and paper patterns, such as gift wrap, that have traditionally always been copyrighted by their creators.

There are certain instances where original works may be used without prior permission. These include situations where the original works are being reproduced to accompany editorial works, as in news reporting or factual writing. But by reproducing the original works of others for commercial purposes you would be breaking copyright laws, so the safe bet is to ask permission in any case. Walking the very fine line between editorial and commercial uses can be dicey at best. You can rest assured that the owner of the work you intend to use will be watching you like a hawk, lawyers at the ready.

Protecting Your Own Work

On the other side of the fence, having created a Web site using original works of your own or works by willing contributors, you stand to be abused by others who could be breaking the copyright laws. How do you protect your own rights? Well, that's a tough one. It's usually not practical to regularly spend time surfing the Web in search of other sites that have copied material from your site.

There are, however, a few things you can do to some of the elements in your site design to at least discourage copyright abuse. Post a discreet copyright symbol on your site's home page that indicates all material on your site is protected under copyright law. This can be as simple as a very small line of type at the bottom of the home page that goes something like this:

```
© ABC Company, all rights reserved.
```

If you suspect there's even the off chance you could be asked for permission to reproduce some of the material found on the site, then make this entire line of text a link. Or, an even more discreet strategy would be simply this:

© Copyright

Make a link to another Web page on the site containing information that's somewhat (or exactly) like this:

All of the material contained on this site is the property of ABC Company, all rights reserved.
Permission to reproduce any material from this site is required, in writing, from Webmaster@ABC_Company.com or by mailing a hard-copy request to:

Webmaster at ABC Company
123 Anystreet, Anywhere
Anystate 12345

Phone: (415) 555-1212
Fax: (415) 555-1213

Offering this information reminds visitors to the site that the material is protected under law, and anyone looking for permission has no excuse for not making an inquiry. Obviously, you're relying on the honesty of people to ask before taking. But, unfortunately, if your material is attractive enough it will tempt dishonest visitors to abuse the law by copying, and there's really nothing you can do to stop them.

Photographic and graphic illustrations at your site are another story, though. One fairly successful strategy for copyrighting photographic digital images includes placing discreet copyright symbols directly on the images as a form of watermarking (see Figure 2-17). This can be done using most any image-editing package and may or may not include the photographer's name and phone number in a discreet size. In fact, some professional photographers demand that they be allowed to include a copyright image when their images are used on the Internet.

Figure 2-17: In order to protect the interests of the owner of the image, it is a good idea to add a discreet copyright symbol to the image.

Placing this subtle hint on your image is by no means going to guarantee that your image won't be used by someone else, but it's the best course to take.

Obtaining Permissions

If copying someone else's work for your own commercial purposes without their permission is wrong, how do you get permission? The quick answer is—*ask*. Permission by way of a telephone call is usually enough, and in most cases is legally binding. But, it's a much safer practice to obtain permission in writing, even by fax. Be sure to identify exactly how you intend to use the images. In cases where you intend to use the image more than once, or over a prolonged period of time (as is usually the case with Web work), you will need to specify this in writing to avoid any unpleasant surprises. Even if you only intend to use a small, seemingly unrecognizable piece of someone else's work, you will still need to get permission in writing.

The best way to avoid having to get copyright permission is to use images you already own, or those you've created yourself from scratch. The next best route is to take advantage of clip art or royalty-free images. It's wise to check the legal fine print before using someone else's image in your Web page designs. License agreements can vary between commercial and non-commercial uses.

There are, however, other issues that surface when it comes to copyright ownership. Often, for various reasons, people aren't sure whether they actually own their images or not. If you are working for someone else and you create a work of art, digital or otherwise, who actually owns the work? The answer is a sticky one that boils down to this: If you were paid as an employee, by someone else to create an image, the person or organization who hired you is the owner of the work and holder of the copyright. This includes cases where you were hired as a contract employee to produce a larger project and created images as part of that project.

If you do own your own images and these images are valuable enough, you might consider obtaining copyright protection. For information on how to go about doing this, contact the Library of Congress, Information and Publications Section, Washington, DC 20559, and request a Copyright Information Kit. Or call them directly at 202-707-3000. Copyrighting your work officially will ensure that you will be in a legal position to sue whoever uses the images you own the copyrights to without your permission.

Moving On

This chapter looked at specific digital typographic issues the Web site designer is faced with when approaching the design and composition of Web pages. While the typographic limitations are severely restrictive to the design in terms of HTML, many other techniques sidestep these limitations. Chapter 3, "Designing Web Pages," discusses Web page design elements, what they are, and how to properly implement them, including shortcuts as a way around HTML limitations.

Designing
a Web Site

3

Designing Web Pages

If you've reached the page design stage, you should have some textual content forged and ready for page "layout."

Diving headlong into a design will get you an "A" for enthusiasm. However, it can also get you into a bit of hot water if you lack a definite goal, start at the wrong point, or simply follow a poor strategy. Since you've chosen to read this book, we'll say you're not in hot water yet. There are plenty of nifty design elements available to help you compose and organize World Wide Web pages and each of these elements plays a different role—so don't let go of that enthusiam yet!

Keep in mind that if you've reached the page design stage, you should have some textual content forged and ready for page "layout." You should at least have a solid outline. If you don't have an outline, you may find yourself making design-driven decisions rather than content-driven decisions. This chapter defines the most common design elements available. In addition, it will help you make some elementary design decisions and provide you with strategies to demystify the design process.

Strategy for Web Design

Beginning the design of anything can be a pretty intimidating task for anyone. It's the equivalent of the "blank page" syndrome most creative professionals are faced with before they begin a project. The burning question you'll immediately face is, of course, where do you begin? The question is rhetorical though, as any creative professional will answer with a sarcastic grin— the beginning.

If you're a seasoned page designer or a highly experienced desktop designer, you might be able to start your design at just about any stage. For novice designers though, the design process can be boiled down to a few basic tasks.

Throughout the process, you'll be faced with some simple decisions to make regarding style and layout, visual appearance, and navigation. Your page design will integrate existing content and structure with things such as headlines, text links, buttons, images, toolbars, and graphic embellishments.

Getting Your Design in Order

In terms of visual design, your Web pages should be created from back to front—the back element being your background design and the front element being the elements that sit on top of your background design. You can organize your Web design using the following steps:

1. **Content and structure:** Write your content and plan your page structure including any text links. Plan as much detail as possible regarding your linked text, before proceeding to the design stage.

2. **Backgrounds:** Decide early whether or not you will be using a background in your design and exactly what the background will be. Your background sets the stage for the remaining design elements. A background can be a uniform color or a stylized image that tiles across the user's browser. Also, any future decisions about colors or graphics will be contingent on the design of your background.

3. **Text format:** Determine a hierarchy of the size and style of your headings, subheadings, and body text according to the standard HTML sizes available.

4. **Navigation:** Consider how you will allow your users to get from one area to another, and back. Decide whether you will be using navigation buttons, toolbars, and/or text links. Determine how you want your navigation elements to appear.

5. **Page alignment:** Choose the alignment (left, centered, or right) of your design elements. This helps you begin your layout decisions. In many cases, you may deviate from a rigid left or center alignment within the body text of your pages, but overall you need to make alignment decisions early on. Left and centered are the most common and workable alignment styles.

6. **Text color:** If necessary, choose the color of your headings and body text. Your choice of backgrounds has a major influence on this decision.

7. **Link colors:** Choose the colors for your seen and unseen link colors. Again, your background color or pattern has a major influence on this decision.

8. **Graphical theme:** Follow a visual theme to help reinforce the environment you are creating. Themes can be anything from simple color schemes to patterns or textures that carry through from page to page. Decide on a theme that is best suited to your subject matter. If your page design features "manufactured" headlines—headlines that have been created as graphics—decide on their size and style.

9. **Graphic embellishments:** If you plan to use separators or graphical bullets, decide on their size, style, and color.

10. **Presentation of images:** Decide whether your images will be color, black and white, photographic or cartoon style, large or small, and so on. Images shouldn't be considered as simply embellishments to your site, but should add value and interest to your actual text. Image characteristics may also include special effects such as GIF or interactive Shockwave animations.

11. **Template design:** Save your first page as a template to make designing the remaining pages of your Web site a more efficient process. If your project contains a number of sub-sites, you're likely to end up with a variety of templates.

What Are My Priorities?

To make the decisions listed above, you need to set priorities for the Web site design. Designing Web pages requires that you:

+ Include well-written content and logical structure.

+ Know who your audience is.

+ Provide obvious links to logical places.

+ Ensure consistency by providing a design theme.

+ Create a seamless environment.

+ Keep your images concise and meaningful.

Achieving these goals shouldn't be a laborious task but a creative one.

Content design should always be your first task. This step in the design process is integrated with the task of writing for the maximum linking opportunities. Be consistent and stick to a theme. In doing so, you will contribute to your user's perception that they are inside a closed environment which in turn contributes to creating a seamless environment. A seamless environment allows the user to focus on the content itself and not the way the elements are put together.

Follow a Design Theme

Creating a theme for your Web pages makes it easier for your design elements to work as a unit. A theme eliminates the danger of your design elements working against each other—especially if the elements you've chosen are strikingly different, in terms of color, style, or even font size.

The Disney site shown in Figure 3-1 shows a theme of famous cartoon characters, bright colors, and a stark white background. One of the most creative sites is the Mr. Showbiz site (see Figure 3-2) that features nostalgic, 50s-style graphics for the background, toolbars, and graphical headline type. The Labatt's beer

Creating a theme for your Web pages makes it easier for your design elements to work together as a unit.

site, geared strictly toward product marketing and awareness, features a theme using beer coasters as buttons (Figures 3-3 and 3-4), reinforcing the fact that nearly anything can create a design theme or be made into clickable buttons.

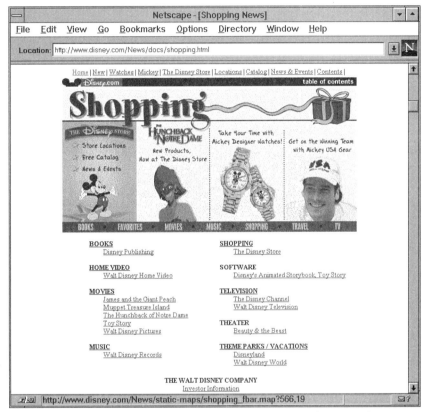

Figure 3-1: Disney's Web site features the obvious theme of cartoon characters taken from their most popular film productions, and used in everything from image maps to product endorsements.

Figure 3-2: The Mr. Showbiz Web site is a self-promotional site developed and maintained by the online design firm Starwave. Its theme is cleverly carried throughout the background and button icons.

Figure 3-3: The Labatt's brewery site's theme is based on the marketing images created for their products. Beer coaster images are used as navigation devices—proving that buttons do not necessarily have to be actual buttons.

Figure 3-4: The Labatt's site also features a similar theme on subsequently linked pages that use beer bottle cap images as buttons.

Work From a Template

Developing a template for yourself not only speeds up your production processes, but also enables you to establish design consistency. Web page headers and footers are the most obvious candidates for inclusion in an average template. These elements can be repetitive from page to page, and may include both graphical and textual elements. Once you have developed a design theme for your site and have produced a few pages, capitalize on the strengths of your computer and the software you are using. Cut-and-paste can be a wonderful thing.

Several of the elements you implement for the first page of your site are likely to follow through to subsequent pages. In a sense, you might even refer to elements such as backgrounds, color schemes, button icons, and toolbars as "master" elements. These images will form the design characteristics of your site.

If you don't keep these elements consistent or similar throughout your site design, you might alienate or distract users. Lack of consistency can also ruin the effect of your design. For example, drastically switching from a graphical background to a uniform-colored background may leave users wondering whether they have inadvertently followed a link to another site. Unless you have a specific reason for changing your "master" design elements, keep them consistent throughout your site by incorporating them in a template.

Creating a template is easy. Simply resave the first page of your final design under the name template.html. If your site involves various deviations from a similar design theme, save each of these themes with a generic numbered name like templat1.html, templat2.html, and so on, or develop your own naming system. Either way, using templates will help immensely in your design and production processes. When it's time to create a new page, open one of your saved templates, fill it with new content, and save it under a new page name. Generic templates can be a safety net, as well. When you create new pages from the generic templates, rather than from live pages, it prevents any inadvertent overwriting of files.

> Drastically switching backgrounds may leave your users wondering whether they have inadvertently followed a link to another site.

Using Backgrounds

As with most elements in Web design, using backgrounds is the designer's choice. This choice gives the designer the power to enhance a design with good backgrounds, or to completely destroy it with bad backgrounds. There are two types of background formats available: uniformly colored backgrounds and image backgrounds. Setting the background to the browser's default color will leave it a neutral gray color. There's one primary advantage to this: Web pages with a default background will load faster than pages with an image background.

> Web pages with a default background will load faster than pages with an image background.

The browser's default color—or no assigned colored background—is a color defined in red, green, blue (RGB) measure as 192, 192, 192, or light gray. It's also the same color used in most program interfaces as the neutral color for scroll bars, selection buttons, and other program interface features.

One caveat to be aware of is that the browser, if so configured, can overrule the Web page designer's background color or pattern choices. While it may seem hard to imagine, some folks may actually prefer seeing the same background color or pattern over and over, no matter the site. Of course, they probably eat a steady diet of white bread, but that's another story, altogether.

Uniform Color Backgrounds

Although the typical uniform background is simple to set up and change, it's still a key element of your design and should be chosen carefully. Determine if your Web pages contain any of the following when choosing a uniform color to use as a background:

✦ Colored text. Any time you change the background color of a Web page, you must consider the color of the text itself. This includes both seen and unseen links whose colors can be separately controlled.

✦ Colored logos or corporate identifications featuring fixed color schemes. For example, if your site features a company logo or product identification mark that is predominantly light colors, your background should ideally be the opposite, or a dark color (see Figure 3-5).

✦ Images that feature transparency masks and uneven shapes. These should appear to float or blend smoothly with the background image or color. When you render the transparent image, you must keep the background in mind to avoid ghosting or jaggies (see Chapter 7, "Common Design Mistakes").

✦ Fixed-color navigation elements such as button and toolbar images. You usually want these objects to stand out. It's imperative to assure proper contrast between the images and the background.

✦ Forms. You may want to restrict the background color of your forms to the default gray, since that's what form elements like buttons and menus use. With a different-colored background, your forms may appear patchwork-quilt style when the form elements are combined with the background color.

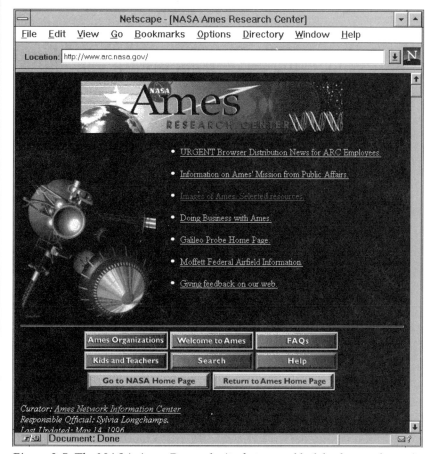

Figure 3-5: The NASA Ames Research site features a black background to suit the text, links, and images on the site.

Image Backgrounds

Using a unique and different image background—or series of similarly designed backgrounds—throughout your site is a sure way to communicate a theme to your users. To display a background image, the user's browser "tiles" the image across the page on the user's screen. The background image can be any dimension and is tiled repeatedly no matter what size is set by the user's browser. Background images contribute to the overall memory size of your page design, but if the same image is used throughout the site, it is cached in the browser's memory and rapidly retrieved whenever the page is renewed.

Well-designed backgrounds can set a powerful tone.

For Web designers coming from desktop publishing backgrounds, the effect of implementing well-designed backgrounds can be compared to printing on colored or textured paper. The special effects give users a feeling of substance and mood, and set a powerful tone for the site design. Figure 3-6 shows that sometimes designers go overboard, causing readers to focus on the background image instead of the content. Other times, designers hit the mark (see Figures 3-7 and 3-8), enhancing the subtle effect of the image and keeping the reader focused on the content.

Background image characteristics should be subtle, somewhat undefined, low in contrast, of a neutral color, and ideally, "seamless" when tiled in the user's browser. By seamless, I mean that the user cannot determine where the tile edges begin and end. It's easy to spot a tiled background that hasn't been designed for seamlessness (see Figure 3-9). You'll be able to see where the pixel colors don't match and cause a distracting checkerboard pattern in the background.

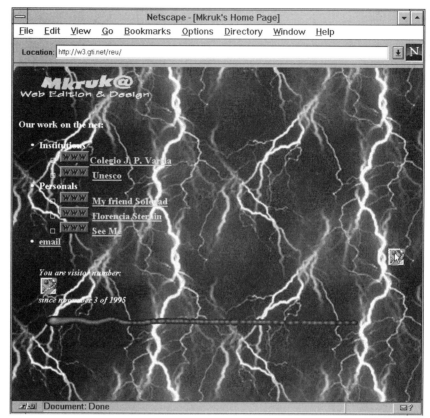

Figure 3-6: Virtually any image can be used as a background, but the effect can be dramatically overwhelming if not used with careful consideration.

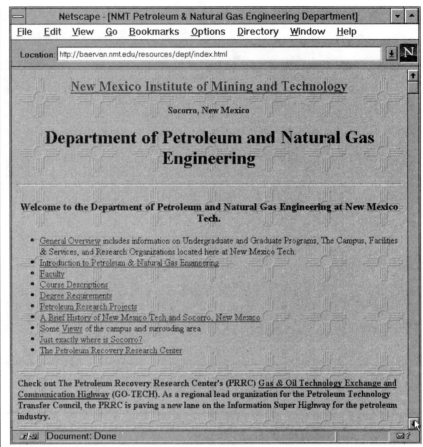

Figure 3-7: The New Mexico Institute of Mining and Technology Web site features a simple and subtle background effect incorporating a graphic symbol.

Figure 3-8: The background in this Web page features the acronym CAREI, but the background image has been muted, subdued, and created in grayscale so as not to visually interfere with any of the other design elements.

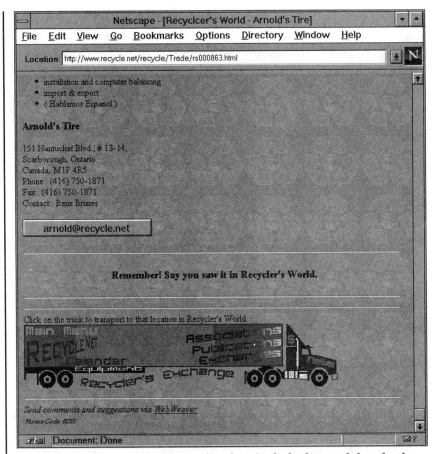

Figure 3-9: This site features a recycling logo in the background that, for the most part, tries to be subtle in a muted green color. Unfortunately, the symbol created is so large that the tile edges appear as vertical and horizontal streaks across the screen.

Background images featuring neutral colors and highly blurred patterns offer the best readability for the text displayed on top of them. The colors found in your background should also contrast any text and images seen in the user's browser. For example, if you are planning to use a multicolor, rock, marble effect, the veins of color found in the pattern shouldn't contain black if you have set your text color to black. Also, if you've left your seen and unseen text links at the default, your background image shouldn't contain large areas of either blue or fuchsia.

When working with portions of a digital photograph, use a small enough portion so that any discernible pattern becomes insignificant. The White House site (see Figure 3-10) did this quite well. Your goal should be to create tight little background files that download quickly and pack a big punch. Figure 3-11 shows how a tall and skinny (10 x 800 pixels) gradation will tile seamlessly to fill an entire page.

Your goal should be to create tight little background files that download quickly and pack a big punch.

Figure 3-10: The White House site features a background that could seemingly be patterned yellow-brown wallpaper. The warm colors and subtle patterns give users a feeling of age, stability, and warmth.

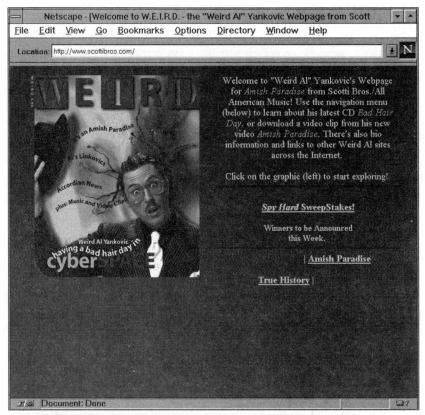

Figure 3-11: The site known as the Weird Al Yankovic Webpage features a clever full-screen color gradation for the background.

Creating Suitable Backgrounds

Designing an image background can be done with nearly any image editing application and a few fresh ideas—the *idea* being the most important part of the process. Once you have your concept in mind, you will either need to scan in a source image or create one yourself by distorting some small part of an existing image. As mentioned earlier though, the trick is to make the image appear seamless when it loads into the user's browser.

The trick is to make the image appear seamless when it loads into the user's browser.

Some image editing applications make this task easier than others. Both Fractal Design Painter and Adobe Photoshop include the ability to offset images. Kai's Power Tools even includes a nifty "Seamless Welder" plug-in.

To create a seamless image, do the following:

1. Offset the image both vertically and horizontally by half the size of the original image.

2. Blend the seams of the image.

3. Lighten or darken the pattern to make sure the background image is subtle.

Using Bullets

Bullets are an excellent opportunity for a design touch that, on a small scale, can enhance your theme and help emphasize content. While HTML includes basic bullets within the List command, the use of graphical bullets opens up your Web page design possibilities. By following a few basic guidelines, you can maximize use of this design element, as follows:

✦ Make your bullets fit the overall design theme.

✦ Make your bullets as compact and concise as possible.

✦ For points that feature hypertext links, make the accompanying graphic bullet clickable to the same link.

✦ Create your bullet graphic to be a comfortable distance (roughly two spaces) to the adjacent text by building transparent white space into the image.

Bullets can enhance your theme and help emphasize content.

Many of the Web style clip-art collections feature ready-made bullets for immediate use. Among these collections you'll probably be able to find a suitable style to match your design theme. But creating your own bullets is a relatively simple task, and the tools in nearly any graphics application will suffice in designing them. Figure 3-12 shows a simple, clean application of colorful, three-dimensional bullets on a well-organized Web site offering product information.

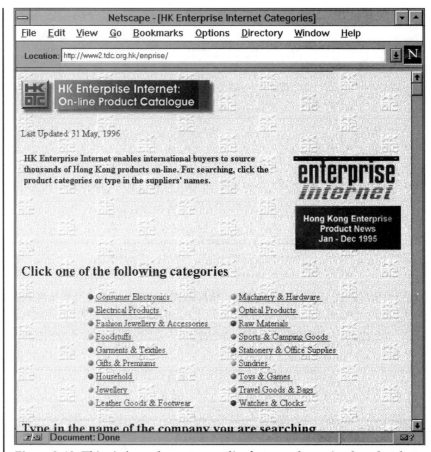

Figure 3-12: This site's product category list features clean, simple, colored bullets to add emphasis to a variety of link choices.

Using Separators

To set one part of a page off from another, consider using a separator—either a basic rule or a graphic separator. These horizontal design elements will divide your pages into sections. Whether you choose a basic rule or a graphic separator will depend on the design of your Web site. While HyperText Markup Language (HTML) provides the means to quickly draw horizontal rules with variable weights and widths, your design may beg for more pizzazz. A graphic separator can be virtually anything from a simple, uniformly colored line to a texture-patterned line or three-dimensional object (see Figure 3-13).

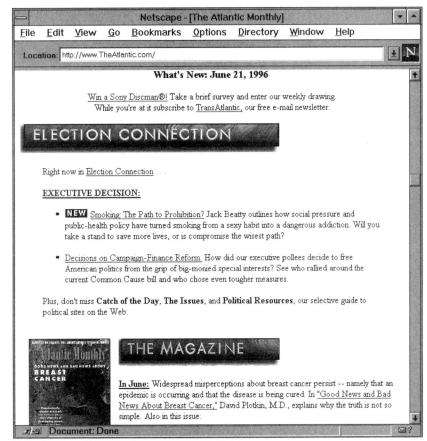

Figure 3-13: The Atlantic Monthly magazine's Web site uses graphic separators as dividing lines between content, as well as headlines. The design pattern in the images is carried on throughout various pages on the site, allowing the separators to emphasize the site's overall theme.

Take heed—separators are one of the most abused and over-used elements in Web site design (see Figure 3-14). Their main function is to put a barrier between two *unrelated* topics. Over-use of separators between *related* topics can destroy the continuity of a page. So, if you decide you need to add more than one or two separators per page, you may need to rethink your Web site structure.

Overuse of separators can destroy the continuity of a page.

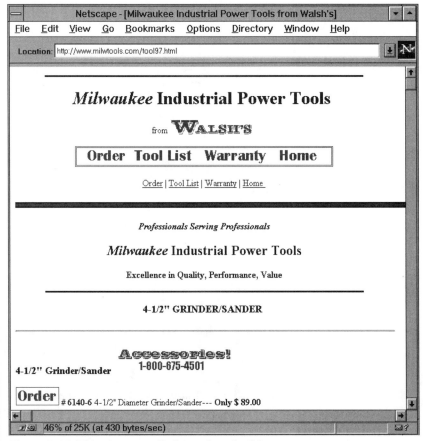

Figure 3-14: This site goes a little overboard with separators.

Most people use the built-in HTML tag <HR> to create separators. The <HR> tag has a variety of options including:

✦ Three-dimensional effects including shaded (the browser default) or unshaded.

✦ Pixel depth or thickness, to a maximum of 750 pixels.

✦ Alignment including left, center, and right.

✦ Width in pixels, or to a set percentage range from 0 to 100 percent of the user's current browser width.

One of the biggest advantages to using HTML separators is that they add virtually no memory size to your page and can resize automatically, depending on the width of user's browser. On the other hand, using a graphic image as a separator can complement a design theme by adding some flair to the design.

When creating an image to use as a separator, 3 pixels in depth and 575 pixels in length is an ideal size. Slimmer images load more quickly and conserve space on the page. As with backgrounds, separators can be virtually any pattern, color, size, or style, but make sure they fit with the overall design and color theme.

Integrating Text & Images

In traditional publishing, laying out photographs and text is considered something of an art. The experienced layout artist is trained at knowing how to manipulate the reader's eye between photos, headlines, and advertising. Once the layout is complete and just right for the type of publication being produced, the artwork is carted off to the printer and that's it. With Web publishing, the layout process is changed dramatically.

Once a Web page is laid out, anything can happen when it finally loads into a user's browser, depending on whether or not the browser is adjusted to nondefault settings or whether or not the image option is turned off. Therefore, you cannot necessarily rely on your graphics alone to communicate your message—your text and graphics must work together to do this.

You cannot rely on graphics alone to communicate your message. Your text and graphics must work together to do this.

Adding Graphics

Graphic images can be placed by themselves, aligned with a line of text, or aligned left or right with the text wrapping around the image. When aligning a graphic image with a line of text, you have the following options:

✦ Align the top of the image with the top of the ascender of the current line of text.

✦ Align the bottom of the image with the bottom of the baseline of the current line of text.

✦ Center the image on the baseline of the current line of text.

✦ Position the image to sit directly on the baseline of the current line of text.

Poor spacing alone can ruin the readability of a page, so be sure to have the correct spacing between text, images, and page borders. Also, wrapping text around an image can create "widows" or "orphans," to use the old typographer's terms. You can avoid this by making sure you have plenty of text to wrap around the picture. Netscape Navigator does a nice job of handling text wrap with the Align command. Unfortunately, other browsers may not be so kind to your pages. Consider setting your wraparounds with a table for more control.

One of the best tactics for avoiding layout problems when combining text and pictures is to *not* combine them. What this means is that you integrate the text and images together in a layout, but keep them separate from each other (see Figure 3-15). This way, none of the intended layout is distorted when it reaches the user's browser.

Figure 3-15: The Shiseido History site leaves the pictures and text separate, but still manages to unify the layout of the page through a smooth design flow.

If your design calls for literally integrating text with pictures or graphics, you'll find that a composition of the two in a single image works best instead of trying some of the more tricky HTML acrobatics. Most intermediate image editing programs allow for treating text, pictures, and graphics as objects. Figure 3-16 illustrates how you can easily combine these elements in a design arrangement that works well with the rest of the page.

Figure 3-16: Nearly all of the design elements on the Epicurious Travel page have been created as text-and-picture images. They have also been designed to work as integral parts of the entire design of the page in terms of color and style.

The most important factor in communicating an idea effectively, especially when integrating text and graphics into a single image, is to keep the layout clean and simple.

If your design calls for integrating images and text to flow together in a loose layout, there are a few basic considerations to keep in mind in order to ensure a degree of control in the page design.

Placing Graphics

Unless the graphic is a logo or an image map, anchor the graphic near the text that it describes. You want your users to believe that the images in your layout are interacting with your text. You want their eyes to flow back into the page rather than some-where else (see Figure 3-17). For example, position a picture of someone who is looking or facing a certain direction to be look-ing at a headline or at a certain point in the text. Images can sometimes even be made to face each other if the subject matter and images are suitable.

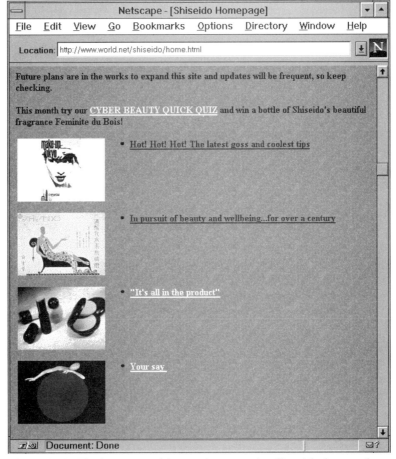

Figure 3-17: The images on this page interact visually with the text they accompany. The effect encourages the user's eyes to follow back into the text.

While positioning your images, you should also keep in mind your other pages. A well-balanced layout is easier to read and follow than one that feels disjointed, jumbled, or weighted to one side or another. For example, one of the most common formats used in Web page design, the flush left format, naturally causes pages to be unbalanced if it is used constantly. When all of your text and images have been pushed over to one side of your page, the effect gives your users a feeling of imbalance. Whenever possible, combine the centered, left, and right formats to create balance in the design of your pages.

Similarly, placing two images featuring an image wrap too close together can also inadvertently turn words or phrases into widows or orphans. Make sure that your images have enough textual content between them to support the text wrapping effect you have applied.

Designing Navigation

The best content in the world isn't worth the electrons it's beamed on if users can't find what they're looking for.

A well-implemented navigational system is at the heart of every successful Web site. The reason behind this is quite clear. The best content in the world isn't worth the electrons it's beamed on if users can't find what they're looking for. While Chapter 1, "Defining Your Web Site," touched on the subject of navigation, this section goes into more depth and will help you determine what, when, and where to link.

When designing a Web site's navigational system, your most obvious intent should be to allow your users to find what they need with a minimum of head scratching. A quick glance at a subject list or toolbar should provide enough information for users to correctly choose the right link on their first click.

There are usually at least two ways around a site, as just about every site includes both a navigational system (in the form of a toolbar) and links within its textual content. The navigational system allows users to jump between the pages of your site, while the text-based links allow them to drill deeper down into your site structure for specific information.

Think of how a newspaper is organized. There may be as many as four sections (or more) to a paper: news, sports, entertainment, and the classifieds. Each one of these sections contains a number of different types of content. The front page of the paper (as well as the Welcome page of your Web site) should include a table of contents that lists the major sections, and perhaps a little teaser of what is contained therein. Once you turn (or jump) to the front page of a section, you're rewarded with the section lead story, along with specific links to what's happening within that section. Navigational systems help readers quickly find what they're looking for on the Web, as in print.

How Should the Link Appear?

Choose your linking phrases carefully, and strive to use only those that are truly meaningful or representative of the "page to come." The phrases should be concise and to the point. And as was illustrated by the "StockTicker" example back in Chapter 1, "Defining Your Web Site," it's always a show of poor form to use the words "click here" to denote a link. Simply highlighting the term, title, or subject will do.

Link From Text, Graphics, or Both?

Your Web site's overall design scheme determines whether you will be linking from either text or graphics (or both). Linking from a text reference is the most obvious and straightforward choice. If you choose to link from a graphic reference, you need to be sure that your users will understand what the graphic infers.

Professional Web developers realize the value of well-crafted illustrations. That's why most successfully designed sites use graphics that were created (or modified) by artists, specifically for use on that particular Web site. If you can't afford the *right*

It's always a show of poor form to use the words "click here" to denote a link.

illustrations, consider whether you need to use *any* illustrations at all. Picking an arbitrary piece of clip art just because it's the closest thing you can find at a moment's notice, is a recipe for disaster.

An abstract or unclear reference will lead to a befuddled visitor. For this reason, you may choose to combine text with your graphics to reap the positive values of both techniques. When you create graphic links, it's especially important to use the ALT field within the <IMG SRC> tag, to properly define the graphic. Should your users hit the Stop button before the graphic loads (or if they're surfing with graphics turned off, altogether), they'll have a clue of what they're missing.

Where to Place Links

Here's a question of both style and substance. When you develop your Web site's editorial style, you must make a determination of where to place links based upon the volume of information to be presented. In particular, you've got to decide whether your content links will appear within text passages or within menus. The sheer volume of links that your pages contain should determine where and how your links are implemented. The more links you have, the more likely that you'll want to list your links in menu form (in a list). It's far more expedient for your users to pick a link from a bulleted list, than it is to dig it out of a chunk of text.

There are plenty of reasons to include your links within text passages, however. If you're looking for a warm, friendly, and informative tone, this method gets the nod. And it goes doubly true when the page is light on content. Half a dozen undefined links don't make a page. A little explanation can go a long way to fleshing things out. With this conversational method, folks will know a little more about the pages you're about to send them to. It may take longer for them to digest, but they'll know what to expect.

The more links you have, the more likely that you'll want to list your links in menu form.

You may want to use a combination of these techniques to determine where to place your links. Combining a long, link-laden text passage with a bulleted list of those same links provides the advantages of both methods. And on heavily text-laden pages, you may want to preface the text with a bulleted list of target links to expedite navigation within the page itself (target links jump to specific anchor points within the text passage).

Belly Up to the Toolbar

The repetitive structure of your pages should include a persistent navigational system (or toolbar). This system should have a similar appearance from page to page and should always be found at the same location on each page. It's usually found at either the header or footer, but it's sometimes both. And some of the most innovative sites have eschewed the conventional "top or bottom" toolbar placement altogether by setting their navigational system along the left side of their pages.

No matter where it appears, however, the navigational elements must be highly visible, clear, and concise. Developing a toolbar is a wonderful exercise in testing the structural viability of a Web site. The form of a well thought out navigational system will follow the function of the site. If a site is poorly structured, the navigational system will always be compromised.

Textual Toolbars

A text navigation interface is the simplest form of toolbar you can possibly implement into a Web site. Experienced designers nearly always make these textual navigation bars the very first elements to appear—even on the home page. If a textual toolbar appears at the top of every page, users are guaranteed instant access to navigation (see Figure 3-18).

Developing a toolbar is a wonderful exercise in testing the structural viability of a Web site.

If a textual toolbar appears at the top of every page, users are guaranteed instant access.

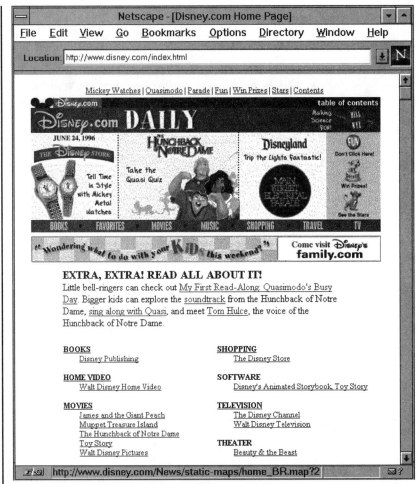

Figure 3-18: The Disney site is one of the most professionally designed and maintained sites on the World Wide Web, and the text toolbar is the very first item on every page of the site.

Don't make the mistake of forcing your users to wait for a navigation tool. If your design calls for a graphical toolbar, make the graphics small and concise.

The text toolbar you provide your users should allow them to reach all the major areas of your site, as well as provide access to critical areas such as Feedback, Search, and Help areas. Because of the nature of some larger toolbars, you may find it necessary to use small-sized text. Separate your text links with spacebars and characters such as the asterisk (*), slash (/), bracket ([ ]), or pipe symbol (|), in this format:

Home * Section 1 * Section 2 * Feedback * Search * Help

Home / Section 1 / Section 2 / Feedback / Search / Help

[Home] [Section 1] [Section 2] [Feedback] [Search] [Help]

Home | Section 1 | Section 2 | Feedback | Search | Help

Graphic Toolbars

There's no question about it—a well-executed graphic toolbar is far more fun than its text-based cousin. While a textual toolbar tells users exactly where a link sends them, a graphic toolbar infers more about what users can expect when they land there. Using images sans text can cause confusion, however. It's essential that the images cast little doubt as to where they lead. The most comprehensive toolbars combine images with text to ensure maximum impact—if users don't grasp the concept behind the design, they're bound to understand the text.

The most comprehensive toolbars combine images with text to ensure maximum impact.

Another approach is to use text *as* graphics, placing the text onto a graphic "button." This can be used to great effect, and can impart a distinctive look and feel to your Web site, without forcing you to go nuts in the quest for imagery. If you're considering using the text-as-graphic toolbar approach, be sure to keep your button bar tight. Big, fat, or gaudy buttons are a sure mark of amateur Web page design.

And what about those folks who cruise the Web with their graphics turned off? A common solution is to use a graphic toolbar, in concert with a separate textual toolbar. This covers all the bases, in allowing for both high- and low-bandwidth users.

Separate Images or Image Map?

Once you've decided on using a graphic toolbar, you'll have to make the call on how to implement your links. There are two ways to convert an image to a hyperlink. The first is to use the <A HREF> tag to create text links; unfortunately, this allows only one link per image. The second method is to use an image mapping application to break one composite image into numerous hot spots. An *image map* is what allows a graphic to carry more than one link. Through image mapping, a number of graphical elements can be combined. This enables design elements, such as site identification, graphical themes, and navigation, to become a single image.

There are pros and cons to both methods, but more often than not, image mapping a larger composite image gets the nod. If you compare the time it takes to download six separate icons with the time it takes to download one image comprising all six icons, the composite image will be faster to load. In addition to the lower overall number of transmitted bytes, there's far less client/server negotiation.

There may still be reasons to go with separate images, however. One strategy is to design your image separately, while assembling them on the Web page to appear as a single unit. Designers have perfected the art of multiple image assembly by compacting several separately mapped images together as a unit.

In addition, there are two kinds of image maps, *client side* and *server side*. Client side maps are the more browser-friendly of the two. When users slide their cursors around the graphic, their browsers provide them with feedback to let them know the Uniform Resource Locator (URL) of each link. A server side map, on the other hand, shrouds this information in secrecy, allowing users to see only the Cartesian coordinates of the cursor within the map.

> There are two kinds of image maps, client side and server side. Client side maps are the more browser-friendly of the two.

Designing Section Icons

Icons are an excellent way to communicate a message graphically. They are instantly read, can cross language barriers (if text is not included within them), and can be less confusing than any other method of communication if used properly. Often, difficult and abstract concepts can be summarized in a situational picture or representative object to convey an idea. Some icons have become standard or "cliché" (for example, a newspaper representing a section on news). If a symbol has been used before, it's because the symbol works and your users will be accustomed to the concept.

When designing icons, though, some designers become so caught up in their own creativity that they lose a sense for what they are designing. Often, designers create icons that are so complicated or so artistic that the original concept is lost.

The quick solution to this is to test the icons. Ask someone the simple question, "What does this look like to you?" Also, don't rely on just a single opinion. Take a sampling of as many diverse opinions as possible. Use this information to shape your icon designs.

Because icons are meant to briefly convey a message, they should ideally be small and simple. An icon may or may not feature color, and should sacrifice style for clarity. The images should be designed to be nice tight packages, ideally in a square or circular shape to fit the typical format of most buttons.

Text is a logical option to create icons for your button style interface. Sure, text buttons may first appear to lack design style, but style can be achieved through the actual design of the buttons themselves. If yours is an English-language audience, there can be no mistaking the destination of the buttons you label with text. Again, with text labels, make sure that your labels clearly identify the area they represent (see Figure 3-19). To remove all doubt as to whether the icons you have designed accurately represent your site, integrate text labels with the icons, but make sure the text is readable even at small sizes. You can accomplish the desired clarity by using either color or contrast effects.

Difficult and abstract concepts can be summarized in a situational picture or representative object to convey an idea.

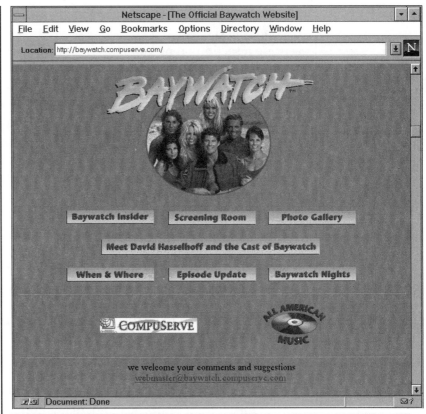

Figure 3-19: This site features highly stylized buttons with only text identification to clearly define their links.

Moving On

Although the content of your site is a good part of the reason your users will visit and revisit your site, the way that you package that content should stir excitement, intrigue, and curiosity. As in print, all of the elements that you integrate into your site combine to give a style and mood to the design and to make the experience memorable. People remember images much more readily than they remember text. Maximize this opportunity to its fullest. The next chapter talks about adding pictures to your Web pages.

Some of the elements discussed in this chapter involve creating specialized files such as image maps, but there are other effects that you can implement that fall into the category of advanced design features. Chapter 6, "Advanced Design Techniques," shows how these effects can add dynamics and vitality to your site design.

4

Adding Pictures to Your Design

As a designer, when you think of a "great" Web site you probably envision a site filled with lively and informative content, a completely intuitive interface, an engaging structure, and of course, some really cool pictures. This chapter provides picture design guidelines that can help you decide which pictures to use and when to use them.

If you're the person responsible for gathering, producing, or preparing pictures for your Web site, you'll need to follow these guidelines to stay focused on your design strategy.

Adding Graphic Appeal

If every page on the Web was perfectly designed, each time your users encountered an image, the image would leap off the screen, convey its idea, and leave users with a lingering and memorable response. In reality, this seldom happens. Strangely enough, many highly regarded Web sites only fill two of the three basic requirements of good design. Namely, well-written content, an intuitive interface, and an appealing yet consistent design theme. All too often, sites are produced with well-written text but poor illustrations or vice versa.

Here are some basic guidelines for rationalizing the use of a picture:

✦ Use a picture when it can tell a story more efficiently than your text.

- ✦ Choose pictures that *directly* relate to your subject matter.

- ✦ Be consistent in your picture selection. Avoid "overmixing" photographs and illustrations that feature a wide range of visual styles.

- ✦ Use a picture only when it complements your design and your text.

- ✦ Tweak your pictures down to a reasonable file size for quick loading.

- ✦ Take the time to adjust the color balance, contrast, and focus.

- ✦ Position your pictures in a logical and consistent manner to create balance and flow of the text around them.

Beware of the hazard of using pictures to simply festoon your site (see Figure 4-1). You're not decorating a birthday cake. Pointless pictures can leave your users frustrated and confused, while they wrestle to make a connection between an unrelated picture and the adjoining text.

As a Web site designer, using graphical appeal to invoke an emotional response from your audience is one of your major goals. The key in adding graphic appeal to your site lies mostly in identifying where your graphic opportunities are. At the start of the design process, you're faced with lines and lines of text. Your challenge is to draw out the logical opportunities and maximize the visual impact based on your creative resources. Use the following list as a guide to drawing out visual opportunities:

- ✦ Significant people, places, or things

- ✦ Rarely-seen or extraordinary situations

- ✦ Relevant information graphics, such as maps, charts, or diagrams

- ✦ Company logos or corporate identities

- ✦ Graphical headlines

Beware of the hazard of using pictures to simply festoon your site. You're not decorating a birthday cake.

Figure 4-1: The bird picture at the Philippines site may leave users wondering what the connection is between the picture and the text.

◆ Graphical bullets with point form text

◆ Image separators

By combing through the text for picture opportunities you'll be able to turn up the visual possibilities. You can then decide which possibilities are worth exploiting. This is often determined by the amount of resources you have on hand, both in talent and in budget.

Coordinating Color Schemes

Choosing a color scheme will depend on the subject matter of your site, your audience, and your content. Coordinating color schemes is an art, and unfortunately, for many people it's a complete mystery. Figures 4-2 and 4-3 show how colors can directly affect the emotion, impact, and beauty of a page or an entire site.

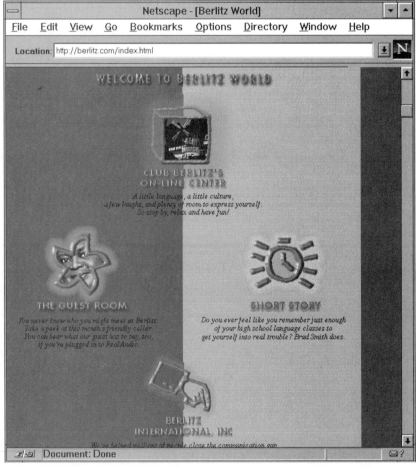

Figure 4-2: The Berlitz International site features vivid and lively colors beginning with red and yellow background bands, and different, metallic outline graphics on top.

Figure 4-3: Inside the Berlitz site, the photographs have all been prepared in black and white with feathering effects around the edges. The background theme continues inside with lively, but varied colored bands.

The color scheme you choose should conjure up a definitive mood for your users.

A color scheme is any combination of colors that complement each other or work together to form a mental "impression." The color scheme you choose for your site can be from anywhere in the spectrum, but ideally should conjure up a definitive mood for your users. The scotch.com site shown in Figure 4-4 features a color scheme with plenty of browns, golds, and bronze colors. These colors provide the impression of time-worn endurance and elegance.

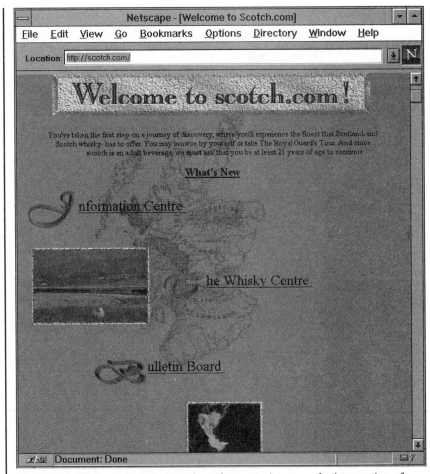

Figure 4-4: The scotch.com site color scheme conjures up the impression of time-worn endurance and elegance.

Some color experts say your users will associate certain colors with specific emotions. This shouldn't be confused with the notion that certain colors invoke certain "physical reactions" in your users. Color schemes are a notorious marketing strategy in both advertising and product packaging. There's a long list of color schemes for certain marketing segments of the consumer market. The following examples may help to get your imagination rolling:

✦ Gem tone colors such as turquoise, red, purple, and gold; and fluorescent colors such as hot pink, yellow, and bright green appeal to the teenaged market especially when they are used with black.

✦ Bright primary colors such as red, yellow, and blue are traditionally appealing to very young children.

✦ Mixtures of shades of red mixed with solid black are associated with powerful emotions such as embroiled passion and deep sorrow.

✦ Bright yellows, bright greens, and yellows in combination with baby blues and white are associated with renewal, growth, spring, and optimism.

✦ Deeper brown-yellow, muddy reds, burnt sienna, heavy ochre, and other yellow-brown-red combinations are colors associated with age, establishment, solidity, and a sense for standing the test of time.

These are just a few of the color scheme strategies used in marketing and other types of communication and are the same strategies available to you as a site designer. If you're looking for more background material on color theory, look no further than Gary Priester's *Looking Good in Color*. It's a great reference guide, filled with sage advice. Although it's subtitled "The Desktop Publisher's Design Guide," much of the book fully applies to online design.

Creating Graphical Themes

The Web site designer's role is similar to that of the interior designer. When you begin to decorate your online abode, you have to visualize how everything works together. Heaven forbid that your electronic wallpaper might clash with the pixel-patterned fabric on your cyber-couch! A well-integrated Web site uses a number of design elements—including backgrounds, thumbnails, icons, and informational graphics—to create a graphical theme. These design elements work together with other graphic features, such as photographs and illustrations, to deliver a consistent look and feel. And as any proud host will tell you, it's comforting to know that everything's just perfect, before you pull off the tarps, open the doors, and welcome in your guests.

Working With Backgrounds

In the last chapter, we covered the subject of solid color and patterned backgrounds. It's not hard to visualize your backgrounds as being the paint and wallpaper on the walls of your electronic cottage—the walls on which everything else will hang. Here's a bit more information on how to use pictures both *with* and *as* backgrounds.

Using Pictures *With* Backgrounds

To be seen clearly, all the pictures featured on your site should sharply contrast the color of the background. A picture that literally pops out of the background delivers maximum impact. There are several common strategies for making a picture pop out from the background:

✦ Make the background and picture colors as different as possible.

✦ Give the picture itself a drop shadow, creating the illusion that it is hovering just above the background.

✦ Give photographic pictures graphic frames to clearly define the picture's edges.

On the other hand, some effects require that the edges of your picture be invisible. This is most often the case with pictures that feature nonrectangular shapes, which need to have edges or borders that are identical to the backgrounds they sit on. This is a technique that can also be achieved through masking effects available in image editors that support the transparency feature in the GIF89a file format.

Using Pictures *as* Backgrounds

Amazing effects can be achieved through the use of background images. But the issues relating to the use of pictures as backgrounds should be carefully considered. Backgrounds are an extremely powerful tool for setting the mood and style of your site. They must be as subtle as possible to ensure that your content stands out. An effective background is one that becomes relatively invisible as users browse your site.

Ideally, background images should be designed to tile *seamlessly*. Your users shouldn't get the impression of an image being tiled. Tiles can take one of four shapes:

✦ A vertical "stripe" that tiles to create horizontal-patterned backgrounds.

✦ A horizontal "stripe" that tiles to create vertical-patterned backgrounds (see Figure 4-5).

✦ A rectangular or square-shaped image that tiles to create a seemingly uniform pattern (see Figure 4-6).

✦ A single image designed to the dimensions of the page that is large enough to file a full page of the user's browser and seemingly creates only a single tile (see Figure 4-7).

While the stripe images can have very interesting effects, the files you create to generate these backgrounds need only be a few pixels in thickness—no more than 6 pixels—and may be created using virtually any image editing program. This type of background tile is quite versatile and files are generally small, making load times quick. Rectangular images can be as small as 50 to 100 pixels in width and depth. Single image backgrounds should be considered only after all other possibilities have been expended, due to their commonly large file size. To make a single image background load quickly, due diligence (in the form of palette-tweaking) must be taken.

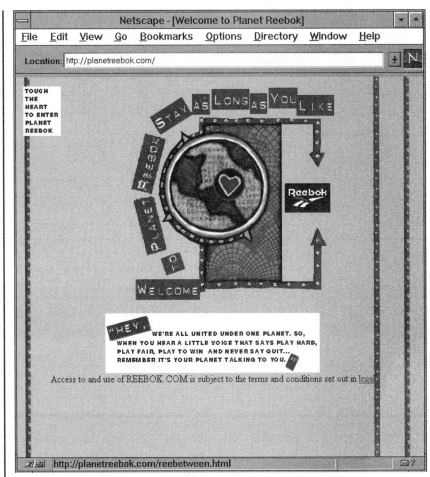

Figure 4-5: The Planet Reebok site features a garish yellow and red colored background, produced using a horizontal stripe that gives the effect of continuously running vertical objects.

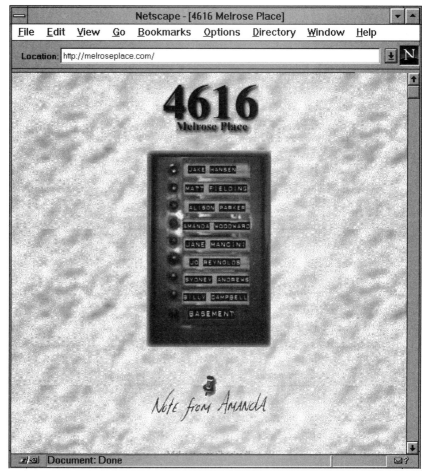

Figure 4-6: The Melrose Place site includes a subtle blurred stucco image as a background, whose tiles can barely be seen, but are still apparent.

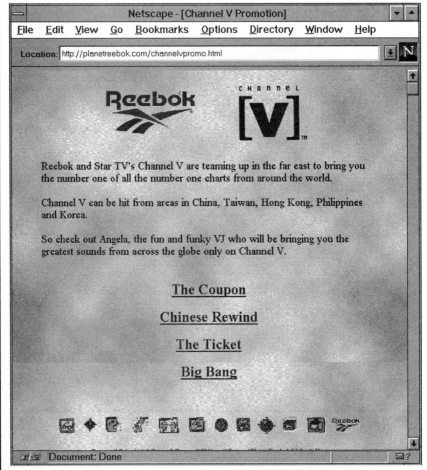

Figure 4-7: A sideline site to the Planet Reebok site features blue and white cloud background patterns, that tile to nearly fill the entire browser.

Implementing Thumbnails

Thumbnail images are small, scaled-down samples of larger illustrations, that link to their full-size brethren. As such, thumbnails both inform and entice. When users download pages that contain thumbnail images, they're quickly rewarded with the visual goods. If one of the little thumbnail images catches their

It's proper online etiquette to annotate your thumb-nails with the size of the larger image.

eye, they can click it and be whisked off to a new page, with a larger version of that image. It's important to note that the proper online etiquette is to annotate your thumbnails with the size of the larger image.

One place this methodology works well is on corporate staff pages. Let's say that your users are highly interested in seeing who runs your company. If they really want to check out a beefy 100K glamor shot of the "president and founder of XYZ, Inc.," they'll click the link. If they could care less about what the big cheese looks like, they'll move on to another page.

If your Web site's purpose is to sell, it's likely that it will feature product photos to showcase the quality and workman-ship of the products. A site such as this can be made or broken by the manner in which the photographs are presented. Delivering lightning-fast pages is critical. Save your users the agony of having to wait while the images download to their browsers. You don't want visitors to leave your site before they get to critical information about your business.

A wise strategy is to feature small, closely cropped, and highly compressed thumbnails that merely hint at the final larger image. For example, Figures 4-8 and 4-9 detail a page on the Lands' End Web site. Lands' End, a traditional mail-order house, features a high degree of site identification, product identification, section identification, navigation, and ordering information on their pages. Adding a large image might make the download time on these pages unbearable. Instead of adding a large product shot to each online catalog page, the designers chose to implement thumbnail images with links to larger, more detailed images. If a customer is interested in a specific product, they can click the thumbnail image and be rewarded with a nice juicy product shot.

Figure 4-8: The Lands' End mail order site features smaller, more compact thumbnail views of products, giving site customers the option of taking a hyperlink to a larger image to get more visual information about the product.

A closer look at the thumbnail image versus the larger, more detailed image shows that the file size of the thumbnail is 10,552 bytes, while the larger image is 26,528 bytes—nearly three times the size. Also, in terms of color palettes, the thumbnail was left at 256 while the larger image was reduced to 41 unique colors to keep file size down. The same file left at 256 colors would likely have been double the size.

Figure 4-9: Taking a link from the thumbnail image leads users to the larger, more detailed image.

Fine-tuning digital photographs and images is a subject unto itself. We'll delve into image compression and other strategies in Chapter 5, "Creating Digital Content."

Using Icons

Icons are the petroglyphs of our time, quickly telling a story or describing an idea.

As you saw in the previous chapter, using icons to describe particular subjects or areas is a popular way to define your Web site's design style. Icons are the petroglyphs of our time. They can quickly tell a story or describe an idea, and have become an accepted form of communication. One obvious example is in international industries such as airline travel, where language can easily be a barrier to communication. Many of the most important things in an airport are clearly identified using universally accepted icons such as exits, stairways, elevators, boarding gates, security, and so on. Icons are commonly used in Web site design to denote different sections, or *subsites* within a site. As such, you'll often find icons in graphic navigation toolbars, as well as in the header or footer of the section's pages.

Icons need to be obvious, eye-catching, and lively to generate interest on the part of your users. When approaching an icon design, follow these guidelines to ensure the highest level of comprehension:

✦ Make your icons clear and accurately representative of the subject or idea they represent (see Figure 4-10).

Figure 4-10: Starting Point features a collection of a dozen well-designed icons that are easily interpreted and are accompanied by text (just in case they aren't).

✦ Design all of your icons using the same style or theme to reinforce your design to your users.

✦ Make your icons interactive by linking the concept they represent to the icon image.

✦ Implement text into the icons if there is any doubt as to whether they will be misinterpreted.

✦ Follow your established design parameters, including color scheme, texture, and illustration style (see Figure 4-11).

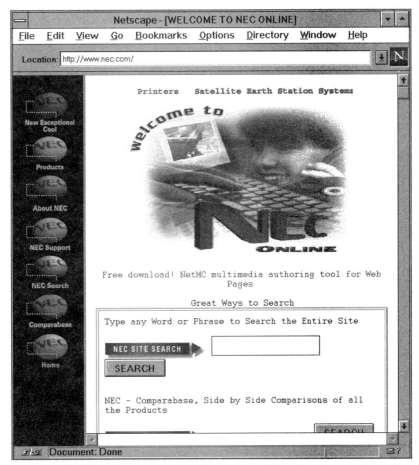

Figure 4-11: NEC features a series of seven colorful and easily read icons that represent the major subsites. The icons sit in a persistent frame and have a high-tech texture mapped appearance, ideally suited to NEC's corporate image.

✦ Position your icons on your site page where they can easily and quickly be seen.

✦ Make them large and clear enough so they can be easily recognized. If there is text that accompanies the icons, ensure that it can easily be read (see Figure 4-12).

Properly designed icons are clear and concise, and are quickly and easily interpreted by users.

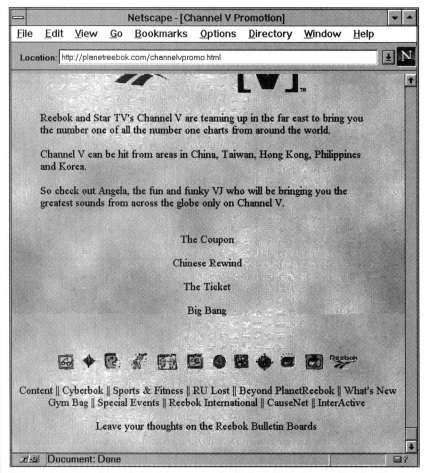

Figure 4-12: PlanetReebok's icons are cute, but a bit on the small side. The text navigation bar is a wise accompaniment.

Informational Graphics

Informational graphics, such as maps, charts, and graphs provide numerous opportunities to present your online information in a graphical manner. Some of the most visually appealing informational graphics in recent memory were introduced by Nigel Holmes in the early 1980s. His talent manifested itself in charts and graphs in magazines and newspapers. Holmes was best known for putting a literal twist on charts in an illustrative way. He was one of the original pioneers in this form of statistical presentation. Holmes used his creative methods to depict data and successfully generate audience interest in otherwise uninteresting topics. This is, of course, the key in presenting data in any medium.

Much of the expertise required to create effective informational graphics is the same, regardless of whether the images are intended for print or online presentation. The artists of Gannett's *USA Today* are among the forefront of current informational graphics development. This team of artists uses imagination, creativity, and artistic license in the creation of maps, charts, and diagrams on a daily basis. The *USA Today* graphics are designed to appeal to the broadest possible audience, and are created in the pressure cooker of a daily newspaper deadline. The Top Weather News by *USA Today* is shown in Figure 4-13.

Most everyday informational graphics on the Web are GIF images. Unfortunately, the format falls short in certain respects. If your Web page maps, charts, and diagrams demand a higher level of detail, you should consider using Macromedia's Shockwave for FreeHand technology. The FreeHand Shockwave plug-in lets you use vector-based illustrations on your pages. While GIF images are fixed resolution (72 dots per inch) files, FreeHand Shockwave images allow your visitors to zoom up to a higher level of detail. This provides the perfect solution for information-heavy illustrations such as street maps.

Much of the expertise required to create effective informational graphics is the same, regardless of whether the images are intended for print or online presentation.

Figure 4-13: The expertise that was required to produce the online version of USA Today's Weather report is much the same as was required for the print version.

When presenting any informational graphics, use these guidelines:

✦ Use a clear, concise title. Don't be (too) cute.

✦ Keep the image uncluttered and easy to grasp.

✦ Give source information regarding research, measurement, or recording method.

✦ Provide detailed labels including callouts or arrows.

✦ Select suitable color schemes to allow your graphic information to stand out against its background.

✦ Use shading or shadowing to give the illusion of depth.

✦ Add reference structure such as grid lines, timelines, and
grid markers.

✦ Include an explanatory legend or symbol key to unlock the
distance scales, colors, symbols, abbreviations, and patterns
used in the graphic.

✦ Use Shockwave for FreeHand to deliver the highest level of
detail.

Moving On

Graphics are meant to add life to your Web site. They should also
inform users, emphasize points in your text, and generate interest on pages. Color, graphics, and information are all important
factors in deciding how to use pictures on your site.

There are plenty of issues surrounding the implementation of
the pictures you may be planning for your Web site. The next
chapter, "Creating Digital Content," takes you through the
design-related decisions and procedures you'll encounter when
preparing images for your Web pages.

5

Creating Digital Content

If you're one of the many traditional print designers making the transition to Web page design, you've likely already figured out that many of the same design and production rules apply. You still need to concentrate on white space, readability, and style when it comes to the overall communicative value of your work. When it comes to working with digital images on the Web, however, the procedure isn't as straightforward as you might think. This chapter takes a close look at the production issues of preparing and fine-tuning digital images for use in Web page design.

Most popular image-editing applications feature the basic tool set required to create or refine Web page images. While the information that follows cites specific programs in some situations, the same basic understanding applies to like applications. Besides the obvious operational differences between vector-based graphics applications and image editing software, there are some significant differences in the technical procedures involved, and some critical hazards and considerations to keep in mind.

For example, although in most drawing applications the procedure for producing a bitmap image of an existing vector drawing is usually by way of the software's Export command, image editors commonly use the Save As command instead. It's a subtle difference, but this slight difference in methodology is critical to the whole process and is something that can easily snag unsuspecting designers. This chapter will explore those issues and provide guidelines for achieving satisfactory results.

When it comes to working with digital images on the Web, the procedure isn't as straightforward as you might think.

Acquiring Images

If most of your digital experience comes from the print production world, you're likely already aware of most of the various ways of converting photographs and graphic images into digital formats. But, if you come from any of the many other areas attracting interest in Web design, how this process comes about might still be a complete mystery to you. There are many ways to acquire an image for use on the Web. Images can be digitized from reflective or transparent artwork with a scanner, or they can be created from scratch, with any one of a number of software applications.

The following are the most common methods for acquiring images using both hardware and software:

✦ Scanners

✦ Digital cameras

✦ Video capture

✦ PhotoCD

✦ Texture creation software

✦ Graphic illustration software

✦ Three-dimensional rendering software

✦ Animation software

✦ Screen-capture software

As a Web site designer, you will probably perform several steps to digitize an image. Hardware such as scanners and digital cameras require the interface of supporting software applications—thus, you may use more than one software application to acquire, manipulate, and save your digital images. The number of steps you take or methods you use will depend on factors such as the physical setup of your computer system, or the special digital effects you wish to achieve.

Image-Scanning Hazards

Perhaps the biggest roadblock you will face in acquiring a satisfactory digital image is poor quality of the original image. If the original has been poorly recorded, physically damaged, is out of focus, or poorly colored, even the most sophisticated scanner will be incapable of improving the image. If the original is poor, you may be out of luck trying to use it "as is," and you may need to choose an alternative.

Continuous-tone, or *contone* originals are good candidates for scanning. Photographic prints, slides, and original hand-produced artwork are a few common examples of contone originals. Once a contone image has been reproduced in print, be it in a magazine, newspaper, or brochure, the printed version is referred to as a *halftone*. In print, colored or black dot halftone patterns create the illusion of highlight and shadow. The finer the printing process, the more difficult the halftone dots will be to discern. Just put your evening newspaper next to a luscious coffee table book, and you'll quickly see the difference.

If your original is poor, you may be out of luck trying to use it "as is," and you may need to choose an alternative.

Scanning a printed halftone image will usually result in an unavoidable checkerboard pattern known as *moiré*. A moiré is created when one dot pattern is applied over another—digital or otherwise—resulting in an undesirable effect. Moiré can cause significant distortion in the scanned image and can be difficult to eliminate without drastically blurring or averaging the digital image. Halftones with coarse dot screens such as those found in newspaper printing are the most difficult to digitize effectively. Scanning printed images with fine halftone dot patterns reduces the effect of moiré considerably. If you have to repurpose prescreened art on a regular basis, it may warrant specialized scanning software, such as ScanPrepPro, which features advanced descreening algorithms.

Image resolution is measured in pixels per inch (ppi). Web graphics feature a relatively low resolution of just 72 ppi, while print graphics can typically be 300 dots per inch (dpi) or higher.

If you find your system crashing every time you open an extremely large image for editing, try rescanning it or opening it at a lesser resolution.

When you scan images for the Web (or create them from scratch), you should always keep the final target resolution of 72 ppi in mind. Scanning large originals—especially color photographs—at high resolutions will result in huge files. If you're working on a high-end computer, equipped with dozens of megabytes of random access memory (RAM), file size may not be an issue. However, if your system isn't outfitted to handle very large images, they may pose a hazard that can be easily avoided. If you find your system crashing every time you open an extremely large image for editing, try rescanning it or opening it at a lower resolution. However, with RAM prices hovering (as of this writing) at an all-time low, an investment in additional system memory may be a prudent purchase.

Strategies for Preparing Images

Once you have acquired and saved your digital image in a bitmap file format of one type of another, you'll need to take a few steps to fine-tune it for the Web. There are some tricky issues involved in getting files into an acceptable state. As mentioned earlier, your images will ideally end up in either JPEG or GIF format, so it's critical that the image editor you're using fully supports both of these. The *Looking Good Online CD-ROM* includes Paint Shop Pro, version 3.11, a Windows-based shareware program that allows you to edit and save to GIF and JPEG file formats.

Using Resampling Options

Resampling is the process of resizing the physical size and resolution size of a digital image. Unless you've been lucky enough to obtain a scanned image at exactly the size and resolution you need it, you'll likely need to resample or "down sample" your image. Under ideal circumstances, it's a wise practice to begin with a digital image resolution higher than 72 ppi, ideally twice that, or 150 ppi.

Most image editors feature menu options to determine exactly the physical size and resolution of images. If you normally work in inches or picas, be sure to change your measurement options to pixels so that you have reference to the de facto Web standard of measurement.

When resampling, be sure your final image doesn't exceed an arbitrary maximum Web page width of 640 pixels. While normally, you wouldn't use an image this large, the final size of your image will depend on the page layout and design. The amount of memory your image occupies will be critical.

When specifying a final resolution, always pick 72 ppi. Choosing a higher resolution will only add wasteful file size to your final image, and most computer screens will be incapable of rendering a higher quality than this. Specifying a lower resolution will cause your image to appear in an undesirable "chunky" or "pixelated" pattern.

Using Anti-Aliasing

The anti-aliasing process can improve or at least maintain image quality, especially if the image contains mostly uniform colors such as graphic images. It's usually applied during the resampling process, although this is dependent on the options available in your image editing application.

Anti-aliasing causes adjacent colors in your image to blend to a certain degree, eliminating the hard, jagged edges known as stair-stepping. Stair-stepping is a result of down sampling images. If anti-aliasing is not used, the results can often be distortion where contrasting colors meet, causing an effect called *truncating*. This is most apparent in resampled graphic images containing uniform color (see Figure 5-1).

If you normally work in inches or picas, be sure to change your measurement options to pixels to check image size.

The anti-aliasing process can improve or at least maintain image quality, especially if the image contains mostly uniform colors.

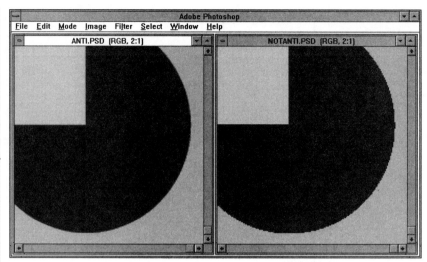

Figure 5-1: Anti-aliasing features can be set as options during resampling and have the effect of "smoothing" areas where adjoining colors meet. The colored circle was resampled using both anti-aliasing (left) and truncating (right).

Consider these rules when resampling an image:

✦ For most digital images, anti-aliasing provides the best possible image sampling technique. Using a stretch or truncate option tends to produce more jagged edges between color shapes.

✦ Avoid repeat resampling. Repeated resampling will degrade your image quality. If you have to resize, always start from the original.

✦ Change the dimension options in your image editor to display in pixels. This way, you'll always know how large your image is in relation to your Web page size.

Following a set of ruthless cropping rules can improve the interest level of your photographs immensely.

Cropping for Speed

Cropping should be as efficient as possible given the physical space you have allotted for your image. Following a set of ruthless cropping rules can improve the interest level of your photographs immensely. For example, when cropping a portrait, you don't need to include much besides the face (see Figures 5-2 and 5-3). To capture emotion, you can often eliminate nearly every other element, without distracting from the effectiveness of the image.

Figure 5-2: This portrait wastes download time and page space. The 272 x 484 file weighs in at 51K as a high-quality JPEG.

Figure 5-3: The same portrait, cropped much closer, accomplishes two goals. The cropped 122 x 186 image focuses on the subject, while reducing the file size to 10K—just 20 percent of the original.

Deciding on a File Format: GIF or JPEG

There are two basic bitmap file formats used in Web page design: the GIF (Graphics Interchange Format) and JPEG (the Joint Photographic Experts Group standard). Most image editors allow you to open and save to both GIF and JPEG file formats. Depending on the characteristics of each image, you'll choose one format over the other.

Choose the GIF format for line art, logos, charts, graphics, screen captures, and cartoon art. Use the JPEG format for photographs and other contone originals.

In general, you should use the GIF format for artwork with large expanses of flat color. Some of the best uses of GIF are for line art, logos, charts, graphics, screen captures, and cartoon art. You'll want to use the JPEG format for photographs and other contone originals, such as paintings.

Working With GIF Images

The GIF format, originally developed for CompuServe, is a compact format, designed for the display of images containing 256 colors or less. While this is a limited palette when compared to the broad spectrum of color offered by JPEG, the format provides excellent results if used properly. One of the most compelling reasons to use the GIF format is that images can be shaped unevenly, through the use of transparency masking.

The GIF format comes in two flavors, GIF87a and GIF89a. Both feature Lempel-Ziv-Welch (LZW) compression, which provides the ability to conserve file space without losing significant image quality. In addition, both GIF87a and 89a formats support *interlacing,* which is the characteristic whereby an image "fades into view." The GIF89a format adds a host of other cool effects:

✦ Transparency masks

✦ Multiple images

✦ Global color palettes across multiple images

✦ Image looping (animation)

✦ Nondestructive text blocks, including comment blocks, plain text blocks, and application blocks

✦ User-definable display and interlace delays limits

✦ User input delays

Transparent Images
The most compelling reason for choosing the GIF89a format for Web page images is its ability to support uneven-shaped images using transparency masks. A transparency mask is a color specified in the file to appear as "no color." This allows the Web page background to show through where this particular color exists.

Any image-editing application worth its salt should include the ability to denote a specific RGB color as the transparent color in a GIF89a file. Figure 5-4 illustrates the difference between a transparent and nontransparent image exported from CorelDRAW! 6.0.

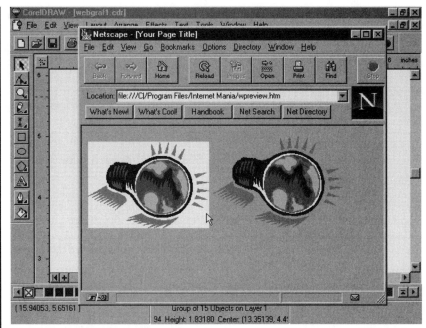

Figure 5-4: The light bulb graphic was prepared in GIF87a format (left) and 89a format (right) using a transparency mask option.

Including Color Palettes

Because you can control the number of colors and the exact color specifications of those colors using a color palette, the GIF file format is very versatile for use on the Web. Color palettes are collections of colors needed to properly display the color information contained in any given digital image. The larger the color palette, the more information is contained in the palette and the larger the file size of the image. Hence, if the amount of color information contained in a file's color palette is significantly reduced, so too is the file size. This is the key to reducing GIF file sizes.

You can use limited color palettes with certain types of images. Limited color palettes reduce file size without harming viewing quality. Be wary of images that feature many smooth gradations of color such as blurred or soft images. This type of image is the

If a file's color palette is significantly reduced, so too is the file size. This is the key to reducing GIF file sizes.

most difficult to render with limited color palettes. Graphic images that feature mostly uniform colors or colors from a specific area of the color spectrum are the best candidates for drastically reducing the number of colors contained in palettes.

On the left in Figure 5-5, a GIF file containing four uniform colors and a complete gradation from black to white was saved using an optimized palette. This image features the maximum 256 colors for the GIF file format. On the right, the same image was saved to GIF using only 60 colors (nearly all of them grayscale) producing an identical-looking image.

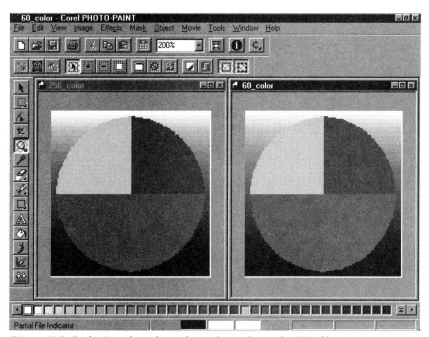

Figure 5-5: Reducing the color palette also reduces the GIF file size.

Some software applications are more efficient than others at detecting and reducing an image to its lowest number of colors. The best tools allow customized palettes that you can use for each graphic. Palette tweaking is strictly manual and can take considerable time—mostly by trial and error—to arrive at just the right palette combination.

The following is a brief description of basic palette options found in most image editors:

✦ **Uniform:** The Uniform color palette includes a complete 256-color spectrum, supplying equal quantities of red, green, and blue regardless of whether they're used by the image. Avoid this option, as it will dramatically alter the appearance of your images (and not in a good way).

✦ **Adaptive:** This option samples the image and uses up to the first 256 colors it finds to create a palette. It allows you to set the maximum number of colors used in your image. If you have to use the GIF format for photographs, use an adaptive palette and experiment with dithering options.

✦ **Optimized:** This palette samples the image to compose a palette based on the most commonly used colors in the image. As in the adaptive palette, you have the ability to limit the number of colors.

✦ **Custom:** The Custom option varies from program to program, but usually provides the option to specify a saved palette in either the standard PAL format or your image editor's proprietary palette format such as in Photoshop. You'll most commonly use the Custom option when converting images into the Netscape 216 palette.

Different image-editing tools use different terminology. For example, Adobe Photoshop uses the term "indexed color" whereas Paint Shop Pro uses the term "decrease color depth." Check your own editing tools to see how they handle the modification of color in an image.

The Netscape Palette

Much has been written, both online and in print, about what's commonly referred to as the Netscape 216 palette. Since the goal here isn't to bury anyone in technical mumbo-jumbo, let's simplify things and get right to the point. Netscape Navigator's internal palette (along with the other most popular browsers)

Netscape Navigator's internal palette uses a common 216 colors across versions and platforms.

uses a common 216 colors across versions and platforms. If you specify any colors in your GIF palette, other than those 216 colors, they will be altered when displayed on the browser, if they are viewed on a system with a 256-color display. What you see in your image editor won't be what you'll see in Netscape.

You can tweak your GIF palettes until the wee hours, trying to shave a few bytes here and there, but the images you'll produce will run the risk of displaying improperly. Here's the tradeoff— Do you value image fidelity more than file size? If so, save yourself the heartache and use the Netscape 216 palette for all of your GIF images. Check out the *Looking Good Online CD-ROM* for a copy of the Netscape 216 custom palette.

Dithering Graphics

Dithering causes an image's pixel arrangement to become patterned to provide the illusion of a smoother transition in tone. Here's a run-down of dithering options:

✦ **None:** Provides no dithering in the conversion. Try this first when converting contone images to GIF format.

✦ **Ordered:** This is perhaps the fastest dithering method. Uses a fixed pattern of dithering to reproduce the various tones in the image. As such, an ordered dither should be your last option.

✦ **Error Diffusion:** Often the best resampling option. Error diffusion develops its own pattern of pixels based on the various tones and colors of the image being converted. This results in a far less obvious effect, when compared to an ordered dither.

If you have to dither an image, the best choice is to go with error diffusion. An ordered dither imparts a "screened" look, which (unless you're going for that type of effect) should usually be avoided.

Working With JPEG Formats

JPEG should be your first choice for contone images. The format supports the maximum number of colors possible—16.7 million—and features varying degrees of compression. With the capability to render more colors, JPEG produces more detail and can render more vivid color depth than the GIF format.

JPEG compression is capable of shrinking your image to a fraction of its original size.

When saving your image to JPEG, you'll likely have two top priorities in mind. You'll want a great image with maximum color depth, crispness, and clarity, and you'll want a tiny file size. JPEG compression is capable of shrinking your image to a fraction of its original size, usually without compromising quality. Again, there are pitfalls to watch out for.

JPEG Formats

In various image editors, options (or settings) involved in saving to the JPEG format can differ quite significantly. In Photoshop 3.0 for Windows, saving to JPEG format involves choosing from only four preset quality settings (see Figure 5-6). The Photoshop settings, Low, Medium, High, and Maximum, make specific fine-tuning of JPEG compression quite limited. More settings are available in PHOTO-PAINT 6, however; the JPEG option categories in PHOTO-PAINT include controls for general JPEG Formats, Sub-formats, and Quality Factor (see Figure 5-7).

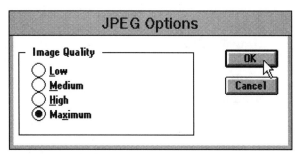

Figure 5-6: Photoshop's options for saving to JPEG are significantly brief, and offer only these four settings for quality and compression.

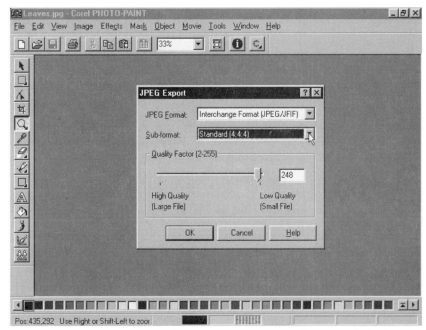

Figure 5-7: PHOTO-PAINT 6's JPEG saving options offer controls for three general JPEG formats, three sub-formats, and a quality factor range between 2 and 255 via a sliding control.

There are these three sub-format standards to the JPEG Interchange: Standard, Option 1, and Option 2. These three standards offer varying degrees of compression, file size, quality, and *lossiness*. Lossiness describes the loss of data of a digital image's color and shape during compression. Each sub-format is described in terms of image quality and lossiness, versus file size in the following list:

✦ **Standard:** The JPEG Standard compression sub-format provides the best-quality image with the least amount of lossiness, but the largest of all the sub-format file sizes.

✦ **Option 1:** The JPEG Option 1 sub-format features the poorest quality images, which endure the highest image lossiness, but yield the smallest files.

✦ **Option 2:** The Option 2 sub-format can be a happy medium between the first two formats.

Compressing Images for Quality

Any image can be compressed to a certain degree, but how far can you continue to shrink an image before it begins to degrade? How can you tell it's degrading? Features that define a clean image include color depth, crispness, and clarity; all of these are sacrificed during compression. Compressed images are usually flatter, more dull, and less focused-looking than their originals. But, because JPEG features various compression levels, the same image can appear differently using different compression levels during the save process (see Figures 5-8 and 5-9).

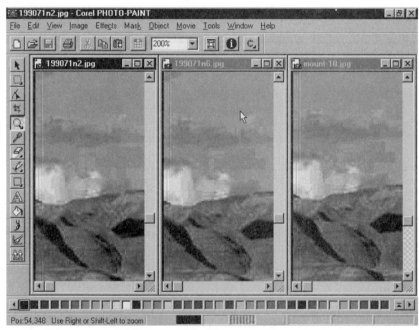

Figure 5-8: A digital landscape created using the three JPEG sub-formats: Standard (left), Option 1 (center), and Option 2 (right).

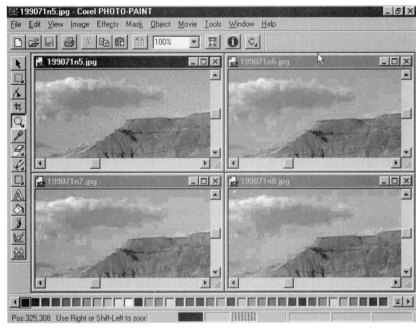

Figure 5-9: Reducing the JPEG quality factor.

Over-compression can cause an image to look as if a thin film of grease has been applied to your monitor. In the worst cases, images can be completely unrecognizable. Most commonly, over-compressed images will appear splotchy, with a posterized, almost underwater look.

Be wary of using JPEG for highly graphic images, with large areas of contiguous color; you'll probably be better off using GIF in these cases.

Be wary of using JPEG for highly graphic images, with large areas of contiguous color; you'll probably be better off using GIF in these cases. The trick with JPEG compression is to use a compression level that is just shy of producing a noticeable degradation of image quality. Once you have arrived at that setting, you can use it in the future for similar images. Various types of images can be compressed to different levels, depending on the image's color, shape, and definition characteristics. For example, a graphic image will use an optimum compression level different from that of a photographic digital image.

Quality Factor

To make your file compression even more controllable, along with each of the sub-formats you choose, you may also choose a Quality Factor setting for your JPEG digital image. The quality of your image is defined as color depth, color accuracy, and *pixelation*. Pixelation is the effect that occurs when a continuous-tone image is mapped to various colored adjoining dots—actually squares, called pixels—in order to digitally simulate a photograph on a computer screen. The higher the resolution of an image the smaller the pixels will appear. An image is said to be "pixelated" if the square areas of color that represent the image are large enough to see, in turn distorting the appearance of the image.

In PHOTO-PAINT 6, the Quality Factor is controlled by moving a slider to values between 2 and 255 in a trade-off between quality and file size. Lower values produce higher quality and larger files, while higher values produce low quality but smaller files. Knowing the exact effects of these controls will come with practice. Digital photographs are much more sensitive to the effects of using lower quality settings and more lossy sub-formats because they contain more color, and it is the image color that usually suffers the most.

Progressive JPEG

The hottest new bitmap format on the Web is Progressive JPEG. Among other features, ProJPEG offers a "fade in" interlacing effect similar to GIF, but with all the fabulous color and compression capabilities of traditional JPEG. Among the browsers, ProJPEG is supported by Netscape Navigator, versions 2.X and up. Image editors have started to support this new format, and export filter plug-ins have begun to pop up, as well. You can check out the speed advantages of the format on Netscape's Web site at: <http://partner.netscape.com/eng/mozilla/2.0/relnotes/demo/pjpegdemo.html>.

Converting Between Formats

Begin preparing your image by saving it immediately in your image editor's native RGB format. Once saved as a native file, you'll have access to any of the formats the application supports.

One of the most confusing riddles you'll encounter is when trying to convert directly from one format to another. In most bitmap editing programs such as Photoshop, PHOTO-PAINT, or Paint Shop Pro, it just isn't possible to convert directly between certain formats. For example, if you open a JPEG file and try to save it directly to GIF, the GIF format is not listed as an option. This throws many designers off, often leading them to think their filters are missing or their file is corrupted. The GIF format won't be available if the JPEG image file currently contains more than GIF's maximum 256 colors. The option won't even show up in the list. In these cases, you'll have to convert the RGB file to indexed color before you can save it as a GIF file. Other programs, such as Fractal Design Painter, allow you to convert to GIF format when you save the file.

Working With 1-bit Images

Bitmap images can be imported into any image-editing package in a number of formats including TIFF, PCX, BMP, and PCD. All bitmap image files contain information about resolution, number of colors, color model used, pixel dimensions, and so on. While a bitmap image's color information may contain up to 32-bit CMYK (cyan, magenta, yellow, black) or 16.7 million colors, in this particular case, let's investigate the possibilities of line art on the Web.

Consider the bottom of the pile—the lowly 1-bit format. This digital file contains the very minimum of information needed to render a digital image—just black and white. Because 1-bit images are so compact, they are ideal for the Web in uses such as simple logos, brand labels, and so on. By starting at the 1-bit level, you are essentially operating in reverse, working your way *up* towards the maximum 256-color restriction of GIF file formats. This way you get to design with exactly the right colors, instead of forcing prepared images into decreased color modes.

The 1-bit image file can be saved to any resolution, but contains only the single color of black. When opened into any image editor, the 1-bit file is a monochrome bitmap containing only black and white. If you've prepared GIF images before, and have

By starting at the 1-bit level, you are essentially operating in reverse, working your way *up* towards the maximum 256-color restriction of GIF file formats.

gone through the process of down sampling a digital image to 256 colors or less, you'll likely realize that the process can also be done in reverse of that. The magic comes in when you discover that 1-bit images are easily manipulated, and carefully changing color composition only marginally increases file size. First, let's back up a little and find out which is the quickest way to go about getting a half-decent, 1-bit image into your computer.

Creative Resources

While there are several ways to create most digital images, there are twice as many available for 1-bit images. The first, and most obvious method of digitally converting an image would be to scan it in. You may also find suitable images at your local software vendor in the clip-art section. If you don't have a scanner, but have fax software, try faxing yourself an image and then copy the resulting image into your image editor using the clipboard.

Cyberspace can be a great resource for digital images. CompuServe, America Online, Prodigy, and the Internet provide a world of opportunities, allowing you to download an image that's already been digitized. In this case, you may need to confirm that the image you select isn't copyrighted or otherwise digitally protected. See the section, "Know Your Copyright Laws" in Chapter 2, "Creating Web Content" for more information. Regardless of the method you choose, the higher the resolution of your original image, the more detail will remain in your 1-bit conversion.

You may find that adjustments to the brightness and/or contrast of the original image are necessary to end up with a satisfactory 1-bit image before performing the conversion. To do this, use the color and brightness commands in your image editor. If you want to apply any distortion or artistic effects filters to the image, you should apply these before the image is converted. Once your images are converted to 1-bit, your editor will likely lock out any filter effects. Carefully applying effects filters to 1-bit images can have positive and dramatic design effects.

If you want to apply any distortion or artistic effects filters to the image, you should apply the filters before the image is converted.

After converting the image, decide exactly how you intend to change its characteristics, if at all. For example, if the image is an artistic rendering of a recognizable object such as someone's face, you may wish to leave it in the 1-bit mode. Eventually, you will need to reduce its resolution to 72 ppi and save it as a GIF format file.

Maximize Your Color Opportunities

Selecting an appropriate image is definitely a key factor for a successful effect. Ideally, your 1-bit image will contain lots of contrast and visual interest, such as the image of a swimmer splashing in the surf (see Figures 5-10 and 5-11). The original image was scanned as a grayscale image at a resolution of 300 dpi. The image was fine-tuned using an image editor's brightness and contrast filters. Then the image was converted into a 1-bit file. Proper tweaking ensured an even amount of shadows, highlights, and contrast. Following the conversion from grayscale to 1-bit, the image was converted to 16 colors, and carefully chosen hues were added.

Figure 5-10: This image of a swimmer has been converted to 1-bit as the first step in producing a 16-color image with the smallest file size possible. The original file size here is 187K when saved at 300 dpi at a size of 579 x 696.

Figure 5-11: This 16-color version down sampled to 290 x 348 takes up only 31K in GIF file format. (The colors do not show in this black reproduction.)

Adding a transparency mask for the white areas creates an interesting effect allowing the background of the Web page to show through.

The areas of the image including the facial features, background, and striped bathing suit all contain plenty of contrast to define the shapes, and add just enough visual information to make their form easily recognizable. Color was added using paint brush and fill tools. The white areas of the image allow the color to show through, while the colors selected hint at highlights, shadows, and depth.

Using Black in Design

The biggest benefit of using simple 1-bit images (or line art) for graphic embellishment is that you can apply all sorts of variations to a single theme or repeated bitmap. This allows you to create design elements for layouts or page designs without adding huge amounts of data to your image files. Simple 1-bit files take only a fraction of the memory required for grayscale or RGB color digital images.

The swimmer image, scanned at a resolution of 300 dpi, takes up a mere 93K of memory. This makes it easier to work with, quicker to save, and even faster to print. When resampled to 50 percent of the original size at 72 ppi, still without color, the image is reduced to a paltry 6K. In your use of 1-bit images you may even choose to leave the images in their native black. Adding a transparency mask for the white areas creates an interesting effect allowing the background of the Web page to show through. When used wisely, black images on a page have a powerful effect that commands attention.

Taking advantage of the power of these versatile little 1-bit images can be just one more of the tricks you can add to your growing collection of design solutions.

Providing Alternate Low Bandwidth Sites

Many sites are implementing what is referred to as *low bandwidth versions* of their Web sites. Low bandwidth versions are provided for the visitor who is accessing Web sites using either a slower-than-average modem, a limited bandwidth access provider, or both.

Encountering a low bandwidth link can be a warning that the site may contain excessive graphics, digital images, and backgrounds. Web sites that have implemented bandwidth links give visitors who aren't interested in visuals an option to take a side road to a similar Web site design that features the same facts and figures.

An example of a Web site design that is well suited for a low bandwidth version is One Color Communications. This print communications company is in the business of design and print so their marketing strategy relies heavily on slick advertising and colorful, splashy visual images (see Figure 5-12). Their Web site features a home page, that contains little in terms of images; high and low bandwidth versions; and advice for using the high bandwidth for access 28.8 kbps and over, and for using the low bandwidth version for access 14.4 kbps and lower. The difference between the parts of this site is substantial. Visual images on the low bandwidth side (see Figure 5-13) are smaller and more compressed, and navigation is provided strictly using text links. The higher bandwidth version features a much more elaborate interface with image maps for navigation, and so on (see Figure 5-14).

Figure 5-12: The home page of this communications company offers a fork in the road for users by offering low or high bandwidth Internet connections.

Figure 5-13: The low bandwidth version of this site still contains graphic images, they're just smaller and there are fewer of them.

Figure 5-14: The high bandwidth version features a no-holds-barred attitude in terms of images and their sizes.

Image Preparation Guidelines

In summary, trying to work with graphics on the Web is a tricky, detailed, and time-consuming business. However, the following guidelines form a basic design-related recipe for preparing any image for the Web:

✦ Use JPEG for continuous-tone images, and GIF for everything else.

✦ Save your images at no more than 72 pixels per inch (ppi).

✦ Use the Netscape 216 palette for your GIF images, to ensure image fidelity across browsers and platforms.

✦ Eliminate any unwanted or unnecessary visual information from your image.

✦ Avoid digitally enlarging poor-quality images.

✦ Always work with a copy of your original digital image.

✦ Apply any filter or image distortion effects prior to saving in either JPEG or GIF file formats and before your final resampling process.

✦ Never resample an image repeatedly. If you have to resample, always do so from (a copy of) the original.

✦ Never recompress a previously compressed image. Once again, always do so from an uncompressed (copy of) the original.

✦ Always choose the interlaced-image option when using GIF file formats, unless you specifically don't want it. The GIF interlaced option adds neither loading time nor significant file size to images.

✦ Alter suitable images to be stylized duotones or grayscale images to reduce their file sizes.

✦ Use uniform colors instead of gradations of color for graphical images to reduce the size of the color palette.

✦ Break up unavoidably large graphics into segments and load them individually.

✦ Partition graphic design elements containing both uniform and full-color images in an effort to reduce color palettes.

And finally, the last two guidelines relate to how you should specify the <IMG SRC> tag within your HTML document:

✦ Allow your text to completely load before your images do, by adding width and height tags (WIDTH="XX" HEIGHT="YY").

✦ Add an <ALT> tag to describe the images (ALT="this is the description") to accommodate those Web surfers who turn off image loading in their browsers.

Moving On

This chapter has closely examined digital image production techniques. As you have discovered, there is a technical side to creating digital content. This chapter describes many critical issues that affect your creative input and design abilities. The design-related decisions and procedures you choose to use ultimately determine the type and quality of images you include on your Web pages.

Just ahead in Chapter 6, "Advanced Design Techniques," you'll learn how to control page loading, organize and design forms, and collect visitor information. This chapter also gets into cool effects including animation and interactivity.

6

Advanced Design Features

Now that you're comfortable with and have had success using the basic design techniques, it's time to take your online design to the next level. This ambitious little chapter covers the more advanced tools in the HTML tool belt—forms, tables, frames, and animation. While the following pages are not intended to be a tutorial, they do provide practical design recommendations and investigate the more advanced features. You'll even learn about a cutting-edge Web design mechanism in the overview of the new HTML 3.2 Cascading Style Sheets standard, as implemented by Microsoft Internet Explorer 3.0.

Using Forms

The HTML form is at the core of the information gathering tools, providing site visitors with the means to submit their particulars (demographic or otherwise) to you instantaneously. The results can then be assimilated into your database without the need for business reply cards, keyboard operators, or telemarketers.

A form allows site visitors to submit their particulars (demographic or otherwise) to you instantaneously.

Forms can also be used to solicit feedback or to provide customized Web pages. They're also essential for entering usernames and passwords on protected sites. And believe it or not, the best forms can actually enhance the user experience. The information gathering form at the AutoWeek On Line Web site is an example of how much fun filling out a form can actually be (see Figure 6-1).

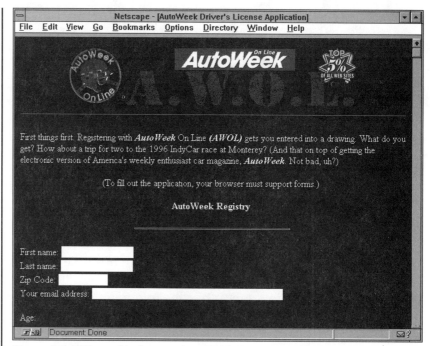

Figure 6-1: Fill out this form at AutoWeek On Line and you're entering a contest to win a trip for two to the 1996 IndyCar race in Monterey, California.

The AutoWeek form is easy to fill out. It merely asks for your name, zip code, e-mail address, age, gender, income, what kind of car you drive, and your three favorite cars of all time. This is a stroke of genius. How could someone not feel camaraderie after reminiscing about their three favorite rides? But perhaps the best thing about this form is the reassurance that it concludes with: "You want info about AutoWeek and AWOL and what we're doing? If so, we've got you covered. Don't worry: We won't sell your e-mail address to the horde of shameless marketeers out there!"

Designing Forms for Clarity

Sit back and think how much *you* hate filling out forms, and get ready for some role reversal. As the Web designer, it's your

As the Web designer, it's your responsibility to entice your visitors into using the forms at your site.

responsibility to entice your visitors into using the forms at your site. To ensure their use, you must design your forms to be simple, clear, and easy enough to be filled out correctly by any user.

Good form design is an art in its own right. If you've never had the peculiar pleasure of designing your own forms, get ready to undertake a joyous endeavor. HTML form design with a decent page editor can actually be fun! Figure 6-2 displays a number of goodies from the HTML form design bag. This simple (yet inelegant) page was created in just a few minutes, using Adobe PageMill.

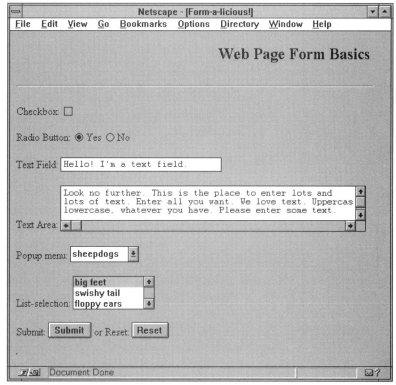

Figure 6-2: An annotated view of all your favorite HTML form tools.

Your goal as a Web form designer is to create an online apparatus that's both easy to use and highly functional. To accomplish such, HTML provides the following form controls:

✦ **Check boxes** for selecting individual items.

✦ **Radio buttons** to select one entry from a group of choices.

✦ **Password fields** to restrict site access.

✦ **Text fields** for single-line text entries.

✦ **Multiline text areas** for multiple-line text entries, such as site feedback.

✦ **Pop-up menus** to display a list of choices. Only one entry is shown until the visitor clicks the menu. They're best used with only a few entries.

✦ **List-selection fields** to display a more lengthy number of entries. They're scrollable and can be configured to accept more than one selection.

✦ **Submit and Reset buttons** to send and clear the form fields, respectively.

With all those form-building goodies, there are a multitude of design decisions to make. You've got to decide how to put things together and when to use one feature over another. For instance, when there are more than a few entries to display, you should choose a list-selection field over a pop-up menu.

The following pointers will help you create successful forms:

✦ Order questions to follow the user's logical progression of thought, not the Web site's (perhaps hidden) agenda.

✦ Don't cram too much information into too little space.

✦ Use HTML's Table command to control alignment and spacing attributes.

✦ Make sure all type is large enough to read.

✦ Avoid building forms over a textured background.

✦ Stay away from dark colored backgrounds, as well. Some features, such as radio buttons, will not display properly on dark backgrounds.

✦ Above all, keep your forms simple and consistent.

What Happens on the Back End?

When a form is submitted by the browser to the Web server, it interacts with a Common Gateway Interface (CGI) script. CGI allows the information to be submitted to a database or used on a customized page. For the Web designer, creating the HTML forms is the easy part. Creating the CGI script to do something worthwhile with the data is what's tricky.

Before you begin to build any form, it's a good idea to consult your Web system administrator. Many of the decisions on how to implement a script are platform-dependent. If your Web server is running on a UNIX platform, the CGI is probably written in Perl. On Macintosh, the CGIs are commonly written in AppleScript. Most of these schemes exist outside of the area of a Web designer's expertise. Thankfully, a number of applications have surfaced to help nonprogrammers create their own scripts. On the Macintosh side, Maxum Development's NetForms is the most popular way to create interactive forms, without becoming a total geek. On the Windows side, O'Reilly's PolyForm holds much the same promise.

Collecting Information

There are three key steps in the information submission cycle. You've got to:

1. Pull your Web site visitors in with some goodies.

2. Ask your visitors the right questions.

3. Complete the cycle by thanking your visitors for their time and effort.

If you miss any one of these three steps, you can risk the whole reason for your Web site's existence (which is, most likely, some type of marketing venture).

Your purpose for collecting data will drive the questions you ask. Consequently, the questions you ask will drive the design of the form. It comes down to the classic battle of *what you need* vs. *what they'll give you.* To be effective, you must spend time looking at it from the visitor's point-of-view. Your visitors should come away from your site feeling good about the experience, not feeling that their personal privacy has been violated. While the questions need to be sensitive to the visitor's psyche, it's equally important to ensure that the answers will fit into the scheme of your database.

Offering Incentives

While many people perceive that everything on the Web is free for the taking, this is most certainly not the case. In the real world of the Web, everything has its price. It's customary to use an incentive to entice visitors to fill out a form. While everyone can't give away a trip to Monterey, there's probably some form of incentive that you or your firm can offer. If you don't want to run a contest, think about what types of promotional materials you can give away. Sometimes, the mere promise of more information is incentive enough.

Asking the Right Questions

If you're going to go through the trouble of setting up an information gathering apparatus on your site, be sure that you're asking the right questions. And if you're working for a big company, it's justification to huddle up with the marketing and MIS folks to determine exactly what the right questions are, and how the data will fit in the grand corporate scheme.

Providing Feedback

What goes around comes around. In addition to soliciting feedback on your site, it's a nice touch to provide feedback to the visitor. If someone sends in a form, there should always be a "thank you for your feedback" page. It's also good to follow up with an e-mail thank you, as well. Without a thank you page or letter, visitors are left with a hollow feeling.

It's important to note that even if you do not have the capability to run CGI scripts on your Web site, you still have the ability to solicit feedback. The HTML Mailto: command provides a quick and easy way to hear what your visitors have to say.

Using Tables

Learning how to effectively use HTML's Table command is a key step in taking total control over your Web page layouts. Coding tables by hand can be the exemplification of HTML-disarray. The high level of frustration—as you search for the one code that's made the whole table go bonkers—is akin to being stuck in bumper-to-bumper traffic on the freeway, with the next exit miles ahead. You know you'll get there—eventually.

The Table command can be used to present multicolumn pages, as well as spreadsheets and other tabular information. Thankfully, second-generation visual Web page editors, such as Adobe PageMill 2.0, make table creation a code-free breeze. Of course, the codes are still there, but they're hidden beneath the surface, as they should be. The goal is not to create beautiful code, but to create beautiful tables. While the former can lead to the latter, it does not necessitate that you spend your days and nights hacking away with a text editor.

Using Tables to Control Page Margins

Tables allow you to effectively set your page margins, and provide for a well-behaved page. Before the Table command was implemented in Netscape Navigator 1.1, Web pages were uncontrollable from a page layout standpoint, as text would always reflow to fit the width of the browser window. With a simple one-column table, however, it's easy to take total control over the page margins (see Figure 6-3).

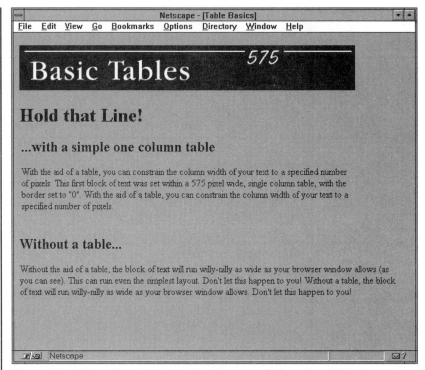

Figure 6-3: Tables allow you to set text to a specified pixel-width column.

Simple one-column tables can be built to hold the text to the width of the widest graphic. This keeps page margins consistent when they're viewed at different browser widths. If users resize their browsers, the text will stay within the column width you've specified. Almost any Web page can benefit from this judicious use of the Table command. A simple one-column table, such as that used in Figure 6-3, is remarkably easy to implement.

Using Tables to Create Multicolumn Pages

Multicolumn pages can help to set your Web site apart from the crowd, without exhausting your financial, physical, or mental resources.

Multicolumn layouts allow you to create more effective Web pages. The options afforded by multiple columns allow for unique, diverse, and interesting designs. And even more importantly, shorter text column widths make text passages easier to read. Conventional wisdom (and countless theses, no doubt) has shown that the less distance the eye has to travel, the greater the reader's comprehension level. That's why just about every publication of note uses multiple columns in print. The same reasoning works online, as well. Multicolumn pages can set your Web site apart from the crowd, without exhausting your financial, physical, or mental resources. They impart a polished feel and sense of order; one which most people come to expect from most forms of communication, whether online or in print.

HTML 2.0 (and up) provides a variety of table controls, including column width and alignment. Table and column width can be expressed either absolutely (in pixels) or relatively (as a percentage of the browser window's width). Horizontal alignment can be specified as left, right, center, or justify, while vertical alignment can be set as top, middle, or bottom. Controls are also provided for the amount of space between cells and the amount of space between the edge of the cell and the contents.

As you design tables, be sure to include enough white space between columns to give the eye a place to stop and rest. Don't jam your columns together, just to "make it fit." Leave enough space so that your text and graphics can breathe freely.

Two- and three-column pages are a little harder to implement than one-column pages but they're really not that tough as long as you take your time and think things through. Figure 6-4 shows a simple layout with a pair of equally sized (285-pixel-wide) columns. Notice that the two columns are almost touching because they lack gutter space—and that's not a good thing! Figure 6-5 shows how additional gutter space aids readability, while Figure 6-6 illustrates how the additional white space was added by using borders to delineate the rows.

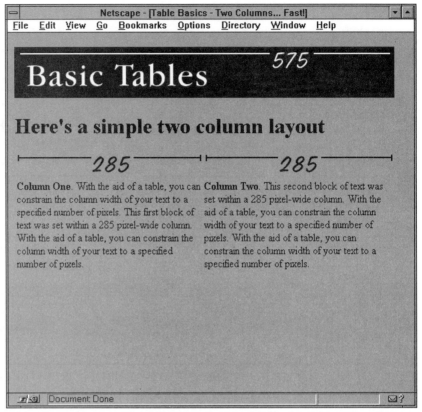

Figure 6-4: A two-column Web page without enough white space between the columns.

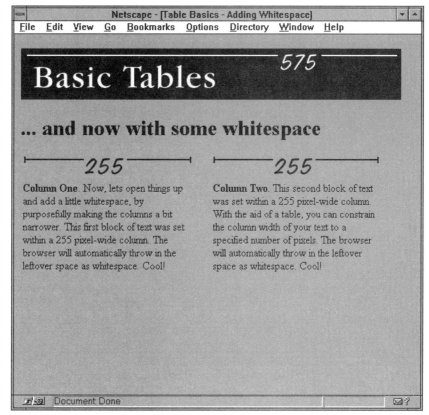

Figure 6-5: A two-column Web page, opened up a bit with a touch of white space.

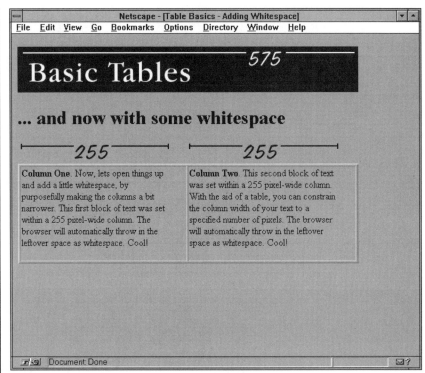

Figure 6-6: A two-column Web page with white space added by using borders to delineate the rows.

Three-column layouts are among the most popular designs on the Web. The first, narrow column is often used for a vertical navigation bar. To implement a basic, three-column layout, starting with a 575-pixel-wide page, divide the page into a 100 pixel-wide toolbar column and two 205-pixel-wide text columns. This leaves 70 pixels to be distributed equally between the columns (see Figure 6-7).

Figure 6-7: Three-column layouts allow for a vertical navigation bar and two columns of text and graphics.

Here are some pointers for creating columnar pages:

✦ Create your page at a reasonable maximum width, say 600 pixels.

✦ Don't use too many columns.

✦ Remember to build enough white space into the design to allow columns to breathe.

✦ Stay away from very narrow text columns. If users have their browsers set with the default type set too large, it will create havoc on the page.

✦ Only use table borders when there's a compelling reason to do so. When you do use them, don't use too heavy a weight.

✦ Don't fret over browsers that can't handle tables. These days, not many browsers *can't* handle tables.

Getting Tabular

Although HTML tables do not provide the total flexibility that you may be accustomed to from spreadsheet applications, such as Lotus 1-2-3 and Microsoft Excel, there's still plenty of power beneath the surface. Before Netscape implemented the Table command, Web page tables were grim little documents, limited to what people could hack out with the <PRE> preformatted text command (see Figure 6-8). The <PRE> command makes everything appear literally as it looks in the text editor. Setting up a table with <PRE> text means that you'll be banging away at the spacebar.

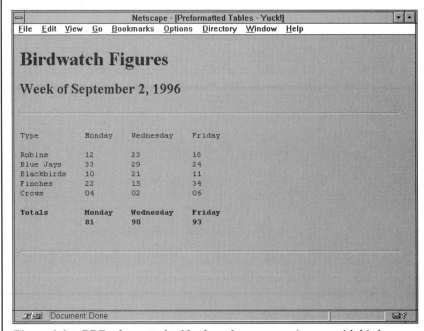

Figure 6-8: <PRE> formatted tables have become passé, even with bird watchers.

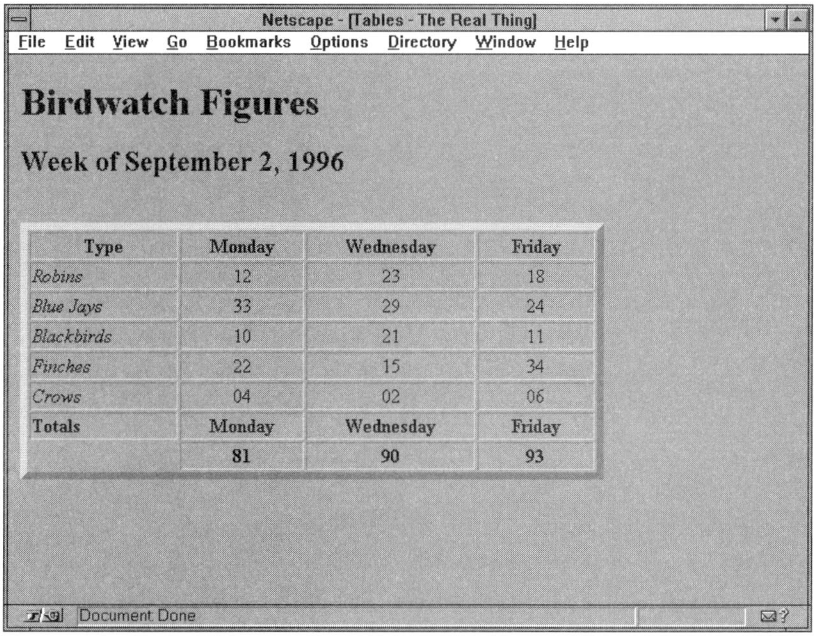

Figure 6-9: The Table command allows you to set alignment and use real fonts, rather than living with a dull, monospaced, typewriter look.

The Table command allows you to set up some rather intricate spreadsheets. Figure 6-9 is an example of how the bird watchers' page might look if the information were placed into a proper table. It was created by saving a WordPerfect table in HTML format. There are a score of different ways to prepare tables. Working in an HTML-aware word processor or spreadsheet is just one option. In general, the higher the level of visual controls an application can provide, the easier your table-building life will be.

Much of what was said earlier regarding multicolumn pages applies to tabular information, as well. Here are a few additional hints:

✦ Experiment with the different alignment commands to achieve the proper look for each row and column.

✦ Use a smaller type size, when necessary.

✦ Be realistic about how many columns you can fit in a table while maintaining readability. You may want to break large tables into two chunks.

Designing With Frames

Frames, introduced by Netscape Navigator 2.0 in late 1995, divide the browser window into distinct areas of online real estate. Framed Web pages have the dubious distinction of being both intensely loved and vehemently hated. But, when they're done the right way (and for good reason), frames will enhance your Web site's user interface.

> When they're done the right way (and for good reason), frames will enhance your Web site's user interface.

Why Use Frames?

Now there's a question that you should ask yourself *every* time you contemplate using a framed design. Before considering frames, examine the reasons to use them. You do not have to add frames just because you can (or because your competition is using them). Instead, you should have valid justification to use frames in your design, before you proceed.

The most compelling aspect of frames is that they allow you to maintain static information, such as site ID and navigational toolbars, while presenting a big window full of variable information. As such, a wide range of Web sites may lend themselves to a framed interface. Placing the navigation bar and site ID into their own (non-scrolling) frames is perhaps the best solution to the "where should they go, and what happens when they scroll off the screen?" dilemma. By putting this information in frames, you're assured that it'll always be right at hand. Chapter 3, "Designing Web Pages," provides other options for where and how to implement navigational tool bars.

In short, a number of page elements may lend themselves to having their own persistent frames, including:

✦ Navigation bars

✦ Site ID banners

◆ Advertising banners

◆ Frequently updated information, such as stock quotes or other market information

Figure 6-10 shows the home page of the mythical "little seaside flower shop." Two of the three frames provide static information. The top frame contains only the banner graphic, while the left frame displays a scrolling selection of flower thumbnails. The flower photos are, in effect, the navigational structure of the site. When a user clicks a flower thumbnail, information or photographs specific to the selected thumbnail appear in the main window (see Figure 6-11).

Figure 6-10: Visitors to "the little seaside flower shop" are greeted by this explanatory front page.

Figure 6-11: Selecting the daylily thumbnail yields a larger photograph and pricing information.

A similar arrangement might work well for a car dealer, furniture manufacturer, or other consumer goods establishment, where quick access to a large variety of visual images is of utmost importance to the audience. A large scrolling frame allows you to present more information on a page, without the worries you'd have of losing the user on a huge nonframed page.

How Frames Work

The mere thought of designing with frames can be intimidating to the untrained Web developer. It shouldn't be. A framed page is nothing more than a container for other HTML pages. It doesn't contain a huge amount of information, other than the size, placement, and specifications of the horizontal (row) and vertical (column) frames. In effect, each frame says, "I'm here. I'm this big. This is the HTML file to use, and here's my name. You can scroll and resize me (or not)."

Once you begin to examine the inner workings of the frames, the mysteries quickly unfold. There's no black magic, just straightforward syntax. The FRAMESET command tells the browser where a frame is located and how large it is, while the FRAME SRC command takes care of the rest. Links can be one of the most difficult things to implement properly for the neophyte frame builder. The first step is to always name each frame, and remember to use the TARGET modifier in the linking command.

Guidelines for Framed Pages

Frames have fostered a wide range of design innovation. And that's a very good thing. In helping to avoid complacency in online design, frames force the designer to consider how users interact with the electronic page. As such, the guidelines for online design are in a state of perpetual revision.

One of the most fascinating concepts is to change the way that people interact with the information by flipping the navigational axis. The Motor Trend Web site uses an intriguing horizontal scrolling scheme to help bring the magazine experience to their online pages, as shown in Figure 6-12. By doing so, Motor Trend's site has literally set online design on end. It can be disconcerting at first, to scroll sideways instead of down, but the interface quickly grows on you.

Figure 6-12: Visitors to the Motor Trend Web site are presented with a unique horizontal interface.

Here are some pointers on when and how to use frames:

✦ Don't go frame wild. Limit the number of frames per page to four at the very most. Three should be sufficient for most applications.

✦ Use frames only when they're appropriate. They're a means to an end, not the end unto themselves.

✦ Place the frames consistently on your pages. Don't vary the placement and size from page to page.

✦ Keep your navigation clean and elegant.

✦ Carefully plan and test your navigation to ensure that all the links function properly.

✦ Clearly label and define each frame.

✦ Turn scroll bars off if they serve no purpose in a particular frame (set SCROLLING=NO).

✦ Do not allow certain frames, such as advertising and site ID banners, to be resized.

✦ Place banner graphics as backgrounds, rather than inline images, to avoid margins.

Provide a Nonframed Version

It's more than polite to provide a nonframed version of your pages—it's practically de rigueur. Unfortunately, this may not always be possible, due to time and budget constraints. If you make the commitment to creating framed pages, without providing a nonframed version, you should be aware that a certain portion of your visitors may become alienated. Frames aren't for everyone, and in truth, some folks just don't like frames in any form, whatsoever.

All too often, you'll see highly framed pages that put gee-whiz techno-skill before good old design talent. And that doesn't cut it in the Web page design business. Once again, if you're planning to use frames, make sure that you have a compelling reason to do so, or play it safe, and stick to using tables, instead.

Cascading Style Sheets

In the Spring of 1996, the World Wide Web Consortium (WC3) set the *Cascading Style Sheets* (CSS) standard into the HTML 3.2 specification. Although you've probably grown accustomed to Netscape's being the vanguard of browser development, Microsoft upped the browser ante when they included Cascading Style Sheets in Internet Explorer 3.0 (IE). Microsoft let out a big cry of "carpe diem" by embracing the standard when they rolled out a beta version of IE that supported CSS shortly after the WC3 announcement. Although some would say that Netscape was left in the dust, it was an accepted fact that Microsoft was involved in the development of CSS for quite a while before the CSS-aware version of Explorer hit the streets.

CSS allows Web page creators to add styles—including specific font, color, margin, vertical alignment, letter- and line-spacing information—to text tags. Although stylesheets are commonly accepted features in the print communications world, they're revolutionary enhancements for the World Wide Web. If you've done much work in a page layout application, such as QuarkXPress or Adobe PageMaker, the mechanism should be quite familiar.

With Cascading Style Sheets, you can create one stylesheet file to apply to all the pages on a particular Web site. By making changes to that one stylesheet file, all the files on the site are automatically updated to the new style. This feature can be of great importance in corporate settings where there are huge volumes of pages to maintain. Designers using CSS can help to ensure a consistency between their pages. The coding within the document remains very similar to traditional HTML, with the big difference being a style tag at the start of the file. Although users can use their own stylesheets, the site designer's styles often take precedence (which is where the concept of "cascading" comes into play).

All in all, the HTML 3.2 standard provides some pretty powerful controls. Here's a rundown of some of its other features:

✦ **Enhanced Tables.** Rows, columns, and individual cells can be assigned specific colors, widths, and styles. There are different settings for inner and outer table borders.

✦ **Floating Frames.** They've broken free of their moorings (see Figure 6-13). No longer will your frames be stuck to the edges of your browser.

✦ **Two-Color Blended Backgrounds.** Blends can follow one of eight compass-like settings. "Give me a due West blend from black to blue!"

✦ **Background Image Tiling Control.** Now you can choose how your background textures tile.

✦ **Fixed Position Backgrounds.** Drop a picture anywhere and make it stick.

✦ **Border Styles.** When a simple 3D border is not enough.

Cascading Style Sheets allow pages to be backwards compatible with older browsers. But CSS backwards compatibility doesn't mean that the pages will look anywhere near the same, or that they'll contain the same information. Figure 6-13 displays a page from Microsoft's Web site, as viewed with a beta version of Internet Explorer 3.0. While this page looks pretty cool, it's not clear exactly how cool it is, until you view the exact same page with Netscape Navigator (see Figure 6-14).

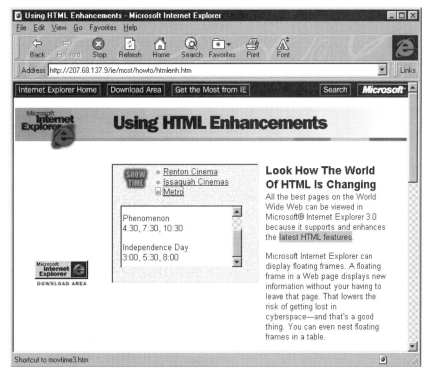

Figure 6-13: This page with Cascading Style Sheets, as viewed in Microsoft Internet Explorer 3.0.

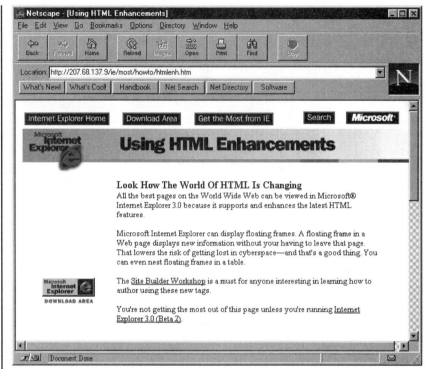

Figure 6-14: The same page, as viewed in Netscape Navigator 2.02.

Notice how the Show Time box is missing in Figure 6-14? That's because Navigator does not support floating frames. And check out the *real* font used for the headline in the Internet Explorer version (not to mention the nifty highlighted text).

Only time will tell if CSS will become commonplace in Web page design. For its part, Netscape has always written its own agenda (and extensions to HTML). Since CSS is an approved standard, however, it's a good bet that it will eventually be implemented in newer versions of all browsers. Regardless, and until that happens, this new standard faces an uphill fight.

Animating Your Web Pages

There's something undeniably compelling about an animated Web page. Onscreen action immediately grabs the viewers' attention, forcing them to take notice. Animation can be as simple as a spinning globe or as complex as a fully-rendered, three-dimensional scene. The possibilities have quickly expanded from the most basic of screen shows into fully interactive online experiences. In the early days of the Web, animation was reserved only for technically astute Web designers. These days, however, anyone can add animation to their Web pages as easily as they can add an inline graphic.

Animation works by displaying a series of images on the browser. The manner in which the images are delivered to the browser is determined by which method you choose for delivery. The four most widely accepted ways to deliver Web page animation are server push/client pull, Graphics Interchange Format (GIF), Shockwave, and Java. Figure 6-15 displays six frames of a simple animation. The individual images were prepared in an illustration program, converted to GIF format, and touched up in Photoshop.

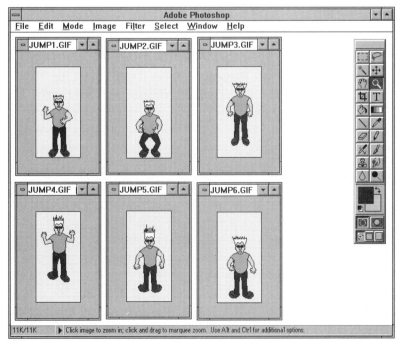

Figure 6-15: Animation, no matter the format, is based on displaying a series of frames to simulate movement.

Every page isn't a candidate to receive an animation. You must determine whether an animation adds to your users' online experience, or whether it just ends up irritating them. This is another situation where alternate demo test pages will serve you well. Try both an animated and a nonanimated page on your test subjects, and pay close heed to their observations.

If you decide that a page should include animation, you must then choose the most suitable method to deliver the goods. The next section takes a look at the four aforementioned delivery techniques.

Server Push & Client Pull

You don't hear much about *server push* these days, as this server-based animation technique has all but outlived its usefulness. Both server push and *client pull* work by displaying a series of files that have been downloaded individually from the Web server. The illusion of motion (or whatever) is created as each subsequent file is downloaded and displayed. The restrictions of file size and bandwidth have everything to do with the speed at which a server push or client pull animation will play.

Server Push

In the days between Netscape Navigator 1.1 and 2.0, server push was the most prevalent form of online animation. With server push, a CGI script opens up the pipe, and continually pushes a stream of new images out to the browser. This continues (and the pipe remains open) until either the sequence of files ends or the browser halts the flow by breaking the connection. This can be done by hitting the Stop button or clicking off to another site.

Server push, by nature, is very bandwidth-intensive and works best with tight little, limited-palette animation. If you decide (for some unknown reason) that you'd like to use a server push animation, consult your server administrator before proceeding too far. You'll have to check to see if a suitable CGI script exists or if one can be written. And even more importantly, you've got to be sure that your server has enough bandwidth to deliver the files at an acceptable rate.

Client Pull

Client pulls are different from server pushes, in that instead of the server controlling the flow of files, it's the browser that actually requests each file. This is accomplished by inserting code into the HTML page that forces the browser to ask for files. Unlike a server push, a client pull opens and closes the pipe each time a file is transferred. Consequently, server pushes are faster, because the connection does not have to be negotiated each time a file is sent.

Although few designers use client pulls for graphic animation, they have a very unique purpose in Web design life. Have you ever been to a Web site that automatically sent you a succession of pages? In all likelihood, that was done with a client pull. One of the most polite ways to implement a client pull is to create a "sorry that page has moved to" page. You can set the page up so that it displays its message and then automatically jumps to the new location after 15 seconds or so. This graciously gives your visitors enough time to read the information, and puts them where they want to be, without requiring any input.

GIF89a Animation

Netscape Navigator 2.0 brought Web page animation to the common user, in late 1995, in the form of GIF89a. Although the format had been around for years, Navigator was the first browser to introduce it to the World Wide Web. As GIF89a animation spread like wildfire, Netscape's competition scrambled to add the playback capability to their browsers. The GIF89a animation format is inherently compatible; you don't need a special plug-in to enjoy the experience (as long as you're using Netscape Navigator or Microsoft Internet Explorer, versions 2.0 or later, that is).

In short, there is no faster, more simple, or inexpensive way to put animation on your Web pages. There's no programming to learn or huge learning curve to master, since GIF animation is implemented by using the HTML <IMG SRC> tag. You can use existing animation files in your Web pages as easily as you use electronic clip art. Or you can create your own animation, with a

Server pushes are faster, because the connection does not have to be negotiated each time a file is sent.

variety of software. And best of all, if you're working on a Macintosh, you don't have to drop a dime on any expensive new animation-creation software. The most popular Mac-based GIF animation tool, Yves Piguet's GIF Builder (see Figure 6-16), is freeware! Windows Web designers get off almost as cheap. Steve Rimmer's GIF Construction Set is affordably priced "bookware." (If you like, and use, Steve's software, he asks that you buy a copy of his novel.) You'll find both programs on the *Looking Good Online CD-ROM.*

CD-ROM

The most popular Mac-based GIF animation tool, Yves Piguet's GIF Builder, is freeware! Windows Web designers get off almost as cheap.

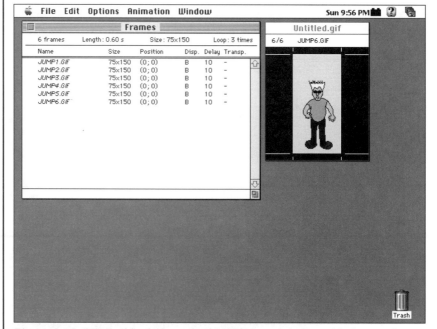

Figure 6-16: GIF Builder lets you build GIF89a animation with drag-and-drop ease.

GIF animation files are extremely versatile, and there are scores of uses for the little critters. Basic animated images can be used as bullets, buttons, and separators. Intricate animated GIFs can even be used as advertising banners and image maps, as long as you keep in mind that the smaller the animation, the smoother it will play.

GIF Animation Guidelines

Animated GIFs are multipart files. In addition to including a number of frames, they carry the information necessary to display those frames at a predefined speed and manner. Knowing how to properly tweak the settings can make the difference between an amateurish- and a professional-looking animation. Here are some things to keep in mind as you build your animation files:

+ Set the proper interframe delay. Avoid using the "as fast as possible" setting, as that results in vastly different playback speeds on different machines.

+ Use animation files sparingly. Perhaps only one or two animation elements per page. Don't let your Web pages turn into a carnival.

+ Keep them tight. Limit the palette, the number of frames, and the image size to assure speedy downloads.

+ Don't use interlacing. It can detract from the quality of the animation.

+ Avoid infinite loops. Set a specific number of loops to avoid hard drive racking at the browser (even though the first round of browsers don't support the loop command).

+ Use the proper disposal method. Throw out each frame, to avoid digital litter.

Trolling for Animated GIFs

While there's a wide range of Web sites that specialize in animated GIFs, there's no one source that can compare to the Tru Realities GIF Animation Gallery. Webmistress Marlina Mahoney has built a staggering site that houses well over a thousand animated images on its server. These range from a raft of rotating buttons and a slew of funky rules, all the way up to scores of full-blown three dimensional scenes. The framed interface, as shown by Figure 6-17 (there's also a nonframed version), packs a ton of images into a tight
little site.

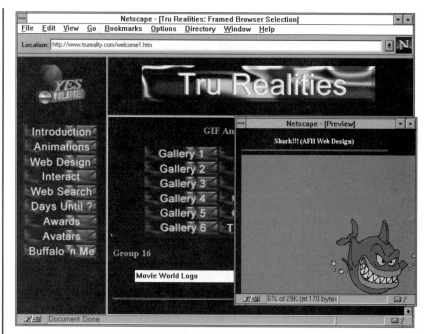

Figure 6-17: Tru Realities is the ultimate resource for GIF89a animation files.

Marlina uses a number of nifty tricks to implement the Tru Realities Web site. Client side image maps and drop-down lists are used to choose between the different galleries and separate collections. And a cool JavaScript hack allows each animation to playback in its own separate preview window. In addition to the exhaustive galleries, Tru Realities is also the home of "The GRAND Competition" for GIF89a animation. The huge GIF89a collection should provide enough animated images for most people, but if you're still looking for more, check out one of the following sites:

+ **The 1st Internet Gallery of GIF89a Animation**
  http://members.aol.com/royalef/gallery.htm

+ **The GIF Animation Thrift Shop**
  http://www.tiac.net/users/stacey/gifshop.html

+ **Rose's Animated GIFs**
  http://www.wanderers.com/rose/animate.html

Shockwave

Macromedia's Shockwave is the most ubiquitous form of interactive animation on the World Wide Web. It delivers synchronized sound, scripting, and a professional level feature set. Shockwave presentations can be created with either Macromedia Director or Authorware (on both Windows and Macintosh platforms). These programs allow for a high level of interactivity that can catapult your Web site from the mundane to the truly shocking.

In order to view a Shockwave animation, you must have the Shockwave plug-in loaded. Once you've loaded the plug-in, the best place to begin checking things out is Macromedia's Shockwave Epicenter (http://www.macromedia.com/shockwave/epicenter/index.html). The Epicenter (see Figure 6-18) features the work of a large number of professional-quality "shocked" Web sites, from cute animation sequences through full-blown games. The Director user base, which numbers upwards of a quarter-million strong, has been proactive in peddling their prodigious talent on the World Wide Web, and Macromedia's been a great cheerleader (or shall we say, ringleader?) for their clients.

Macromedia's Shockwave allows for a high level of interactivity that can catapult your Web site from the mundane to the truly shocking.

Figure 6-18: The Macromedia Shockwave Epicenter showcases the talents of many professional Web development efforts.

When you build an animation sequence in Macromedia Director, you're given total control over what happens online. Figure 6-19 displays our little jumping guy on the Director stage. The program allows you to tweak an infinite number of settings, with control over stereo sound, fades, type, and more. There are so many floating palettes that you'll go out looking for a bigger monitor.

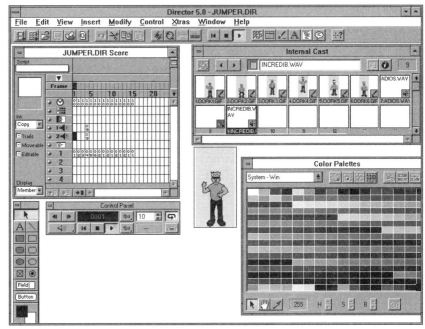

Figure 6-19: Creating an interactive animation in Macromedia Director is akin to scoring a movie.

Check out these Web sites for some cool Shockwave goodies:

✦ **Marc's Shockwave Shop**
   http://mediaband.com/shockwave/index.html

✦ **Shock-Bauble Showcase**
   http://www.pcslink.com/~sbullock/abtboble.htm

✦ **Pop Rocket's Game Arena**
   http://www.poprocket.com/shockwave/

Java Animation

Java animation is several notches above GIF animation, in that it can include sound and conditional responses. Since Java is a full-fledged programming language, it opens up an entire world of animation possibilities. The earliest Java animation efforts were hacked out the old-fashioned way—in code. It didn't take long for the software developers to figure out that Java animation was a hot ticket. Although the tools are just beginning to come to light, Java animation holds great promise.

> Since Java is a full-fledged programming language, it opens up an entire world of animation possibilities.

Sausage Software's Egor Animator (http://www.sausage.com) was the first Window's program to deliver Java animation-creation capabilities to the masses. Egor Animator, version 2.0, offers a number of impressive features. The program allows you to assign URLs and sounds to individual animation frames, as well as providing an overall animation soundtrack. For a mere fifty bucks, you could do a lot worse. And, if you don't have the time or desire to create your own animation frames, Egor Animator also comes bundled with a slew of canned animation files, in a special "Weenies" pack, for an additional 25 dollars.

Macromedia's PowerApplets (http://www.macromedia.com/software/powerapplets/index.html) are another good choice for adding Java animation to your Web site, without resorting to code. PowerApplets are little Java programs (they're also available in Shockwave variants) for creating animated banners, bullets, image maps, icons, and logos. Macromedia's AppletAce allows you to quickly customize the animated images by simply filling out forms. And best of all, Macromedia has made their PowerApplets and AppletAce freely available for download on their Web site!

How to Decide Which Type of Animation to Use

With four different types of animation to choose from, you might be confused as to which type of animation you should use. You'll probably want to make these decisions on a case-by-case basis, rather than as a generalization, but here are some guidelines:

✦ **Server Push.** Put this one out to pasture. Its days are pretty much over.

✦ **Client Pull.** Great for sending down a series of pages or for automatically updating a page on a set schedule.

✦ **GIF89a.** Use for most general purpose, silent animation files.

✦ **Shockwave.** Best used for interactive pieces, including synchronized sound and streaming audio. While it requires a plug-in, it's one of the WWW's most popular.

✦ **Java.** Falls somewhere between GIF89a and Shockwave. Allows for interactivity and sound, but user-level (non-programmer's) tools are just beginning to surface, as of this writing.

Moving On

Advanced design techniques can put your Web site into a whole new realm. But, don't get sucked into tacking on the technology, just for the sake of the technology. There should be solid justification for implementing the latest and greatest gewgaws and wizardry. Keep in mind that the technology was created to work for you, not vise versa.

And along those same lines, Chapter 7, "Common Design Mistakes," takes a look at some widespread faults that have befallen many a Web site.

7

Common Design Mistakes

The road to Web site design success is filled with potholes and detours. This chapter helps you plan your route, and avoid the common maladies that can sidetrack a Web site. By learning about the mistakes that others have made, you'll be forewarned about the rough road that lies ahead.

On a successful Web site, *everything* is done by design. As such, design mistakes go beyond what one might think of as purely design-based problems. Most flaws fall under one of four broad categories: promotion, design, performance, and maintenance.

Promotion Issues: Make Sure They Find Your Site

The greatest site in the world will be ineffective and unproductive if the intended audience can't find its way to the site's front door. Therefore, it is essential to make your Web site as easy to find as possible. There's a wide range of ways to promote your site without incurring huge additional costs. All of the suggestions that follow are either low- or no-cost endeavors. As your site is under development, it's essential to keep your promotional opportunities in mind. And once your site is up and running, you've got to keep up with the public relations (PR) assault.

Mistake #1: Having an Obscure Domain Name

Does your Web site warrant its own unique domain name, such as http://www.littleflowerstore.com, rather than something obscure like http://www.users.bobslittleisp.com/commercial/mall/littleflowerstore.html? Of course it does! A unique domain name helps your audience find (and remember) your site, and it fits more readily on your promotional materials and other printed matter. It also gives your site the added panache it deserves, helping it to stand out among its competition.

InterNIC, the regulatory agency responsible for doling out domain names, charges $50 to register a domain name. You can reach the InterNIC Directory and Database Services by calling 800-862-0677; once you've selected a domain name, you can register it with InterNIC by calling 703-742-4777. Then you'll have to shell out another $50 for the yearly maintenance fee. If your site is running on someone else's Web server, they can probably help you get your own domain for an additional fee. All things considered, registering your own domain is a minuscule expense when compared to the benefits it brings.

No doubt, you've noticed that many domain names for your favorite companies end with ".com." Such suffixes denote the type of organization that an address is for. In the United States, Web addresses fall under one of the following categories:

◆ .com—commercial enterprise

◆ .edu—education, such as colleges and universities

◆ .org—nonprofit organizations

◆ .net—network service providers

◆ .mil—military operations

◆ .gov—government

Unfortunately, unique domain names are getting increasingly hard to come by. If you intend to use a popular or common name, there's a good chance that it will already be in use. For

Registering a unique domain name gives your site the added panache it deserves, helping it to stand out among its competition.

instance, when Acme Markets decided to put up a Web site, they were locked out of using www.acme.com, as it was already registered by Acme Laboratories (see Figures 7-1 and 7-2). Software developer and consultant Jef Poskanzer uses ACME Laboratories as his business name, and notes on his home page that "the only affiliation between ACME Laboratories and Warner Brothers is that I've been a fan of Wile E. Coyote for thirty years."

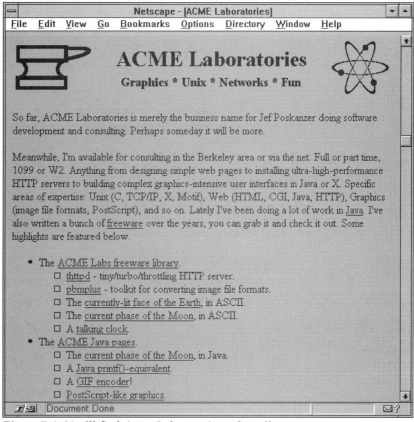

Figure 7-1: You'll find Acme Laboratories at http://www.acme.com.

Figure 7-2: If you're looking for Acme Markets, you'd better try http://www.acmemarkets.com.

Unless your company is instantly recognizable by its acronym, think twice about using one as your domain name.

When users need to look for a company on the Web, they may start by probing the search engines, or they may just try opening a location by typing in the company name in various combinations. While it's very cool to have your company name and domain name in synch, it's just not always possible. As such, you may be forced into choosing a different option.

It may take some inventive thinking to come up with a suitable alternative. Acronyms are one possibility, but they can raise more questions than they answer. Unless your company is instantly recognizable by its acronym, think twice about using one as your domain name. Consider a related word or phrase instead. One of the best examples is Ragú's eat.com, as shown in

Figure 7-3. Hungry users are greeted by a wise (and wisecracking) Mama. As she leads you into the living room or the kitchen, Mama shares some recipes and teaches you a little Italian, too!

The shorter your URL is, the better off you'll be. As with eat.com, users only have to recall three letters to land at fun.com, shown in Figure 7-4. Virtual Office, Inc., the company responsible for fun.com, shrewdly snapped up the domain name, along with such easy-to-remember addresses as bank.net, hospital.net, mobile.office.com, school.net, shop.com, today.com, and virtual.office.com. The Virtual Office site goes into depth on the subject of the mad URL grab. In the rush to reserve domain names, there have even been reports of people registering common names and words, simply to hold them hostage.

Figure 7-3: If you're hungry, stop into Mama's kitchen at eat.com, courtesy of Ragú.

Figure 7-4: When the kids are ready to play, check out Virtual Office's fun.com.

Keep in mind that your domain name may not be your Web site's complete Web address. You may be running multiple servers off the same domain, as with mobile.office.com and virtual.office.com.

Mistake #2: Lack of PR

Launching a Web site is similar to the marketing roll out of any important new product. As such, it's important to be properly prepared so that you aim at your target market, before you fire off the public relations' cannons.

In general, you should make sure that your press releases go out in a timely manner. Be realistic and don't waste your time filling them with superfluous drivel. Savvy press people see through the hyperbole. While this might seem like obvious

Don't fill your press releases with superfluous drivel. Savvy press people see through the hyperbole.

advice, you'd be amazed at the sheer volume of garbage that's shoveled out to the press. Here are some hints for the efficient use of electronic press releases that apply to large and small entities alike:

- ✦ Try not to send out your press release until your Web site is up and running. If you absolutely must send it out before-hand, include the date when the site will go live.

- ✦ Consider using PRNewswire or Business Wire to distribute your press release online.

- ✦ E-mail your press release only to relevant press people. Don't be overzealous and send your press release to every-one on the Internet (i.e., don't broadcast it in a willy-nilly bulk mail fashion)—it's bad NetKarma.

- ✦ If you don't have an e-mail press list together, scour the mastheads of pertinent publications. Just about every magazine or trade paper will print their e-mail address there. And don't forget the e-zines!

- ✦ Include the direct URLs of some of the most important pages, as well as the front page URL, when highlighting site features.

- ✦ Always include an e-mail address.

- ✦ Post a polite little (nonpromotional) note in relevant news-groups, announcing your site's arrival. Don't post the press release.

- ✦ Add your Web site's URL to your e-mail signature.

Put your URL on everything your organiza-tion prints, from brochures through business cards.

In addition to sending out press releases, there's a world of tactics to get your URL out there. You should include your URL on everything your organization puts in print, from brochures through business cards. When printing the street address, fax, and telephone number, include your online address as well.

Consider these places that allow you to include your URL, without incurring significant extra costs:

✦ Stationery, including letterheads, envelopes, and business cards.

✦ Promotional items, like pens, notepads, t-shirts, and trade show giveaways.

✦ Print advertisements, including trade publications, local newspapers, and the yellow pages of phone books.

✦ Marketing collateral, such as capabilities brochures and sell sheets.

In short, examine all your print and promotional projects to see if it's appropriate to add your URL.

Mistake #3: Not Registering With the Search Engines

Who said there's no such thing as a free lunch? Registering with the search engines is key in creating an increased level of Web site traffic. Do not overlook this opportunity to gain the maximum exposure for your site. Getting your site listed doesn't have to cost a dime, just your investment in time, as you make your way from engine to engine. A properly listed site will pull in an infinitely higher number of hits then an unlisted site. Here's a short list of the most pertinent search engines:

✦ **AltaVista**
http://altavista.digital.com

✦ **Excite**
http://www.excite.com

✦ **HotBot**
http://www.hotbot.com

✦ **Infoseek**
http://guide.infoseek.com

✦ **InfoSpace**
http://www.infospace.com/

Registering with the search engines is key in creating an increased level of Web site traffic.

- ✦ **Lycos**
  http://www.lycos.com

- ✦ **Magellan**
  http://www.mckinley.com

- ✦ **Open Text Index**
  http://www.opentext.com/

- ✦ **Point**
  http://www.pointcom.com

- ✦ **Yahoo!**
  http://www.yahoo.com

Each of the search engines has different registration methods. The majority of them ask you to fill out an online form. But others, such as Infoseek, ask that you send e-mail with your Web site's URL. If you don't have a morning or afternoon free (as that's all the time it should take to get the job done, on a cursory level), there are alternatives to registering your site, one by one.

Submit It!

Submit It! (http://www.submit-it.com/) refers to itself as "the fastest way to publicize your Web site" (see Figure 7-5). This is a free service that lets you submit your URL to the following search engines, in one session: AltaVista, Apollo, ComFind, Infoseek, InfoSpace, LinkStar, Mallpark, METROSCOPE, Nerd World Media, New Rider's WWW Yellow Pages, Starting Point, WebCrawler, What's New Too!, What's New UK, Yellow Pages Online, and Yahoo. Using Submit It! will save you time and effort, and best of all, it won't affect your budget.

PostMaster2

PostMaster2 (http://www.netcreations.com/postmaster/) is the Godzilla of Web page posting services (see Figure 7-6). The service allows you to submit your URL to well over 300 search engines, hot lists, and publicity sites in one fell swoop. This power does not come cheap, however. PostMaster2 charges a respectable fee to deliver the goods, with one address account costing $500. Thankfully, NetCreations, the parent company of

PostMaster2, offers substantially reduced rates for multiple addresses. If you're a professional Web site developer, Internet Service Provider (ISP), advertising agency, or PR firm, who's regularly called upon to provide site registration, you can expect to save 50 percent or more on PostMaster2 fees when "buying in bulk."

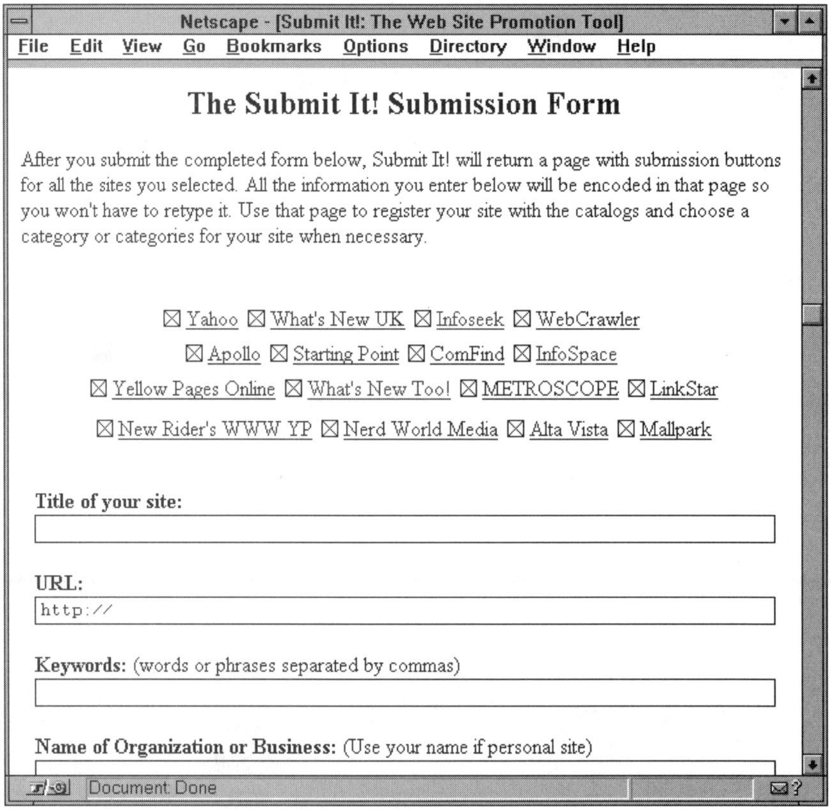

Figure 7-5: Submit It! simplifies the search engine registration process.

Figure 7-6: PostMaster2 delivers a comprehensive search engine and PR blitz at a very fair price.

Ryan Scott, of NetCreations, Inc., explains: "The main reason to use PostMaster2 is that if you don't get listed in all these spots, you may as well not even be on the Net. It's like opening a business, but not hanging a sign out, or not listing yourself in the yellow pages. People spend tons of money and effort putting up their sites. If you don't promote it, you may as well not even build the site. The old adage is wrong, it should be, 'If you build it and *promote it*, they will come.'"

NetCreations has scored swift and impressive results for its clients. The alt.culture Web site won InfiNet's "Cool Site of the Day" two days after submission. IBM's site grabbed *USA Today's*

Hot Site the very next day. Scott states that, although "other sites might not be that cool, 'you gotta play to win!'" And there are plenty of players in the game. PostMaster2 has been used by big names, such as AT&T, Intuit, Intel, New Line Cinema, MCI, Yahoo!, and ZDnet.

PostMaster2 was designed to be comprehensive, efficient, and easy to use. "PostMaster2's engine does the actual posting for you. Other services make you press the button, and they use your browser to do the submission," says Scott. "With our service you'll find that you have to do the least typing. Every place we can, we've already filled in everything for you. With our autosubmission feature, you can automatically submit to hundreds of spots without having to type anything at all. It really couldn't be much simpler."

Regardless of the method you use, it's essential to register your site. If you can afford to spend the bucks, give serious consideration to using a submission service. Then you can just sit back and watch your server get hammered!

Attacking Design Issues

Pure graphic issues are at the root of many a Web site's design failure. The best tack, as stated back in Chapter 2, "Creating Web Content," is to keep things simple. Sites that "go over the top" with wacky backgrounds, poorly rendered 3D type, and cheesy animation are on route to design failure. Be realistic about what you can achieve on your budget and with the graphic skills at hand. Accept reality and scale your efforts to what's within reason.

Good Web design practice uses plain old common sense. But you'd be surprised how many Web designers lack it. Thankfully, the Web is full of places to get the gospel of good design. Jeffrey Glover's site, "Top Ten Ways to Tell if You Have a Sucky Home Page" (www.winternet.com/~jmg/TopTenF.html) explains the most prevalent Web blunders in a whimsical manner (see Figure 7-7). Jeffrey lambastes such design faux pas as huge pointless graphics, JavaScript marquees, construction signs, and the blink tag, among other things.

There are a number of Web sites that take great joy in blasting poorly designed sites. Rather than flaming bad design attributes in a general manner, Mirsky's Worst of the Web (http://www.mirsky.com/wow/) (see Figure 7-8) happily picks a new (and hideous) site each Monday, Wednesday, and Friday. Every fledgling Web designer should pray that their site never appears on Mirsky's list.

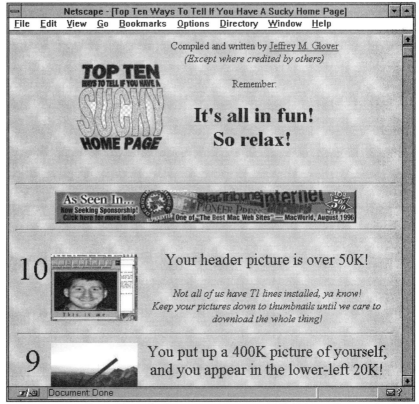

Figure 7-7: Jeffrey Glover's "Top Ten Ways to Tell if You Have a Sucky Home Page" is one of the best places to go to see what not to do!

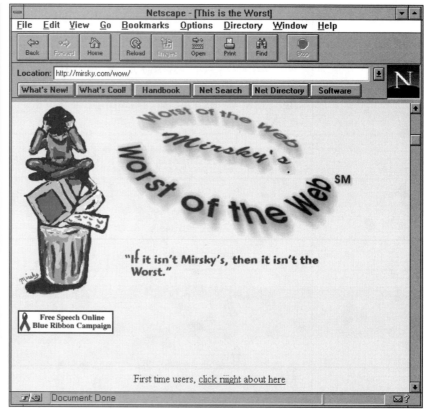

Figure 7-8: Mirsky's Worst of the Web is the one hot list on which you don't want your site to appear.

On the Web, as in the real world, there are plenty of folks who are more than eager to tell you what is and isn't acceptable. Good design is an objective process, even if the audience interprets the design in a subjective way. It's enlightening to learn *why* a Web page *does* or *doesn't* work for different people. This is one of the secrets to designing for a specific audience. Keep this in perspective, for once you've learned what works for your audience, you should always design for *them,* never for *yourself.*

Reaching your audience is key. Don't waste your time worrying about the rest of the world. If one sector of the population has been proven to absolutely hate a design, you have not failed—just as long as it was not the intended audience. On the other hand, if your intended audience hates it, it's time to look for a new design (or a new job).

Mistake #4: Not Bringing the Right Resources to Bear

Are you bragging to your peers about how cheap it was to have your Web site designed? Are they snickering behind your back, because the design flat out stinks? Bargain-basement Web designers, such as the mythical firm shown in Figure 7-9, do a disservice to everyone, including themselves. While bad lawyers are disbarred and crooked politicians impeached, lousy Web designers merely go without work.

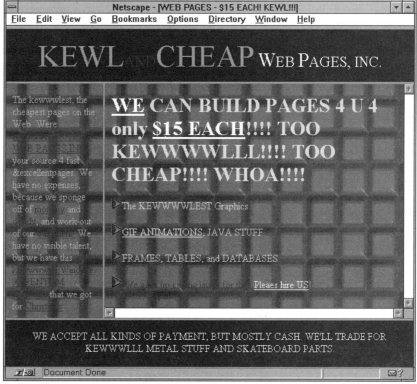

Figure 7-9: Needless to say, this isn't the firm you should consider for outsourcing your Web site design.

One excellent strategy is to have a professional create your basic templates and navigational structure, while you handle all the daily maintenance tasks.

This not to say that every Web site should cost a zillion bucks to produce. And it shouldn't infer that you can't design a perfectly good Web site yourself. But if you realize that, for whatever reason, you don't have what it takes to do it right, you should enlist the help of a skilled practitioner. A professional designer needn't produce your entire site. One excellent strategy is to have a professional create your basic templates and navigational structure, while you handle all the daily maintenance tasks.

Mistake #5: Improper Graphics

Poorly created graphics are the mark of an amateur Web design effort. While Chapter 4, "Adding Pictures to Your Design," and Chapter 5, "Creating Digital Content," discussed online graphics, the subject is worth revisiting here. There are a number of ways that bad graphics can bring down your site.

Don't Shovel Your Pages Full of Graphics

Web users eschew sites that use too many graphics, with little or no purpose. Besides the added download time, an overabundance of graphics can lead to visual cacophony. Use the least number of graphics necessary to get your point across. Don't allow your Web pages to look like a five-and-dime store. Simplicity, when implemented properly, leads to true elegance.

Avoid the Pitfalls of Anti-Aliasing

Everyone loves a beautiful, drop-shadowed graphic. Out on the Web, however, poor drop-shadows are the rule, rather than the exception. You've seen the results—jagged, chunky ghosting around the edges of drop-shadowed images. Fortunately, this is easily preventable by using a simple technique. To avoid jaggies (stair-stepping) and ghosting (visible fringes), always render a transparent anti-aliased graphic on a background similar to the one it will be displayed on.

Figures 7-10 and 7-11 show the same graphic rendered in Adobe Photoshop on both a white and a neutral gray background. Since Netscape uses a default gray background of 192/192/192 (when expressed in RGB terms), those exact colors were used for the gray background. Notice how the graphic rendered on the white background exhibits an objectionable level of ghosting, while the other graphic blends smoothly into the background.

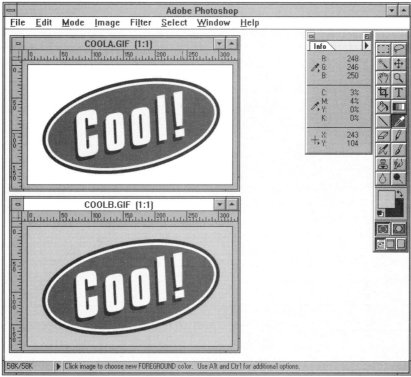

Figure 7-10: A transparent graphic created in Photoshop on both a white and a gray background.

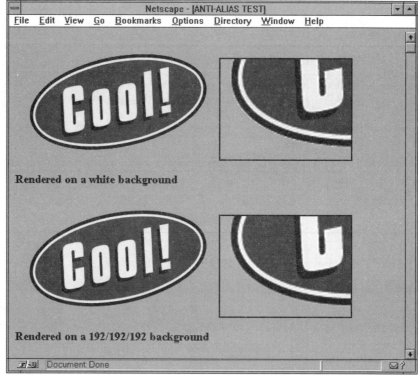

Figure 7-11: By rendering the graphic on the same value background as the Web page, jagged ghosting was avoided.

The edges of a transparent graphic are not transparent as they blend into the background color. The eye is fooled into believing that the graphic is truly transparent because the graphic was rendered on the same background it was going to be displayed on. Consequently, if your page background is dark blue, you should create your graphic on a dark blue background before exporting it with transparency. Working with background patterns can be a bit trickier. Depending on the pattern, you may choose to either render the graphic on the background pattern itself, or on a background that matches the most prominent color in the pattern.

Keep Graphic File Sizes Down

Let's hammer it home again. Always strive to make your graphic files as small as possible by using the proper file format and palette. If it's a photograph, use JPEG. If it's a graphic, use GIF and limit the palette to the smallest number of colors without affecting the image quality. Professional-level, palette-tweaking tools, such as Equilibrium DeBabelizer, are indispensable. Chapter 5, "Creating Digital Content," covers the subject of image compression.

Mistake #6: Unreadable & Unintelligible Text

If you've succeeded in attracting users to your Web site, but they can't read your message because it's truly unreadable, you deserve to be flogged. Readability is paramount; unintelligibility is inexcusable. This applies to both the graphic and textual integrity of your presentation. Save your site (and your hide) by following these basic rules:

- ✦ Avoid busy backgrounds. Stick with muted tones.

- ✦ Take care in choosing type and background colors.

- ✦ Use large enough type to ensure readability.

- ✦ If you set type in ALL CAPS, do so sparingly.

- ✦ Make use of tables to break up your copy and to present it more effectively.

- ✦ Have your text edited and proofread by a professional.

Unless the sole purpose of a site is to create a wacky online environment, the readability of text should always rank as the first priority. Your goal should be to help users focus on the information being presented, not on the presentation itself. Check back to Chapter 2, "Creating Web Content," for details on typographic matters.

The readability of text should always rank as the first priority.

Mistake #7: Confusing Web Site Identity

Have you ever gone looking for information on a search engine, only to follow a link that lands you on a generic and unidentifiable page? Having an unidentifiable Web site is a common problem for site designers, but it's one that's easily avoided. Keep the big picture in mind—take a step back from the design of your individual pages, and look at your site as a whole.

Your visitors should always know, without question, that they are on *your* Web site. This can only happen if you build a strong site identity and stick to it. Additionally, as users move about your site, they should encounter a smooth transition between pages, with a consistent look and feel.

Since the majority of pages are accessed directly from search engines, rather than from a Web site's front page, a number of precautions should be taken. Each one of your Web site's pages should be instantly identifiable as belonging to your site. At the very least, site identification should be included in the title bar (see Figure 7-12). You should also consider including it at the bottom of every page. And once again, every page should have a navigational toolbar of some sort. If someone hits a deeply buried page from a search engine, you'd probably like them to take a look at other parts of your site. Without a navigational toolbar, you're likely to lose them as they hit and run.

Each one of your Web site's pages should be instantly identifiable as belonging to your site.

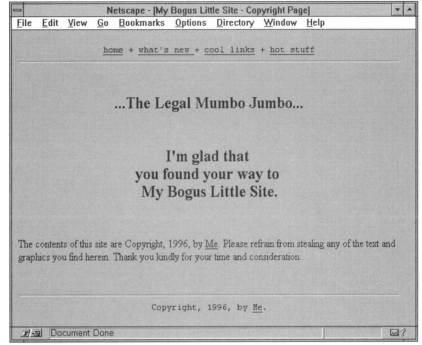

Figure 7-12: Don't overlook adding the site ID to every page.

Mistake #8: Inconsistency in Graphics & Navigation

You might recall that back in Chapter 2, "Creating Web Content," a 'sense of seamlessness' was stressed. That's another point worth revisiting. Once you've established a graphic—be it a bullet, separator, or other embellishment—reuse it on subsequent pages, rather than using a different graphic for the same purpose. This reduces download times and helps to invoke a seamless experience for users. In addition, try to keep the following elements consistent from page to page:

- ✦ Navigation toolbars
- ✦ Color schemes
- ✦ Backgrounds

✦ Graphic identity, such as corporate logos and typefaces

✦ Writing style, formatting, and tone

While it's not imperative to maintain the same backgrounds and standing graphics from page to page, it can help immensely in providing a sense of seamlessness. Think twice before you swap out the background texture or a recurring graphic.

Navigation

Site navigation should be consistent from page to page and from section to section. It can take a good bit of time to arrive at the best possible navigational metaphor for your Web site. Start by carefully planning and implementing your navigational scheme. Then, make a few test runs and fine tune as necessary. Once you've gotten the basic structure together, it's time to enlist the help of an Internet neophyte or two. Have them test drive the navigational system before the site goes online. Utilize their input and make whatever changes necessary to enhance the online experience. Then, try out the new design on some users.

Once the navigational structure has been tweaked to perfection, implement it thoroughly throughout the site. Every page should include a bare bones navigation toolbar, at the very least.

> Every page should include a bare bones navigation toolbar, at the very least.

Dealing With Performance Issues

When users reach your site and experience their very first page, they're left with an indelible impression. That impression is not limited to how the pages look or to the information that they contain. It also has to do with your Web site performance on a purely technical level. As such, you've got to be cognizant of how your Web site behaves from a performance standpoint. And the best way to really check things out is to put yourself in your users' shoes. The speed at which you connect to your internal server is likely to be far faster than what your users will experience. Try accessing your site from ISPs, CompuServe, or other corporate connections.

Mistake #9: Slow-Loading Pages

A slow site is
the kiss of death
for impatient
users.

A slow site is the kiss of death for impatient users. How many times have you bailed out on a Web site, because of its lethargic response time? Plenty of times, no doubt. No one likes to sit there and wait for pages to load. And everyone appreciates a fast, responsive site.

There's no magic involved in having a fast site, just a number of gating factors. As the designer, one of those factors is your responsibility. Another two are likely to fall into the jurisdiction of the techies responsible for running the server. In short, there are three basic reasons why your Web site may be performing sluggishly:

✦ **Poorly Engineered Pages.** This should have been drilled through your head by now, but it's worth reiterating. It's your responsibility to build the fastest pages possible. Cut them down to size. Keep text files well under 40K and limit the number and size of the graphics. Reuse as many graphics as possible from page to page.

✦ **Maxed Server.** Check the usage capacity of your Web server. If there are multiple Web sites running on the server, it may be possible that they are affecting the response time. If the server is maxed out, see what can be done to increase its capacity or consider moving your site to another server.

✦ **Clogged Pipe.** What kind of Internet connection—28.8 baud modem, DS0 dedicated high-speed telephone line at 56K, ISDN (Integrated Services Digital Networks) telephone line, T1 (1.5 million bits per second), or T3 (45 million bits per second)—is the Web server sitting on? As hit rates climb, so do the bandwidth requirements. If you're doing your job right, and attracting lots of traffic, it may be time to upgrade your connection. You may want to talk to your system administrator, for example, to see if moving from an ISDN connection to a T1 line is a feasible option.

Mistake #10: Browser Incompatibility

Browser compatibility has historically been a thorny issue. While Netscape Navigator set the standard for all other Web browsers from its inception, its market dominance has run into a serious threat in the form of Microsoft's Internet Explorer. Although Explorer's effect on Navigator's huge market share is debatable, it seems as though Mosaic and the other browsers are rarely mentioned these days.

The big question *used to be* "but will it play on Mosaic?" That question is rarely asked these days. Since Microsoft wisely mimicked the capabilities of Navigator, browser compatibility is ensured for the vast majority of the market, as long as your Web site has been designed for Netscape. As of this writing, Microsoft is still playing catch up with regard to market share. It would be wise to avoid using any features that are supported only in Microsoft's Internet Explorer, lest you risk losing your audience.

The real question now is "which version of Netscape should I design for?" The most prudent answer is to never design for features contained in a beta version. Always design for the released application. Stay behind the bleeding edge, and let the other guys take the arrows in the forehead. There are two major reasons for this advice. The first is that most users are *not* using the latest and greatest versions of browsers. If you build in advanced features, there's a good chance that most people will never get to see them. The second reason is that the browsers can change while they're still in beta, breaking any workarounds or tricks you may have built into your pages, based on pre-release software.

The ultimate way to provide complete browser compatibility is to build a core of text-only pages. Unfortunately, this shoots for the lowest common denominator, and is only possible if time and budget allow. If you choose to create a set of text-only pages, be sure to add a link to the front page of the site, as well as on every full-featured page that is mirrored with a text-only page (and visa versa). The White House Web site, profiled in Chapter 11, uses this technique, as well as a sly server trick to automatically serve up the proper version for each browser.

What About Plug-ins?

Keeping up with the latest developments in the Netscape Navigator plug-in world is perhaps more important than worrying about browser compatibility. There are scores of software companies that have jumped on Netscape's coattails, and there are more plug-ins out there now than anyone could possibly know what to do with. The best place to find all the latest plug-ins is Netscape's Web site (see Figure 7-13). You'll find plug-in listings for 3D and Animation, Audio/Video, Business and Utilities, Image Viewers, and Presentations.

Figure 7-13: Can't find that new plug-in? Netscape has a link to all the latest goodies.

Deciding
which plug-ins
to use on your
Web site can be
a complex
issue. But if
there's
good reason to
use special
features, by all
means: *go for it!*

If your Web site requires the use of a specific Netscape plug-in, be sure to include a link to Netscape's site on your front page, so that your users can quickly obtain the plug-in. And since many people won't hit your front door on the way into your Web site, it's even more polite to include the link on every page that requires the plug-in.

A handful of plug-ins are considered de rigueur. Three of the most prominent examples are:

✦ **Adobe Acrobat**
(http://www.adobe.com)

✦ **Macromedia Shockwave**
(http://www.macromedia.com)

✦ **RealAudio**
(http://www.realaudio.com)

Deciding which plug-ins (if any) to use on your Web site can be a complex issue. Much of the equation has to do with your intended audience. If you're aiming for the lowest common denominator, you probably want to avoid using any, as boring as that might seem. But if there's good reason to use special features, by all means—*go for it!*

Site Maintenance Issues

Putting up a Web site is one thing, but keeping it running in top condition is quite another matter. It takes diligence and a bit of hard work to ensure proper operation on an ongoing basis. As you plan your site, think past what the site will look like when it opens its doors. Think how it will evolve over its first year of operation. Put a plan in place to help it flourish and stay relevant as times change. Target the areas that will take more attention than others, and implement procedures to allow those areas to grow without constant weeding.

Think of building a new site as planting a new garden; you never know exactly how it will develop! The best changes will happen organically, as your site reacts to its audience. If you find out, two months into the project, that they're looking for a specific piece of information that you're not currently providing, provide it! Plant it, water it, fertilize it, keep it weeded, then sit back, and watch it grow.

Mistake #11: Stale Material

Nobody likes a stale Web site. While you may not be able to change your content on a daily basis, you should endeavor to keep your site as fresh as possible. Target at least one or two areas that will change regularly. This will help to attract your visitors back on a routine basis. You might time the changes to calendar or industry events. Certain company information, such as press releases on quarterly earnings, will be easy to predict. Other occurrences, such as product announcements or personnel changes, will happen on a more unpredictable basis. Here are a few quick ideas on keeping your site fresh:

✦ Don't overlook getting the word out when something new happens on your site. Be sure to list the very latest happenings on your what's new or front page. If the event warrants the attention, consider sending out e-mail press releases.

✦ Set up an editorial calendar, as you would with any publication. Get your staff in tune with the schedule. Aim for those target dates, but take joy in the fact that they don't have to be hard and fast, as they would be in the printed world.

✦ Remove old information promptly. No one likes to read a page announcing an event, after the event has already happened. Once the event takes place, have someone write a summary and post that in its place.

Mistake #12: Broken Links

To avoid broken links within your site, use a link-checking software package such as Adobe SiteMill.

Don't let your links go 404 (File Not Found)! With a little time and effort, broken links are completely avoidable. It's a good idea to assign someone the responsibility of checking for bad links on an ongoing basis. Although this isn't a full-time job, it's certainly worth doing on a periodic basis. To avoid broken links within your site, you could also use a link-checking software package such as Adobe SiteMill. These programs allow you to quickly identify and fix bad internal links, without opening up a single HTML file.

Adobe SiteMill (see Figure 7-14), is an invaluable aid in keeping your links current. In this example, two of the graphic files in this little Web site were renamed after the pages were built (a common malady). SiteMill allows users to automatically fix the broken links by simply dragging the renamed file onto the broken link. It couldn't be easier.

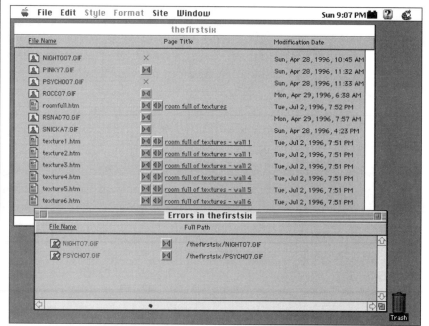

Figure 7-14: Adobe SiteMill quickly identifies broken links, and allows you to fix them with drag-and-drop ease.

While you have total control over the internal links on your site, unfortunately you have no control over what's happening with your external links. There can be a number of reasons why an external link may go bad, including:

✦ The other site's server may be down or swamped with traffic.

✦ There may be problems with either your Internet connection or the other site's.

✦ The other site may have moved (or killed) the page your link is to.

The best strategy is to try revisiting a bad link in an hour or two. In the first two cases, the page may magically reappear. In the last case, however, you'll have to put your nose to the electronic grindstone and find out where the page has gone. A polite Webmaster will always leave a forwarding page if something has to be moved.

Mistake #13: Not Being Ready for Growth

The Web is the most dynamic publishing medium yet invented. At the core of its power is its ability to metamorphose at a rapid pace. As a Web site developer, it's your responsibility to ensure that your site can be quickly expanded and altered to fit your changing needs. This demands that you design both the file structure and the structure of the files themselves so that each change does not require that you start from scratch.

When you build your site with expansion in mind, you use a modular approach to page building. This allows you to swap in new images and text by running batch search and replace routines against all the pages on your site. In one fell swoop, you can update navigation bars (both text and graphics), site identification, and other features. Perhaps the easiest way to do this is by using a high performance ASCII text editor, such as BBEdit, which provides directory-level search-and-replaces.

It's your responsibility to ensure that your site can be quickly expanded and altered to fit your changing needs.

Moving On

Before you take any trip, it's wise to plan out your route and avoid the obvious obstacles. This chapter presents common problems encountered in putting up and maintaining a Web site. By following these common sense guidelines, you'll ensure that you have a pleasant voyage.

In the Professional Web Site Design section of *Looking Good Online*, take a look at some of the most impressive sites on the World Wide Web. Hear how their professional designers built those sites, and learn about the trials and tribulations they went through.

Section III

Professional
Web Site Design

8

Design Case Study: Online Version of *USA Today*

Site: *USA Today,* http://www.usatoday.com
Design chief: Jeff Dionese
Design firm: Gannett Publishing, *USA Today*, Arlington,
                 Virginia

Founder Al Newhart established *USA Today* in 1982. Since then, it's been getting larger and stronger, in terms of circulation. Gannett currently owns the largest chain of newspapers in the world, with competitor Knight-Ridder running a close second.

USA Today is Gannett's flagship daily. It is distributed virtually everywhere. It's colorful, informative, accurate, and credible— the four magic ingredients that make a newspaper successful. As far as newspapers go, *USA Today* is one of the most reader-friendly daily publications around; it appeals to a large and diverse audience across the United States, North America, and around the world.

As with many print publications, *USA Today* is now available online. The online portion was launched April 17, 1995. It stands apart from other publishing sites because it hasn't just been repurposed to exist online. The designers of its Web site have managed to do something quite extraordinary. They've success-fully captured the essence and flavor of a newspaper, online, through an effective design. This is something that's hard to do well on the Web.

Taking Apart the *USA Today* Web Site

The site features design elements similar to those used in the printed publication. The home page includes the newspaper identification nameplate, which integrates a secondary news story in it. This is immediately followed by a photo relating to the main feature and an unrelated news headline (see Figure 8-1). You'll notice plenty of image mapping on the GIF graphics, including access buttons to the newspaper's News, Sports, Money, Life, and Weather subsections.

Included in the top area of the home page is direct access to sections including Top News, Feedback, the Search engine, and the *USA Today* graphic called a Snapshot. Snapshots are nearly a *USA Today* trademark, and characteristic of the newspaper's graphical emphasis. Snapshots feature quick-read summarized bits of news data translated into easy-to-interpret pictures. In addition, the first page also includes graphic and text links to indexes listing online sponsors, hot stories, a Baseball Weekly supplement, and a searchable index to the entire contents of the paper.

The home page has been designed to occupy exactly two Netscape browser pages whose options for toolbars and direc-tory buttons have been turned off. The second full page (see Figure 8-2) contains links to the most newsworthy stories second-ary to the main front-page feature. Finally, the last two elements of the home page show the front page sponsor and a navigation toolbar in the form of an image map that provides access to the items found at the top of the first page. In all, the home page offers 37 links to interior areas of the online newspaper, while still conveying news headlines and story information.

Figure 8-1: The USA Today *home page is structured to provide as much access to breaking news, core news, and subsections as possible.*

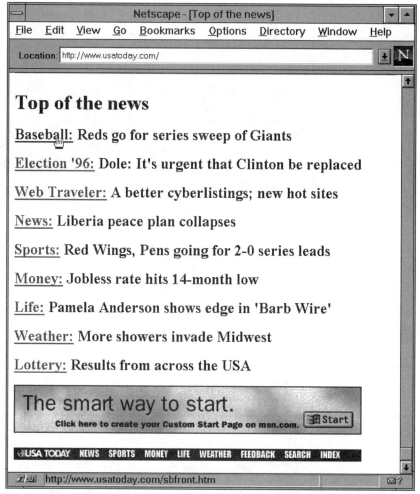

Figure 8-2: Page two of the home page contains text links only to the top news stories covered throughout the paper, a front page sponsor, and links to more areas through a navigation bar.

Designwise, that's a considerable number of direct links to lower-level content that have been integrated into the first page, without causing the page to become fragmented or cluttered. This organizational structure relies largely on image maps, but it's more than just that. A close examination of the design elements shows many related elements integrated together to form well-packaged units. For example, the newspaper's logo, an interest photograph, link buttons to five subsections, and the Top News, Feedback, Search, and Snapshot items have all been made into a single unit (see Figure 8-3).

Figure 8-3: The first GIF image file to load is the most critical in terms of catching the visitor's attention. The USA Today *design team avoids clutter and confusion by integrating multiple links into a complete package.*

The subsections of the site—News, Sports, Money, Life, and Weather—each feature an introduction page structured after the design of the main page. It's a model that reflects the character of the newspaper itself. Each subsection features a top-of-page color GIF that mimics the design of the top design element on the site's main home page (see Figures 8-4 and 8-5).

Figures 8-4 and 8-5: Each of the main subsection title bars of the USA Today *site have been designed identically for easy identification.*

The individual design elements have been structured the same for all sections, even down to their naming conventions. The purpose of this is twofold. First, it makes editing, updating, and replacing each of the elements much easier whenever the news changes. Next, by using the same image filenaming conventions, image files are easy to locate and can be updated without having to adjust any of the paths specified in HTML markup for the pages. Files may be updated and saved to the same system directories or folders and with the same filename, without any complicated page re-engineering.

This naming convenience does have its drawbacks, though. One hazard rears its ugly head when you look closely at how some browsers operate. The problem comes to light when users viewing what they think are fresh news pages see pages they've already seen, and news they expected to be new is actually old. This can happen when browsers cache-load images. Most of the time, cache-loading works to the browser's advantage, allowing faster load times for images previously cached. However, in the case of a news site, where the information changes constantly but the filenames do not change, the user is forced to manually flush out the old cache to see the new information. Fortunately, this is characteristic only of older browsers.

TIP

During the design of a site, naming files with logical names can make organization much simpler. Using a lettering or numbering system in your naming conventions makes locating files for updating or replacement easier. This works just fine if your site images change infrequently. But if you are planning a site in which the files are likely to change daily or hourly, you'll find that updating files using the same filenames may do more harm than good.

The design team also uses a naming convention that self-organizes the files within their system directories. Each file begins with the same letter as the section it applies to. For example, the Life section images all begin with the letter "L," Sports images begin with "S," and so on. It's a very basic concept that avoids using a numeric cataloging system, which many Web sites can become tangled in.

The section images are split into chunks, each of which contains a single element or multiple elements. The JPEG format is used for the larger and strictly photographic digital images, while GIF, with its limited number of color display capabilities, is used for images containing uniform or limited color. It's also interesting to note at this point that, as many site designers have chosen to do, the *USA Today* team uses digital images for headlines and subheads instead of relying on the limitations of HTML markup. This allows them the typographic freedom of placing emphasis where it's needed by using their headline typeface at various sizes. It also gives them full control over the appearance of their Web pages, regardless of which browser a person is using.

Finally, all pages are equipped with a navigation bar (see Figure 8-6) that includes access to the *USA Today* home page, each of the subsections, and secondary site features such as Feedback, Search, and Index. The navigation toolbar has also been designed as an image map.

Figures 8-6: The bottom of each and every page features a slim, image-mapped navigation bar providing access to each of the main subsections of the site.

Special Site Features

The site itself is extensive and presents an array of specially designed features, including an interactive crossword puzzle—one of the staples for any avid newspaper audience. But under the category of special features is where the *USA Today* site flexes its muscles as a high-caliber news and information site. Two of the most successful features include the news snapshots borrowed from the newspaper version, and the immense accumulation of weather information.

The Famous News Snapshots

Snapshot is the name *USA Today* has given to a self-explanatory graphic that depicts a collection of facts or figures in an easily readable form. The newspaper's artists and illustrators are masters at designing these informational graphics. The Snapshot format is unquestionable proof of their expertise.

Figures 8-7 to 8-9, sample news Snapshots taken directly from the site, show the simple, basic format of these graphic images. All Snapshots are saved to JPEG format, and all are produced in full color, using both 2D and 3D graphic software—sometimes both. Snapshots range in physical and file size and are highly compressed using the JPEG standard compression. File sizes range between roughly 17,000 and 40,000 bytes and take anywhere from 10 to 20 seconds to load through a 14.4 modem.

Each of the subsections of the site gives access to Snapshots dealing with a particular subject, but an entire library of all the site's Snapshots is available through a page of text links describing the subject matter of each graphic (see Figure 8-10).

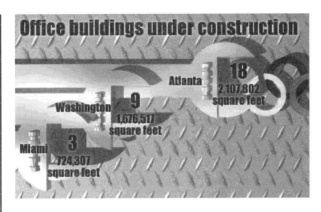

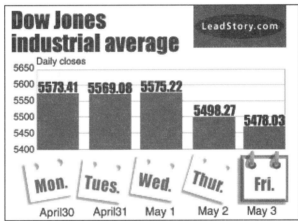

Figures 8-7 to 8-9: Sample news Snapshots show the simple, basic format of the site's graphic images.

Figure 8-10: With just two clicks from the main home page of the USA Today *site, you have access to the entire collection of News, Money, Life, and Sports Snapshots.*

Defining the Weather

People often turn to a daily newspaper for information about the weather. The *USA Today* site spares no effort in offering descriptions of everything from what "drizzle" is to how tornadoes form. In fact, like it or not, talking about the weather is how many people begin polite conversations with others. Weather talk provides a common platform of "safe" topics to help people relate to each other, whether or not they actually care about weather phenomena. Figure 8-11 shows how efficiently a simple graphic can offer a vast amount of information at a glance. This JPEG image of the continental Unites States air temperatures takes up a mere 328 pixels wide by 224 pixels deep and is 38,642 bytes in size.

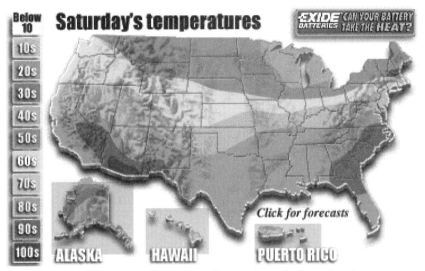

Figure 8-11: A picture may be worth a thousand words, but when it comes to information graphics, the USA Today *designers exceed the limit. With this graphic of continental temperatures, a huge amount of data is conveyed to the reader in a short period of time.*

The *USA Today* design team uses its illustration skills to explain daily weather conditions across the nation, and supplies access to past weather information graphics that depict actions and reactions caused by weather. Figures 8-12 to 8-14 demonstrate some of the strengths of using illustrations to relate concepts in graphic form that would otherwise take the average reader several minutes to read and digest if the information were presented in text form.

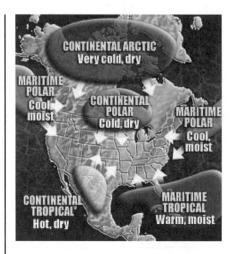

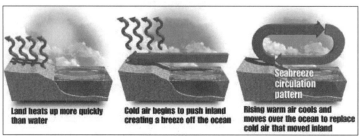

Land heats up more quickly than water

Cold air begins to push inland creating a breeze off the ocean

Rising warm air cools and moves over the ocean to replace cold air that moved inland

DRIZZLE: *Drops with diameter smaller than .02 inch falling close together.*

RAIN: *Drops with diameter larger than .02 inch or smaller drops, widely separated.*

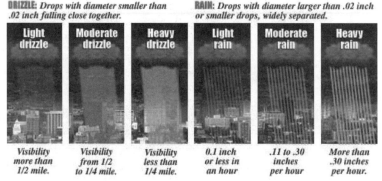

Light drizzle	Moderate drizzle	Heavy drizzle	Light rain	Moderate rain	Heavy rain
Visibility more than 1/2 mile.	*Visibility from 1/2 to 1/4 mile.*	*Visibility less than 1/4 mile.*	*0.1 inch or less in an hour*	*.11 to .30 inches per hour*	*More than .30 inches per hour.*

Figures 8-12 to 8-14: These weather-related informational graphics show the potential for using efficient graphics to portray difficult ideas and concepts.

Emphasizing Graphics & Images

In the *USA Today* site, as in the printed publication, graphics become a focal point for the editorial stories. If readers choose to skim the paper, they can read the headline of an article, look at the graphics, photos, and captions, and get the basic thrust of the story without actually reading the text. It's a model mimicked even in traditional publishing. The reason for this is reader-driven. In modern-day business, a person who's on the move just doesn't have time to go in-depth. This rule alone gives the *USA Today* editorial team a philosophy they follow religiously: Engineer all content to be easily digestible.

In following this model, the newspaper has had its share of criticism from competitors in the industry. Some have even branded it McPaper. But journalistically *USA Today* doesn't pretend to be anything it's not. Regardless of this criticism, its priority continues to be maintaining a "quick read." Its graphics do just that, better and faster than text. "One of the rules we follow here is that all graphics must be capable of holding their own," says design chief Jeff Dionese. "At the *USA Today* site and in the printed newspaper, you'll likely notice you never have to read the whole story to understand the graphic."

Dionese points out that when he started working with the *USA Today* Web site team, its design looked very scanned-in and flat. As an artist, his first goal was to produce specially tailored graphics for online use. He found that although the existing designers were using some of the content and concepts from the newspaper, improvements needed to be made to many of the visuals. His strategy was to recreate the graphics using 3D modeling software similar to what you'd see in animation work. The reason for this was to give each graphic a fresh online-specific look and to gear the dynamics of the site toward movement and animation. In the end, his strategy paid off. "Even though we're producing *USA Today* for the Web," says Dionese, "it still really has to have the same feel as its printed form. It's the same content—just a different type of execution."

The Online Production Team

A team of approximately 80 professionals puts together the site on a daily basis. The team includes journalists, reporters, researchers, editors, artists, designers, and technical online personnel. Their division has been set up as a separate business unit within Gannett Publishing in Arlington, Virginia. Essentially, they are a Web site design unit whose core product is online service. They simply use the *USA Today* newspaper editorial content—a daily wealth of information any news network would envy.

Jeff Dionese, design chief at the *USA Today* Web site, is responsible for the look and feel of the site. Dionese insists that the title "design chief" is more or less another name for art director. Like many professionals who have made the transition to the Web, his professional background is rooted in graphic illustration and design in the traditional sense. For the most part, his experience came from working with information graphics in the printed version of *USA Today* back in the early 1980s. Dionese also worked for Knight-Ridder, producing broadcast animation. There he used 3D modeling techniques to supply television news stations with animated graphics dealing with breaking news.

"I was one of the senior artists at *USA Today*—the newspaper—from 1988 until when I left in 1992," says Dionese. "I worked with Webb Bryant, Sam Ward, Bob Laird—some of the strongest artists who are still there at the paper. Those early days were an exciting time for the newspaper industry." When *USA Today* came on the scene, it really changed the whole newspaper landscape. By raising the importance of visuals in communication journalism, designers working in art departments of publishing firms everywhere became more important. They were no longer just sitting in the corner, waiting to be asked to fill a hole with a cartoon or comic. Graphics became viewed more as journalistic content. Once the trend toward informational graphics was under way, even their competitors began integrating them with written editorial.

"I think *USA Today* has become the de facto model for all other newspapers," says Dionese. "My past experience producing broadcast graphics helped immensely with my online work. I try to use the broadcast as a model for the look of the graphics and design as opposed to it feeling like print online. We found, just as with stories, we just can't take a *USA Today* story or graphic and slap it online. It's just not very appealing."

Size & Makeup of the *USA Today* Site Team

At any given time, the site covers roughly 22,000 browser pages. A small portion of these pages are created through automation, but the majority are actual HTML pages. Now, it's not practical, or even humanly possible, to manage this volume of pages simultaneously, so the design team needed to make some choices as to which areas of the site would get the needed extra-special attention.

The Weather and Sports sections were two sections they targeted initially for improvements. These are the two areas of *USA Today* that most readers go to first on a daily basis. "At times, you'll likely see more content in our Weather and Sports sections than in the Life section," says Jeff Dionese. "We just can't throw all our resources at everything all at once. We're lucky enough to have a fantastic weather editor, Jack Williams. He's done a fantastic job. He's even written a book called *The USA Today Weather Book* that's done real well and is said to be one of the easiest guides to understanding the weather ever written."

The majority of the staff members are content creators and editors with experience in reporting and journalism. They're responsible for adapting or adding to the existing *USA Today* content. Their job is to package the content and get it ready to go online, including editing, writing, and HTML markup.

Next, the *USA Today* online division has a group they call stringer-managers, who are responsible for managing a small army of college and entry-level reporters. These local reporters attend and write about local sporting events across the country. The content they produce gets to the stringer-managers by whatever means possible, including fax, e-mail, and FTP. For the readers of both the newspaper and the Web site Sports section, this provides live reporting at a local level, giving sports hounds current news about what's happening in their own home town.

There's also a marketing crew working right alongside the Web site news team. Gannett made a special effort to have these people in close proximity. They gutted an entire floor of the Gannett Tower in Arlington, Virginia, to make space for them. The marketing crew is responsible for researching and selling all the online advertising space on the site.

Designing & Redesigning

The designers were given plenty of freedom in the design of this site. But, it didn't begin that way. Before Jeff Dionese came on board, Gannett had already contracted Roger Black to do the first *USA Today* site design version. Black is the design-grid evangelist who is credited with the success of *Esquire* magazine.

Following Black's initial design, the *USA Today* team continued the design internally. "We find outside designers really don't have a feel for *USA Today*," says Dionese. "It was a good lesson for Gannett to learn. The Roger Black group has an excellent reputation and they've produced some exceptional Web sites. But, we found the real key to a successful design—especially with a site like *USA Today*—was that the designers had to have a complete understanding of the flavor of the newspaper. The contract designers we've seen so far just don't seem to have that.

"When I came on board this project," says Dionese, "I and two other designers, Marry Badman and Steve Coney, did our own design and it seemed to just click from day one. Marry and Steve have each been with the paper a long time. We also had editors Chris Fruitridge and Warren Springer involved in the planning. In terms of news graphics and news presentation, they developed a lot of how that came across in the newspaper and continued that with the site design. I think we had the right people. We also didn't begin with a structure that limited us in terms of what we could try. We knew we could do just about anything, but it was just a matter of trying something. I actually came up with the basic shell during one of those creative, middle-of-the-night brainstorms, but it was the genius of the whole crew that turned it into what it is now. The more we all worked on the site, the better and better it became.

"I think the reason for our design success was that we approached the site without any preconceived ideas," says Dionese. "We just knew the original's design extremely well, and it wasn't our intention to simply force-fit *USA Today* into an online version. Even after just a few short planning sessions, we felt the site was just screaming *USA Today*. We were confident that readers would feel as if they were inside *USA Today*. We weren't getting that feeling with the work our outside designers were first doing.

"Roger Black eventually helped us immensely with technical issues like font licensing and HTML training," says Dionese. "But, the actual design ended up being done in-house by me, two designers, and two editors. We just locked ourselves in a small room and hammered it out. It took about a month of hardcore and constant flushing out of ideas and preliminary planning before we ended up with what launched a little over a year ago. Of course, it's changed since then, but it's remained amazingly similar to what we first came up with."

Visually Oriented Content

The philosophy of the *USA Today* Web site design team is to reflect the structure and image of the newspaper. Their aim is to hit their audience with what they believe is the news of the day and, editorially, take a stand on what is important or significant. At the same time and on a slightly lower level, they also needed to leave availability for the rest of the content. "For us," says Dionese, "it evolved as a belief that any waiting we put the audience through has to be worthwhile." In a nutshell, if a large graphic was used, the waiting time needed to be justified by how content-rich and important the story was.

This brings up the issue many designers struggle with when approaching the design of a site. How much time is too much to expect users to wait, and how do you translate that into file size? "The top strip of our site that contains the *USA Today* logo, navigation buttons, promotional advertising, and the home front is a rather large GIF," says Dionese. "We had to justify that for its usefulness. To do this, we continued reducing its size until our audience wait time didn't outweigh the image's usefulness. We're against using graphics just for decoration. Our graphics have to be extremely useful and full of content."

"We're against using graphics just for decoration. Our graphics have to be extremely useful and full of content."

The structure of the site is extremely well organized. It presents itself as the front of a newspaper, where you have the hottest news and the most access to interior subsections. The Web site also brings in some other factors that give you the ability to look at an index and search for things. As the site designer, it's a heavy consideration.

The *USA Today* site has effectively capitalized on its strong visual identity. This would have been impossible if it were a radio or TV station, where identity is harder to translate in terms of design. Certain parts of the site are *very USA Today,* and the design team tried to prevent those areas from being lost. The most critical feature to the site—the one that makes the *USA Today* newspaper exciting on a daily basis—is the 1A, or front page, photo (see Figure 8-15). It's the newspaper's way of saying to its readers: This is *USA Today*'s version of what's going on right now, today.

Figure 8-15: The front page photo critically states what the newspaper editorial staff claims is the most important or most interesting event happening in the nation that day, that moment.

Planning Navigation

"After we had our initial approval, we took it a step further and did a working rough that had a couple of links coming off of it," says Jeff Dionese. "We did it this way so we could start to get a feel for the navigation of the site." The challenge is to make sure that the right design elements come forward and what remains is visually secondary. Again, for the first draft of the site the team took a very nontechnical approach. Dionese says his team didn't find a lot of success in doing a whole tree of the entire content in the site right from the start. "We found it just starts to get so abstract," he says. "We had more success with just sitting down and trying things over and over again by literally clicking on the mouse to see how it worked."

Helping Users Make Easy Choices

Minimizing the amount of drilling down users have to do for the information they are looking for is one of the most important considerations for the designer. Site visitors find that it becomes more and more frustrating for them to have to hunt and click throughout a site to satisfy their needs. The entire time their hunt is going on, they're never quite sure whether their efforts are going to be fruitful or not. They've put all of their trust in the designer and the organizers of the site. They're putting their trust in the fact that the designer has done his or her job correctly in terms of navigation controls.

This is where much of the human nature of Web site design comes into play. If there's one thing people hate, it's being made to feel foolish or inadequate. The shame of it is that this is often the case if the user takes a wrong turn somewhere and ends up having to backtrack or, worse, leave the site permanently never to return again.

One of the biggest mistakes you can make in site design—and you see it done all the time—is to give the user too many choices right from the start, at your home page. If all of the elements on the page are given the same weight, everything becomes the same level of importance. For example, in traditional or desktop publishing, layout artists often make the mistake of setting all major headings at the same point size, or all photographs the same size. When readers first see a page, they should be attracted by something that interests them. It's often up to the designer and the editors to put a focus on what's important for the reader. The last thing you want to do is force your reader to struggle through a page of monotonous text or graphic images and try to decide what they "should" read or what they need to know. Many Web sites make that mistake. It's a leftover practice from the days when type size couldn't be easily changed.

To Dionese, as with many designers, a good Web site is one that narrowly targets a specific niche market but does it *well*. That's the strongest feature of the Web. It should allow site visitors to get to one specific niche or area and find out everything they'd ever want to know about a particular subject. At *USA Today*, it's one of their biggest daily challenges. But, they also have to weigh this against the fact that they're appealing to a general-interest audience. In other words, if someone is a movie nut, are they more apt to go to a site that deals only in movies or come to the *USA Today* Life section and go to movies? "We try to look at each section of the *USA Today* site as its own niche Web site," says Dionese. "We're competing directly with other niche sites out there that are covering the same topics and aimed at the same market of readers."

Loading Pages in Parts

One of the more curious things you might notice when visiting the *USA Today* site is that the order in which elements load into the pages appears to have a planned, logical sequence. And, there's an interesting story behind that. When these site designers first started working on their design, the plan was that it be a *paid* subscription service. It wasn't until three months after the site's initial launch that the business plan changed and Gannett decided to release everything free for Internet users at large.

In the beginning, all of the design and HTML markup was limited to viewers using Mosaic. Because early Mosaic was so much more limiting in terms of design, it meant they were really aiming for the lowest common denominator. When using Mosaic, instead of bits and pieces of the site gradually loading, users see an icon while they wait. When the items on the page are ready to pop, the whole page pops in at once.

Since users had to wait for each graphic to load one at a time, the site was designed to have elements sequentially build on the page, like a storyboard. But even now that it's designed for Netscape, this building-block strategy still works well (see Figure

8-16). Loading pages in parts works well if you structure the loading process in the same way people naturally read, or when a storyteller tells a story, which is exactly the plan the *USA Today* site designers had in mind. "I like it because it turns a negative aspect into a positive quality," says Dionese. "The fact that your audience has to wait for graphics can be turned into a pleasant experience if you look at it as an entertainment tool."

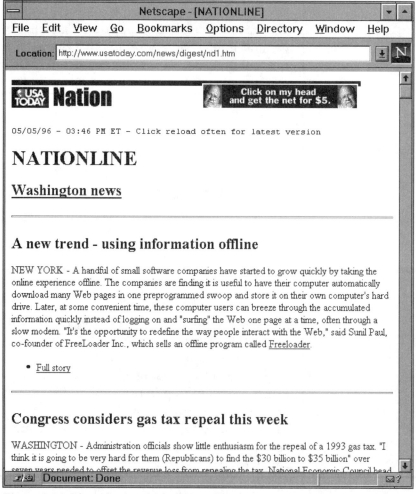

Figure 8-16: The order in which design elements, images, and text load is a leftover from when the USA Today *design team was forced to design for an early version of Mosaic's browser.*

Look Who's Watching

Knowing your audience is a critical factor in the design of any Web site, and the marketing crew at *USA Today* is on a constant watch for who's reading the paper and who's visiting the Web site. They've discovered that their site visitors tend to be slightly younger than the readers of the newspaper. However, the content for both publications remains targeted toward the hard-core business users. They continue to market toward the core *USA Today* reader, the male business person who travels frequently for business.

Knowing your audience is a critical factor in the design of any Web site.

The revenue from the site is currently generated solely from advertising. But the big question is, "Why would a company choose to buy advertising space on the Web site as opposed to the printed newspaper or even television or radio advertising?" The answer depends purely on demographics. The current audience surfing the Web is a specific type of crowd—for the most part well educated, well paid, and technically savvy—while the portion of this crowd who surfs a specific site on a regular basis could be considered the cream of the crop. For advertisers, what's even better is the fact that advertising on the Internet is generally less costly than other forms of advertising.

The Design Tools of Choice

Most of the site designers at *USA Today* use Macintosh computers. In terms of production, Jeff Dionese describes it as a three-step process. "We begin by creating our graphics using 2D drawing software and etch out the basic sketches for our graphics. For that part we're using Macromedia FreeHand. Those basic graphic shapes are then imported into one of our main 3D modeling tools, which can be either Specular Infini-D or Strata StudioPro. Then, those images are brought into Adobe Photoshop, where we drop in the text on the information graphics. From there, each image is saved to either GIF or JPEG—at whichever file format makes sense for the job. Then they go directly online."

With the software industry offering various tools for "no brainer" HTML page creation, it's often tempting for companies managing large sites, like that of *USA Today*, to use site management software. This type of software can often cut down the amount of time needed to manually manage internal and external page linking and avoid locking out site visitors who become discouraged by "nowhere" links—links that are invalid because the link destination either doesn't exist or because of some other reason.

One of the designers on this particular team has specialized in site management and has been dealing with Java scripts and HTML. But the page editors and reporters are actually responsible for doing the HTML work. "In terms of an HTML editor, we're talking about going with NaviPress," says Dionese. "That will allow us to do a little more than what we are doing now by using Internet Assistant. It's basically just a temporary choice until we know the majority of our audience is working in Windows 95. Who knows what we will end up with down the road. In the beginning, though, Internet Assistant was adequate for us."

Moving On

The online version of *USA Today* demonstrates a critical design approach—engineering an electronic version of a traditional publication. The team's approach demonstrates the need for designers to be not only fully aware of subject matter of the site, but also to have a realistic understanding of the target audience and a fine-tuned sensitivity for the medium. This is a design model that can be used for many types of online information publications.

The next chapter looks at the National Football League site.

9

Design Case Study: National Football League

Site: National Football League,
                     http://www.nfl.com.
Project manager: Michael Nanfito
Design firm: FreeRange Media, Seattle, Washington

If you're considering running out for beer and chips, now's the time to go. The National Football League's official Web site is the next best thing to being at the game. This is one of the busiest Web sites on the Internet. The traffic here is consistently heavy. This particular site combines many different types of Web sites in one, but each and every corner of the site is saturated with American football.

Now, here's an interesting concept. Take a sport that's traditionally attended in person and that has been largely adapted to broadcast media such as television and radio, and put it up on the Net. At first, you might ask, "Who needs football online?" But taking a close look at this site will show you why it's so popular. By the grace of the computer, avid fans can monitor not only their local hometown games but *all* games nationwide at any given moment. They can also check back into history to see team standings for any given year, check out the exact rules on penalties, and plan their schedules against upcoming game times. Wondering where to get team jerseys or other football paraphernalia? No problem. It's truly a football fan's dream come true.

It's also a tribute to the planners and designers of the site. They've successfully capitalized on nearly every aspect of this particular subject, making it a niche-market site. It offers so much information that it's nearly unimaginable that they've missed anything. To many designers and audiences, this is the epitome of good Web site design and a model for all niche-market Web sites to follow. Information, news, history, commerce, reference—it's all found at this site.

The Football World Online

The NFL home page features quick access to a veritable almanac of football information. An NFL Newswire area lists the latest happenings on recent games and significant team strategies.

As in many areas of the site, the problem of presenting enormous amounts of statistics was solved by using large textual documents navigated with text anchors. This is done by placing links at the tops of the pages, which are then linked to their respective document counterparts.

A roomful of football information is contained in the NFL Library, which includes an NFL Record Book, NFL Rules of the Game, NFL Bookstore area—and, yes, you can even find out about your favorite NFL Software titles.

Like any full-featured Web site, you can shop for items you'd likely never get anywhere else. The NFL site features a shopping area called Pro Shop, that allows site visitors to browse images of selected products and merchandise, such as jerseys, jackets, sweatshirts, and various other official NFL products. At the time of this writing, direct purchase from the site was not yet available, but at the rate change occurs on the Web, more than likely this will soon be possible. Instead, products are purchased via a toll-free hot line, where the transaction is handled by an operator. In case you don't see something you like online, a full-color printed catalog is also available through an online request.

A Locker Room section of the site features a live chat area dedicated solely to football-related conversations. Both current and historical information about the leagues and their teams is available from the Extra Points section, which includes areas such as Sunday Ticket; Timeline, a summary of significant football events from 1869 to 1995; the NFL Football Hall of Fame; NFL Team Mates (more associated Web sites); and links to alternate information sources, such as television, through an area named Broadcast Networks.

For those avid sports fans who need to satisfy an urge immediately, the site also features a Search function that combs through all information on the site, and an Index in text format. Search and Index functions are contained in a simple yet colorful image-mapped toolbar at the bottom of each section's page. The toolbar also provides navigation back to the Calendar, Shopping, and main home pages.

Several of the text-heavy reference pages exist as very long HTML documentsdesigned to be navigated using text anchors. Text anchors are a design solution for information that can't easily be chunked down to smaller pages, and in cases where breaking up and separating information might cause confusion for the user.

In comparison to other Web sites, the NFL site has a very clean design look on the upper levels in terms of visuals. Most of the pages feature white backgrounds. But looks are deceiving, and that clean appearance is actually a carefully tailored balance between content value and user wait time. What pages lack in surface images is made up for in quicker access. Much of the navigation is through quick-loading text links, while a persistent toolbar produced with image mapping takes care of the users' main navigation needs.

Consider Tables for Organizing Information

Much of the appeal of the NFL site is its ability to keep its visitors up-to-date on scores, schedules, players and team statistics, and so on. The design strength of tables is their ability to organize reams of figures into neat little packages. Tables can be engineered to interact automatically with data coming from outside sources such as internal or remote servers. If it weren't for tables and their ability to package information, much of the information being presented about the game of football just wouldn't be possible.

"Before tables existed as a design feature," says Michael Nanfito, a senior project manager at the Seattle-based Web site design firm of FreeRange Media, Inc., and mastermind behind the design of this Web site. "There were only two ways to control information across the screen horizontally. The designer had to either create a special image to have nice parallel body groupings of information, or you had to use a preformatted tag that would convert everything to the Courier font. Unless that's the effect you're looking for, it usually gives terrible results. Tables allow designers to control the flow of information horizontally across the screen in a presentable fashion."

About the NFL Site Designers

Michael Nanfito heads up the Information Management division at FreeRange Media, Inc. During its first two years in business, FreeRange quickly developed an enviable reputation for doing high-profile, well-executed Web site work. The NFL site is one of the firm's more recent achievements and embodies the spirit of one of America's most popular spectator sports.

A Designer's Web Philosophy

Michael Nanfito's background is in the information sciences. His specialty is providing the best and most efficient information possible with the aim of improving productivity. His main focus is information management and communication technologies, rather than the typical art, design, or publishing background of most who have migrated to the Web.

Nanfito comes to the Web with his own personal experience as one of the pioneer users. "I very much see the Web as a communications device, an information and communications device," he says. "Years ago, when there were about 5,000 of us on the Internet, we used to communicate through the Web using only the most basic of software tools. But now, the mechanics of the Web are hidden behind a nice comfortable browser and, in many cases, a very graphical environment. Thankfully, no one needs to know that kind of stuff anymore.

"The Web is a much more humane, accessible environment now. I think that's where my personal area of expertise is. My challenge is in how to make information accessible to people, *real* people. Many people get excited about the multimedia aspects of the Web, but essentially it's just another way to communicate. Whether you're using HTML, Java, or Shockwave, it all boils down to communication.

"For example, the NFL site is mostly statistics and data about football, the Microsoft site is about specifications for back-office software, and the Christian Science Monitor site is a daily news site. That's just the core information, and that's where the Web comes in. Think of it as the 'universal translator' used on Star Trek. It's the ultimate communication facilitator."

About the Design Firm

Based in Seattle, Washington, FreeRange Media, Inc. was started by Andrew Fry in 1994, and was originally established as a CD-ROM and multimedia company. At that early time, when the Web was just emerging, FreeRange became involved in media development. From there, FreeRange landed several large clients, including corporate computer giants Microsoft, IBM, and Hewlett-Packard, as well as commercial companies such as MCI, CBS, McGraw-Hill, the NFL, the Westin Hotel chain, and Price-Costco. A formidable track record for a company in business less than two years. "Shortly after we established FreeRange Media, the Web sort of blew into everybody's reality," says Nanfito. "It was becoming apparent that Internet Web site design was a good direction to take the organization."

And it's lucky they did. Like other design firms who sniffed a change in the wind at the beginning, FreeRange Media grew at an incredible pace during the first two years of corporate development. "Two years ago I was the thirteenth person hired here, and now we're roughly eighty people," says Nanfito. "Our professional inventory of resources includes experts in HTML design, graphic design, software development, database development, network engineering, and project management."

But like any good entrepreneurial-minded company, FreeRange doesn't intend to stop at Web site design, according to Nanfito. They've already established three other growth areas for the company to nurture future opportunities, beginning with product development for the Web (meaning software tools and software products to use with the Internet). Next, their Intranet Solutions Division is developing tools for TCP/IP Web technology and database integration for internal corporate environments, which is expected to be the next big growth area for Web technologies. Finally, they've formed a Properties Group that involves more of a sponsorship arena for Web sites. For this area, FreeRange intends to develop an environment that is not really a product but more a matchmaking organization, to marry advertisers with Web sites for sponsorship.

For more information on FreeRange Media, Inc., visit their Web site at http://www.freerange.com (see Figure 9-1). For design tips, see the Builder Page at their site.

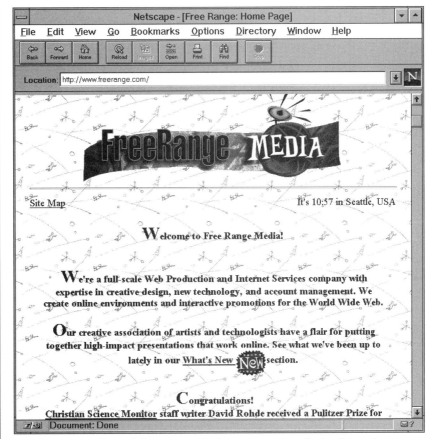

Figure 9-1: FreeRange's home page design appears to reflect a fun and easy-going attitude toward Web site design, but their many successes speak for themselves.

Kicking Off the NFL Site Design

The project began when FreeRange landed a design contract with Ann Kursnir, senior vice president of New Media Technologies at the National Football League in New York. For a design firm just starting out, landing a client of this size and stature is bound to be a bit overwhelming. But, it didn't come at all as a surprise. Being selected as the Web site design firm for this site took a lot of preparation, planning, and hard work.

Once they knew they wanted a Web site, the NFL executives hired their own consultant to scout out potentially qualified Web site design firms around the globe. FreeRange was among 15 companies selected to participate in the bidding process for the design. The round-up of competition was formidable, including firms from cities like New York, San Francisco, and Seattle. But, what gave them the edge they would need to seal the deal?

At that point FreeRange already had a fairly good reputation. They'd already done a large publisher's site and were involved with projects for Microsoft. Some of their staff were involved with Internet World. FreeRange had also put out their own Internet training video, and company president Andrew Fry had published his own book on Web publishing. These are things that help immensely when trying to start up any type of business. But that usually isn't *all* it takes. "When I was discussing site strategy with some of the other staff here," says Nanfito, "I realized this site was going to be complex, sophisticated, and technically challenging. We knew we needed to present a proposal that showed we were prepared for all of those factors."

FreeRange realized early on that they needed to be very up-front with all the background technical issues. Nanfito put together a team of five to develop a proposal that outlined the marketing, sales, and communications aspects of the site. It needed to address specific technical issues and yet give a feel for how the site was *really* going to work. The natural inclination of prospective clients is for them to focus on their site's look and feel. "Frankly, I think that's what got us the job," says Nanfito. "We had a very detailed proposal, which recognized that it was much more than a look-and-feel project."

Present Solid Ideas

FreeRange presented a firm and focused approach in their client proposal. The secret to being selected lay in how they pitched their ideas and how they positioned solutions to the challenge of providing sports information to Web surfers at large. Nanfito says his firm recognized early what they thought was the real thrust of the site. Even though the NFL site is essentially a professional sports and entertainment site, they concluded that the technical function of the site was to manage the flow of information. The site itself would include everything from daily news stories to transmissions of live data from the stadiums where the events were taking place.

As part of their original proposal to the NFL, FreeRange mapped out a strategy for advertising, commerce, and sponsorship opportunities. The NFL makes money on selling sponsorships to big sports promoters such as Coke and Nike. Experienced designers and design firms know the client must be convinced that the site will make money. Nothing speaks louder to clients. It puts them at ease and reassures them that the designers are working for the client's best interests.

FreeRange decided that a key aspect of the NFL site would be selling official NFL logo merchandise. Basically, if it has the NFL logo on it, it's for sale on the current site. "The NFL doesn't sell tickets directly from the site," says Nanfito. "They're not quite ready for that. But each of the team areas provides information on local ticket sales outlets. Online ticket sales will be coming eventually. You will be able to log onto the site, go to the Seattle Seahawks, buy your tickets online, and have them delivered to you the very next day."

The rest of the FreeRange's approach to the site was simple. The philosophy they communicated to the NFL was that they would not make Internet users out of football fans, and they would not make football fans into Internet users if they weren't already. FreeRange saw their audience as football fans who were already surfing the Net. Based on that hypothesis, they worked with the client to bring together the providers of all the information that makes up the current site.

In reality, all of the NFL's teams could be thought of as information providers to the main site: 30 organizations, with each team separate unto itself. The real challenge in putting together a successful site was to work with each team to provide a concise, coherent communications protocol to allow them to provide information to the fans on a daily basis. The site would become an information news service, and because the information changed daily, many areas of the site would be rebuilt on a daily basis. Eventually, a portion of that building process would become automated, and the rest would be done by dedicated staff.

Plan & Follow a Thorough Strategy

Michael Nanfito on project strategy in general: "Once the proposal is accepted, I create a detailed design specification document roughly 30 pages in length, which looks at the structure, graphic design, and technical specifications of the site. The design specification then becomes the guidebook for the actual creation of the site. Next, I create a project timeline, including time for graphics, with at least three distinct design styles for the project. To do this we create mock-ups in the form of screen shots. We literally produce graphics and rough HTML pages and pop them into a browser so the client can get an idea of the look and feel. Occasionally, we'll build a dummy site online to act as a basis for the design. We either present this at a client site, or devise it in such a way that it can be on a CD-ROM or floppy disk and mailed to them. In some cases, we've built a dummy site on a server and passworded it so that only the client has access. That way they can sit in the comfort of their own city and review our ideas."

During the initial design phase of the NFL site, Nanfito assembled a Web site team specifically for the project. During various stages of the project, this dedicated staff consisted of between 6 and 14 people, including graphic designers, layout people, software developers, database designers, and network engineers. Technically, the contents of the site would become very large and would eventually consist of data being handled by five Sun Microsystems Sparc machines. It would also require a dedicated information manager for the huge volume of daily information from the league received from the individual leagues.

FreeRange knew they immediately needed to develop a close working relationship with their client. In fact, even from across the country they were in contact several times a day by phone, e-mail, and fax. The client was—and had to be—very much involved with the site and had to take an active interest in its development. In many regards, the site designer needs to get under the skin of the client and find out exactly what makes the client's business tick. As project manager, Nanfito needed to study all he could about the *business* of football, not just the game itself. More than that, he needed to *understand* the client's business and in a sense become a part of the client's organization during the production of the site. And, at the same time, the information management process requires that the designer hunt for the information needed—and from their own perspective, not the client's. Most organizations typically focus on information from a marketing perspective, and the trick for the project manager is to see through that. The designer will essentially be focused on the information aspects of the site.

The designer needs to find out as quickly as possible what the client's needs are and how to satisfy those needs in a Web environment. The first step in the NFL site design was to develop a basic architecture on paper to fill those information needs. But relying heavily on current technology can be dangerous in terms of design. In the case of this site, much of the basic structure was designed with the understanding that the Web is a changing environment. The technologies, like the HTML used to design it, are highly changeable. This potential for change should be a key design consideration in the architecture for any site.

Keep in mind that six months after any site design is put in place, it's very likely the client will come back to the designer and ask that a new feature be implemented. In theory, it could be something that seems easily implemented from the client's perspective, but it could actually change the entire site structure. As you surf the Web it's easy to spot out-of-date sites that use old design limitations or older technologies. As the design community on the Web moves up the ladder of technology, so too does the appearance of the average site. It's up to the designer to plan for expansion later on. One key might be to keep things simple from the start and avoid designing yourself into a corner.

Michael Nanfito suggests that designers structuring a new site should imagine the site as if they were building a house. "If you are having a new home built, you're going to be thinking about paint color chips, wallpaper, and carpeting—all the things that

> The site designer needs to get under the skin of the client and find out exactly what makes the client's business tick.

make a house *pretty* inside. But while you're dreaming about what to hang on the walls, or how to position furniture, the house still has to be erected in a way that suits your needs in the first place. In reality, the most important part is to logically think out the foundation—how to pour the footings, erect the supports, and construct the frame—in order for your house to eventually look and feel right. That's what designers do; they build solid information environments."

Successful Web sites have to be engaging. They have to provide the ingredients for interactive energy. Without this, users lose interest quickly. Your visitors will simply go away and find something else to do. When you create information environments, they have to be coherent and keep your users interested. Do this, and they'll not only come back but they'll stay as long as they possibly can. They need to think of your site as a place they can go and get something in return. Consider the addictiveness of video games. They're engaging and challenging. Challenge your visitors and they'll stay longer.

Clients look to the designer for advice, and they should be included in the design process as early as possible. It's important that they feel their site is being designed appropriately for them, either in a business or corporate sense. It's similar to advertising agency work in designing corporate identities and logos. It's very important that the site designer be creative and present an accurate portrayal of the client.

Web Site Acrobatics

Currently, the NFL site handles live data coming from 30 stadiums. During peak game seasons, on any given Sunday, there are 15 games with live data coming in. That data is translated by a custom software application every 10 to 30 seconds and updated every 15 seconds, then converted to a database. From that database, information is extracted by another custom software application, which then converts it to HTML and automatically places it in the appropriate table on the site. If data-crunching were an Olympic sport, this data-juggler would be a medal contender.

The size of the NFL site varies, depending on the information the visitor is requesting and the football events currently or recently in progress. In terms of actual pages, the site exceeds 4,000 individual pages. Many pages are created dynamically. Much of the site is automated and involves sophisticated, behind-the-scenes software programming and linking to external data-bases and information servers across the country.

According to Michael Nanfito, much of the information seen on the site is supplied by the NFL's official statistical reporting company, SuperStat, in Minnesota. "We worked with SuperStat to coordinate the flow of data from the stadium to the Web site. We developed a custom software application to translate the data into a form the Web can understand, and the site then dynami-cally creates those Web pages. For me, the most amazing part of the site is the live data. It was a tricky task to perform but it worked beautifully. We presented the very first Internet broad-cast of the SuperBowl, and it was technically flawless. We're very proud of that."

Get to Know the Audience

What sort of content appeals to a football fan on the Web? To illustrate the importance of audience targeting, FreeRange did their homework even before approaching their potential client. As it turned out, the NFL already had their own idea about who the market was, but the FreeRange design team needed to be on top of that long before they ever reached the client.

Through their own demographic research, FreeRange knew the site would likely be accessed by a mostly male audience, roughly between the ages of 25 and 45. They also knew these were either young professionals or college students, and they knew this was a slice of the Internet public that had access to fairly sophisticated computing technology. They were also confident this group was using at least a 14.4 modem at work or school, and most likely a 28.8 modem at home. This was a key consideration in the design of the site and gave them the ammu-nition they needed to proceed with several key design elements.

Armed with the knowledge that most users were accessing the site via faster-than-average modems, the FreeRange team decided to prepare their graphic images slightly on the heavy side. After the site's initial launch, custom software was used to track visits to the site. By doing this, they discovered something very interesting. "Everyday, there was a spike in site traffic," says Nanfito. "It started at roughly 10:00 in the morning and jumped up until about 1 or 2 in the afternoon and then plummeted. We discovered that 90 percent of visitors were either from educational institutions or commercial institutions. The remaining 10 percent came from miscellaneous connections. That meant to us that the audience was composed mostly of students on their breaks at school on a T1 or T3 line or they were employees at work.

"For site designers, this is valuable knowledge. This allows the design team to decide whether they can beef up the graphical look and feel of the site without throwing off their audience. They don't want to shut out the portion of their audience browsing with America Online or CompuServe browsers; but looking at these statistics FreeRange knew that most of the people that were accessing this site were on a T1. It's not a situation you find with every site, but in this case it was true. So that information significantly impacted the design.

"The NFL had already tried one Web site called NFL Sidelines that was available through Prodigy, which didn't work out. From the start, it was a very poor name selection for a football site, partly because sidelines is a metaphor for being out of the game. Prodigy at that time was a big NFL sponsor and they heavily promoted the site. As a result, when they did their design research it was skewed toward Prodigy users, which prompted them to make some limiting design compromises. Unfortunately, politics can often be a part of the design process.

"The Internet audience generally knew nothing about this Sidelines site," says Nanfito. "In fact, none of us had ever heard of it. My understanding of the browser market was that Netscape was going to dominate. Netscape supported tables, and it was critical that we implement tables, given the nature of the site. It was a difficult design issue we had to deal with. On the one hand, their consultant was saying the exact opposite—and he already had a lot of pull with them. On the other hand, we had a mandate to properly design the site. It took us two weeks of our own marketing research to convince our client that the statistics proved our standpoint."

Use Frames for Flexibility

One of the true beauties of the World Wide Web is its ability to easily adapt to change, unlike other types of publishing formats. Imagine for a moment that your local phone book is already riddled with errors the very moment it's sent out for printing. Correcting printed materials traditionally means expensive rework, time delays, and added labor and material costs.

With the Web, you need to make changes and alterations only to the site itself. Textual pages can be edited while images can be replaced, and links can be updated, changed, or eliminated altogether. Implementing a complete format change such as adding frames may be done offline, and the switch can be made when everything is ready. Distribution is essentially instant.

Designing with frames has many advantages when structuring a site, and it was an option that FreeRange seriously considered implementing initially. FreeRange has used frames in many of the sites they have created, says Nanfito. The biggest problem with frames is that they aren't yet available in most browsers, including Netscape's prime rival, the Microsoft Internet Explorer. But frames are very useful. They allow users to look at several different locations at a time.

The NFL site doesn't yet use frames, but frames haven't been ruled out as a possible growth area. Nanfito endorses their use as a highly valuable design tool. "For example," he says, "If you're running a law firm and you want your paralegals to do legal research, you can keep them on your site by having a table of contents in one frame window while allowing them to link to other sites using an adjacent window. This setup provides multiple scrollable windows in the browser interface. The advantage is twofold. First, you can retain users on your site while providing them access to remote services. Next, you can have navigation

"With many sites, as you scroll the page it's easy to lose navigation. Frames allow you to have a navigation always present."

continuously present on the screen. With many sites, as you scroll the page it's easy to lose navigation. Frames allow you to have a navigation always present."

For a commercial site, designing with frames gives you the design freedom of keeping something like a company logo in the view of the user. You can guarantee that the logo will be in front of the user all the time. In terms of business, this is certainly a distinct advantage of frame technology.

Reducing Load Time by Limiting Image Sizes

As a design issue, load time for pages can make or break the attractiveness of a site.

As a design issue, load time for pages can make or break the attractiveness of a site, no matter how appealing the images are. As a professional designer, Nanfito limits the total file size of any page to absolutely no more than 40,000 bytes. Setting a limit on the amount of information on any given page is a common design dilemma. It's tough to take a potpourri of elements, throw them together, and try to make sure that they're less than 40,000 bytes. A quick calculation of page size can be done by adding the size of the HTML document that creates the page together with any of the linked elements.

According to Nanfito, the typical image size should fall in the range of 10,000 to 15,000 bytes. Most full-featured graphics packages such as CorelDRAW! or FreeHand allow you to export to a range of file sizes, depending on the image's contents. Likewise, image editing packages such as Corel PhotoPaint or Photoshop allow you to take elaborate graphics and reduce their file size significantly by fine-tuning color palettes. Equilibrium DeBabelizer is perhaps the most highly regarded application for image tweaking. The program, which is widely used for both multimedia and Web development projects, allows you to radically reduce graphic file sizes for GIF and JPEG. Unfortunately, unless you have access to a Macintosh, you're out of luck. DeBabelizer has always been a Mac-only app.

"DeBabelizer has been around for awhile and we've been using it for a couple of years," says Nanfito. "We turned the NFL onto it because we have a lot of graphics coming to us directly from NFL properties in Los Angeles. They were sending us these wonderful photographs, but digitally they were huge and totally unusable. So, we coached them into doing some media preparation. They have a huge photo and image library. Now they're able to edit down these images before we even get them."

Web Site Design Hazards

As a designer producing high-profile sites, Nanfito has his own hit list of design strategies to avoid on the Web. "One of the biggest mistakes made these days," he says "is for designers to create sites that are too graphical. It impacts significantly on download time. I think the reason for this stems from designers looking at Web sites from a media point of view instead of an informational point of view. Creating a site that is graphically overloaded is a big mistake.

"I think designing a site to be an electronic page turner is also a big mistake," he says. "It's looking at the solution on a page-by-page basis, rather than an environmental basis. Some sites tend to be created on a piecemeal basis, and unfortunately it's the wrong approach. A Web site should be looked at from an overall perspective and should be designed with several different angles in mind. I think that most designers tend to create pages, tweak them until they like them, and then move to the next page. What you end up with is a site that is incoherent across the spectrum."

Another big mistake is putting up "under construction" signs, says Nanfito. If it's not finished, don't put it up. Don't even make any mention of it, except maybe as a news release. It's a big mistake that many designers make. They think they're communicating something, but all they're really doing is frustrating their audience. It's the kind of thing that makes the audience say, "You made me come here to tell me that there is nothing here? Why are you doing this to me?" This isn't just poor design, it's poor site management.

The reality of this lies in human nature. If you put up a site and by chance users make their way to it and see all these under construction signs and poorly formed graphics, all they're going to remember is that the site is not very good and not to come back. They don't know *or care* when it'll be ready. All they know

One of the biggest mistakes made these days is for designers to create sites that are too graphical.

is that you just wasted their time. It's not as if people surfing the Web check back frequently to see if the site's ready yet. There's just too much else to look at out there. That's where many designers make their first mistake. They don't think about the site from the perspective of the audience.

Moving On

Consider for a moment that while Web site design involves art, technology, niche marketing, and information management, it demands that the designers have a total understanding of the subject matter as well as a sensitivity for business. FreeRange's NFL site not only engages users but it allows them to hit a single location for all aspects of the sport. It's not only a tribute to the sport but an excellent example of a fully exploited subject.

Chapter 10, "Design Case Study: American Airlines, AA On Board," takes a look at the American Airlines' site.

Design Case Study: American Airlines, AA OnBoard

Site: American Airlines, AAOnBoard,
http://www.amrcorp.com

Designer: James Hering, account supervisor

Design firm: Temerlin McClain, subsidiary of Bozell,
Jacobs, Kenyon, and Eckhardt

About the AMR Corporation

As the parent company of American Airlines, the AMR Corporation is one of the largest business icons of America. Their high profile air travel business, American Airlines, is a world wide company in the truest sense of the term. It seems only natural they have a presence on the World Wide Web. The AMR Corporation site is a multipurpose site for both the company and their customers.

The airline business is a turbulent one to say the least. Competition, economics, politics, and customer service all play key roles in the success of any airline, and in recent years only the fittest have survived. To appreciate the magnitude of operating an airline, consider that on an average day, American Airlines will:

- ✦ Receive more than 343,000 reservation calls.

- ✦ Handle more than 304,000 pieces of luggage.

- ✦ Serve more than 196,000 meals and snacks.

- ✦ Fly more than 2,200 flights.

- ✦ Transport more than 270 animals.

- ✦ Change more than 70 airplane tires.

The company maintains its own fleet of more than 648 aircraft totaling over 100,000 passenger seats, and it also provides various airline-related services to more than 100 other airlines companies across the globe. Its business dealings reach into more than 160 different countries, involving over 300 individual travel destinations.

Overview of the Web Site

American's main Web site was launched on May 14, 1995. Although much of the daily maintenance of the Web site is maintained internally, the design is handled by the advertising agency Temerlin McClain, based not far from the Dallas/Fort Worth area of Texas.

Here is a company with an interesting, multifaceted corporate image. The parent company is likely the least prominent and least well known. The airline side of the company is the highest profile and most service oriented, but not necessarily the most profitable. As with many large corporate sites, the site itself is a literal reflection of the overall corporate structure of the AMR Corporation.

The welcome page (see Figure 10-1) highlights the AMR Corporation and serves as the hub for the four key areas of the company. These areas represent the business units of the company including the parent AMR Corporation itself, the Air Transportation Group, the SABRE Group, and the AMR Management Services Group. Each of those areas can be considered a Web site in its own right, having links to various other Web pages intertwined within the company's structure. Although the site is growing constantly, it originally featured roughly 300 pages. Its initial launch was accomplished at an estimated cost of $100,000.

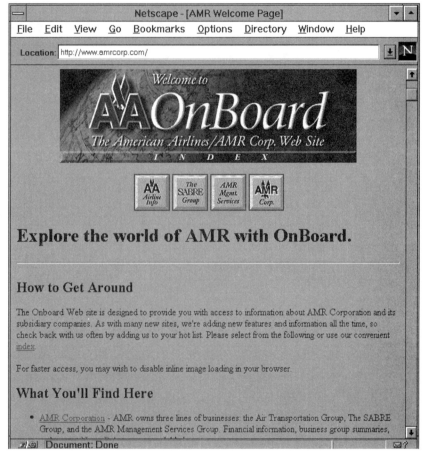

Figure 10-1: The welcome page of the AMR Corporation Web site is actually the "hub" for the four key company business units.

The site is spread throughout a number of unique domain names and physically resides over multiple servers. Information available at the site is also collected from various systems. For AMR customers and high-profile business interests, the most significant area of the site is the airline operations side of business. By clicking the AA Airline Info button on the AMR welcome page you can access the American Airlines home page shown in Figure 10-2. From the customer's perspective, it's a site within a site.

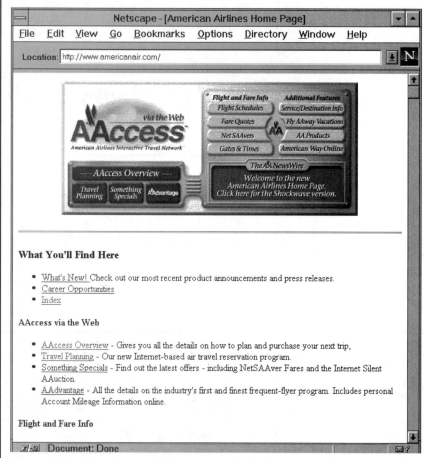

Figure 10-2: The most popular area of the AMR site is the airline service and information site that features access to schedules, quotes, and various travel-related information.

The rest of the site will be of interest mostly to AMR's other existing and potential customers including services marketed to other airlines, and management and technology services.

About the Designers

Temerlin McClain is a full-service advertising agency headquartered in Los Colinas just outside of Dallas, Fort Worth. It is one of the largest advertising agencies outside of New York or Chicago.

The AMR Corporation site project is headed by one of Temerlin McClain's account supervisors, James Hering, who has been working closely with their American Airlines account for more than six years. As with most agency account representatives, it's Hering's role to know what clients want *before* they do. It may seem unusual for an advertising agency to be handling Web site design; but, as is the case with many different media professions, Temerlin McClain considers the Web merely another business frontier.

"Some people in the industry originally thought advertising agencies were doomed," says Hering, "but, recently, I think those same experts have done an about face. Now they say some of the most innovative Web content being done is by advertising agencies. If it's not being done by agencies, it's being done by people who work at agencies or who are freelancing after having gained agency experience. I think it all boils down to understanding clients and their business objectives, and designing something to meet those objectives. Good design is more than just throwing together a splashy Web site."

According to Hering, his agency had been eyeing the Web as an agency opportunity since the Web's infancy. "Temerlin McClain has been involved in interactive media for roughly 7 years now," he says. "We started tinkering with the Internet and looking at it as a potential new medium opportunity as early as 1994."

To Hering personally, being involved in Web site design is a marriage of two of his loves. "I come from an advertising background," says Hering, "but, I also have a love for computers, and I've always been a self-taught person. I've never had any specific training in the computer area other than simply my own enthusiasm and interest. When the World Wide Web was introduced, I felt it was an opportunity for me to put these two interests together."

> "We started tinkering with the Internet and looking at it as a potential new medium opportunity as early as 1994."

The Web site designs that Temerlin McClain produces are driven by its clients' needs and its own need for communication consistency. "The true value of an advertising agency is to cross all types of communication media," says Hering. "We provide—to coin the big buzz word of the early 90s—*integrated communications*. As an analogy, you might say it's like speaking with one clear voice across a number of different channels."

Hering says big businesses are constantly searching for ways of tapping into their customers' lives and the Web is a perfect way to do that. "Interactive media has become another tool for our clients to reach their customers. So, if there's continuity on the Web, there should be communication continuity throughout the campaign, including the TV spot, the newspaper ad, the radio spot, and the billboard ad. With a clear client image there's synergy and you have an image campaign." When you have communication continuity in all these media, the client speaks with one voice and the message is crystal clear.

"Interactive media has become another tool for our clients to reach their customers."

With that in mind, designers at Temerlin McClain have become experts in identifying their client's message or objective and presenting it so that it is continuous with their advertising in other media. "In terms of our design role," says Hering, "we never approach a site design simply because it's a Web site. It's because there's a strategic business goal behind doing the site. If it's to bring people to the Web site to sell something, then there's a very specific objective that we want to work towards.

"There are a lot of great designers out there producing fabulous work," but, says Hering, "I think the time has come to use the World Wide Web as a tool to reach a very specialized, upscale, and highly-educated audience. Fed Ex's package-tracking site is a good example of this. Talk about a perfect mix of the right media to provide customer information! This is exactly the type of approach we have with the flight schedules on the American Airlines site."

Designing the Site Structure

Because the AMR site features four main areas, "This site turned out to be one of those balancing acts in appealing to a variety of audiences," says Hering. "In terms of site structure, on the very top layer we named the main site AA OnBoard, because of the different audiences involved. We wanted to provide a structure and a focus that would work well based on each audience." The most recognized and visited part of this site is the AA Airline Info area. American Airlines is a subsidiary of the AMR Corporation, and AMR is its stock ticker symbol, but many financial analysts and industry watchers track AA by all of AMR.

"What we did was provide an overall structure, so that if the financial industry wanted to take a look at AMR as a whole, they could start on the top level," says Hering. "The areas other than American Airlines, such as the SABRE group, each have their own audiences, and so this overall structure provides access for these audiences."

Specifically, the information contained in these different areas is structured in this way:

AAccess Via the Web: This American Airlines Interactive Travel Network site includes information pages featuring What's New!, flight, travel and frequent flyer points information, schedules, fare quotes, and online arrival and departure information associated with consumer air travel. Additional features include a multi-airline service and destination guide, vacation planning and accommodation reservation service, duty-free shopping details, and access to the online version of American Way, the internally produced in-flight magazine.

SABRE Group: This reservations systems unit site includes access to four of SABRE's own internal divisions including its travel information network, Decision Technologies, Computer Services, and SABRE Interactive divisions.

AMR Management Services: This home page features access to five smaller areas including AMR Services Profile, TeleService Resources, Inc., AMR Training Group, Business Jet Solutions, and AMR Investment Services. Each is a part of the management services needed to support other airline-related services within the company.

AMR Corporation: This is the corporate site featuring general upper-level information about the company, news releases, financial information, president and board of directors profiles, and news of kudos won by the company including their corporate environmental initiatives and corporate awards and endorsements.

When Temerlin McClain designers first presented their concept, they focused heavily on the organization of the content. They knew they had several different audiences to attract. Their challenge was to design a structure that would not only provide an easy way for users to navigate through the site, but would also be organized in a way so that different audiences could access the information they needed without having to dig through multiple layers on the site.

"If it's a travel agent audience who wants to access information about the SABRE travel information network, we send them right to that page," says Hering. "This way, they feel as though they're in their own Web site. Customers accessing the site for airline information also have access with this flat structure."

Selling the Web Site Concept

For many Web site designers and their clients, concept presentations can be a tricky maneuver. Clients are often mystified by the technology and terminology that revolve around the World Wide Web. Temerlin McClain designers knew they were dealing with a technology-savvy client and elected to take a straightforward approach to sell their ideas.

"Following the structure development," says Hering, "we actually compiled the Web pages complete with text and artwork. We used finished pages to show the main concept.

"Then," says Hering, "we indicated with colored text how the links would work, complete with designed buttons and visuals. We sketched up large-sized boards that showed each Web page, and demonstrated how the site would look and operate. Finally, we just walked them through the rest of the presentation process.

"For the identity of the site," Hering says, "we had a brand development or name development brainstorming session to choose the name AA OnBoard. Following that, we had more name branding, graphic design, and organization discussions. This isn't a unique approach. In fact, in our usual advertising business, this is in line with how we approach *all* of our communications and creative work. We followed these sessions up with a final review process to make sure everyone was sure about the design, all the way up to AMR president and chairman Bob Crandall.

"At the top," says Hering, "Crandall was mainly concerned with how AMR would be presented as a whole. His main responsibility is answering to shareholders, so he wanted to make sure that the audience was taken care of. The other executives were interested in each of their own areas. So, through the use of a nice tree chart, we demonstrated how subsequent Web pages would tie the entire site together through integrated linking.

"Once they agreed on how the structure would work," says Hering, "we went into our production phase and the information-gathering phase to put all the pieces together. The Web site was about 300 pages when we launched it in May 1995. Back then it was strictly information, there weren't any interactive parts; but even before we got the thing out the door to launch it, we were already focusing on how we could link together various databases and information systems in the company to provide added value.

"That's how American Airlines arrived at the interactive flight information," Hering says. "The route map (see Figure 10-3) provides a wide range of flight-related information. There, users can get destination information, specifics on flights, baggage claim, and live online arrival times."

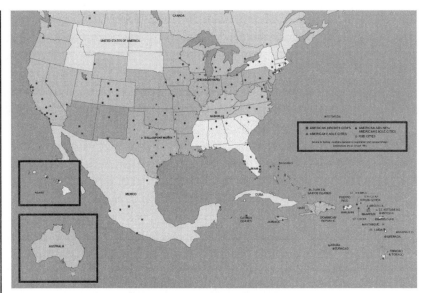

Figure 10-3: This clickable image map of North America enables AMR Corporation's users to simply point and click at their intended destination.

A Closer Look at the Site Design

For Temerlin McClain designers, the way they represented the client visually and the way they imparted their client's information was the easy part—they'd already been doing that for years. Their design challenge was how to put a wrapping around a very complex company, while exposing its most valuable assets.

Hering says that it's important for the designers to have an understanding of the client's content and how it can be organized. "The content should be reflective of the products and services the company is offering. Your site has just got to be intuitively easy to navigate. Use indexes and make it easy to go back to start if somebody is lost or confused. Make it easy to go back a page and go forward a page. Use indexes and search engines help in this area."

The site design was also a result of familiarity with the client's content. By using the AMR Corporation as a main hub that leads to four sections, Hering's group had the option of treating each of the four main areas differently. The more corporate areas were designed with a more traditional, conservative look and feel (see Figure 10-4), while the more commercial areas, such as service information pages, used a livelier, more sales-conscious design (see Figure 10-5).

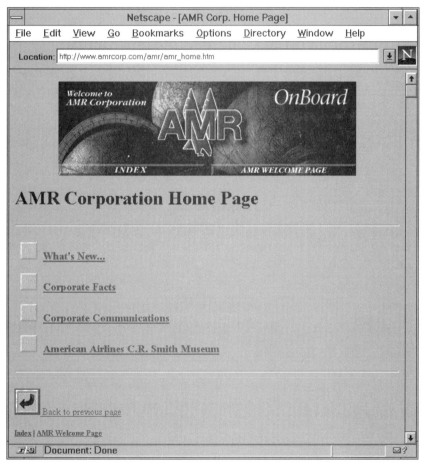

Figure 10-4: The heavily corporate areas of the AMR site feature very conservative, traditional-looking banner images and text on plain default backgrounds.

Figure 10-5: This FlyAAway Vacations Planner page features lively graphic toolbars, colorful photographs, colored image backgrounds, and graphic embellishments.

The American Airlines section is the only commercial section, so the overall design of this site is very traditional in its appearance. The three other main areas were designed with the more corporate-looking design.

Navigation tools and buttons at the site have been designed in various ways, depending on the audience appeal. The corporate site areas, which are smaller, feature few backgrounds and conservative graphic banners and buttons for navigation. The more commercial area of the site features highly stylized image map navigation using graphics modeled after aircraft control panels.

"The relationship we have with American is really nice. We develop, create, and deliver various parts of the site to them, but they maintain the actual servers," says Hering. "It's a very good relationship. It's been extremely productive. Both sides support each other and it's made for a much stronger site."

Measuring the Success of the Site

Measuring the effectiveness of this site would be a difficult and time-consuming task if it weren't for the very nature of the site. "One example of the strength and usefulness of this medium hit me the first winter our Web site was up," explains Hering. "A series of severe snow storms had completely locked up air travel through the East coast. During that time, our Web site server traffic and access to flight information pages spiked off the map. We received hundreds of letters from people thanking us for providing this service.

"Using the Web site," says Hering, "our audience knew they could check when flights were coming in at a point when reservation phone lines were jammed. It saved them having to trudge through the snow to the airport to wait hours for friends' and relatives' flights to come in. It's a prime example of how we not only help the customer, we were helping ourselves by giving this information out on a broad basis."

Temerlin McClain and American Airlines both recognized early that visitors to the Web site were potential customers. It was easy to see the appropriateness of including a fare quote page (see Figure 10-6). The primary business focus of any airline is the frequent business traveler. "These are folks who take a lot of trips and they're the airline's best customers," says Hering. "They're people who qualify for American's AAdvantage Platinum and AAdvantage Goldelite program memberships. They rack up 25, 50, 100 thousand miles a year on the airline. And, they're also the ones who use the site the most."

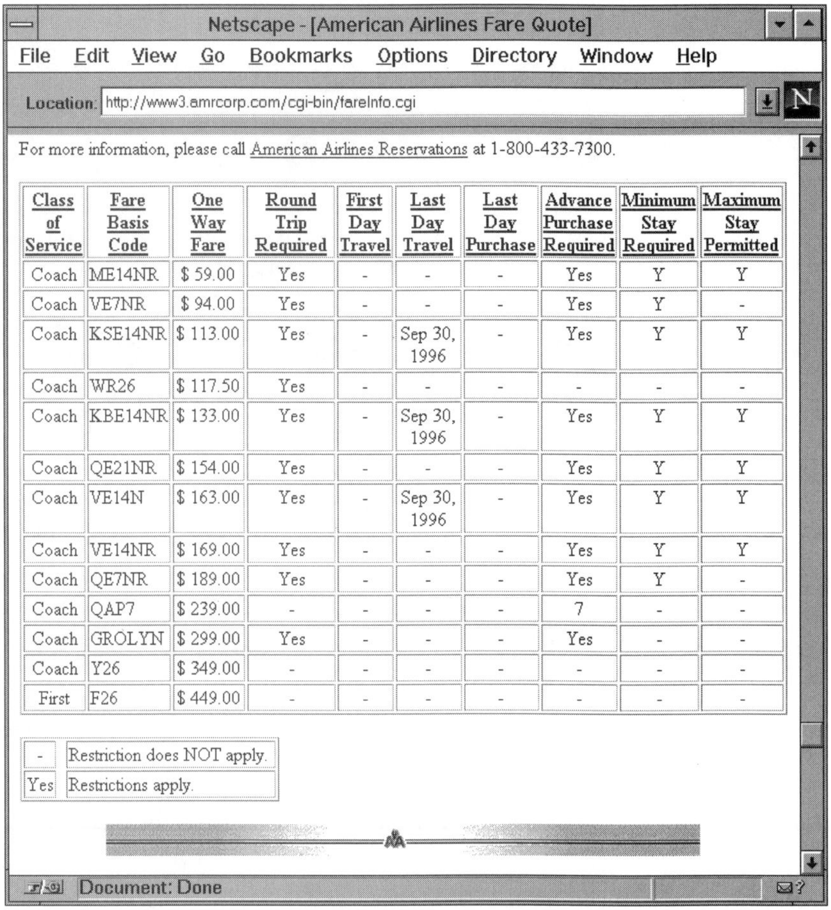

Netscape - [American Airlines Fare Quote]

File   Edit   View   Go   Bookmarks   Options   Directory   Window   Help

Location: http://www3.amrcorp.com/cgi-bin/fareInfo.cgi

For more information, please call American Airlines Reservations at 1-800-433-7300.

Class of Service	Fare Basis Code	One Way Fare	Round Trip Required	First Day Travel	Last Day Travel	Last Day Purchase	Advance Purchase Required	Minimum Stay Required	Maximum Stay Permitted
Coach	ME14NR	$ 59.00	Yes	-	-	-	Yes	Y	Y
Coach	VE7NR	$ 94.00	Yes	-	-	-	Yes	Y	-
Coach	KSE14NR	$ 113.00	Yes	-	Sep 30, 1996	-	Yes	Y	Y
Coach	WR26	$ 117.50	Yes	-	-	-	-	-	-
Coach	KBE14NR	$ 133.00	Yes	-	Sep 30, 1996	-	Yes	Y	Y
Coach	QE21NR	$ 154.00	Yes	-	-	-	Yes	Y	Y
Coach	VE14N	$ 163.00	Yes	-	Sep 30, 1996	-	Yes	Y	Y
Coach	VE14NR	$ 169.00	Yes	-	-	-	Yes	Y	Y
Coach	QE7NR	$ 189.00	Yes	-	-	-	Yes	Y	-
Coach	QAP7	$ 239.00	-	-	-	-	7	-	-
Coach	GROLYN	$ 299.00	Yes	-	-	-	Yes	-	-
Coach	Y26	$ 349.00	-	-	-	-	-	-	-
First	F26	$ 449.00	-	-	-	-	-	-	-

-	Restriction does NOT apply.
Yes	Restrictions apply.

Document: Done

Figure 10-6: American Airlines Fare Quote page.

Most of the airline's communications strategies are focused toward these frequent business travelers. They are the people who are getting on corporate local area networks to get access to the Web. Access to flight schedules such as the one shown in Figure 10-7 has consequence, and for some, the use of this schedule information page is a daily requirement. Hering says American Airlines is also targeting the academic, collegiate, and university crowds, who are natural users of the World Wide Web.

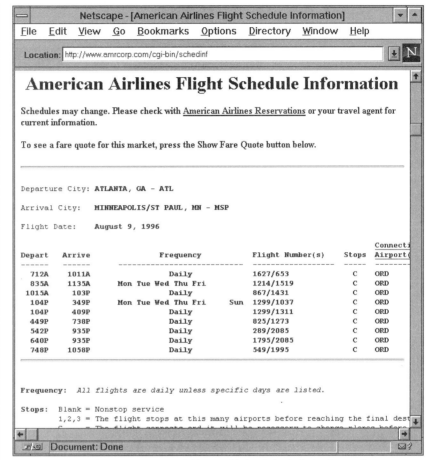

Figure 10-7: The American Airlines Flight Schedule Information page exemplifies how the Web site design firm literally puts flight schedules at your fingertips.

"We often receive site feedback actually thanking us for putting flight schedules at their fingertips so they don't have to thumb through a flight schedule."

"When you consider the corollaries between personal computer sales demographics, our target market, and World Wide Web users in general, they're all pretty close," says Hering. "We often receive site feedback actually thanking us for putting flight schedules at their fingertips so they don't have to thumb through a flight schedule or be put on hold on the phone. They also thank us for putting their American Advantage air miles account online so they can track their own points. That's one way for us to measure the usefulness and payoff of the site."

Measuring a Return on Investment

Pinning down an overall return on investment for most sites is a tricky thing to do, especially in this case. "I think we know intuitively, by the type of traffic we have through a Web site, that we're providing a distribution medium for information that we believe lowers American's overall cost and reservation costs in terms of phone calls to the airline.

"From a business judgment sense, I think this Web site is very viable," explains Hering. "Comparatively, the American Airlines Corporation site wasn't that expensive to create and maintain.

"The largest portion of our initial cost of the site was the photography usage rights for a lot of the images at the site," adds Hering. "We wanted to make sure we had a balance between usability and image. AMR is a worldwide leading corporation so, while we could have gone with very basic graphical treatment, the site had to be inline with the corporate image. We chose a format that had a lot of nice images that we felt accurately communicated the company's corporate culture."

Avoiding Web Site Design Mistakes

As a professional agency making part of its business Web design, it's often overwhelmingly obvious to Temerlin McClain where mistakes are being made in terms of structure, aesthetics, and visual appearance of sites. Hering's opinions in this area come as no surprise.

"I think losing focus on ease of use and navigation is the biggest design flaw out there on the Web."

"I think losing focus on ease of use and navigation is the biggest design flaw out there on the Web," says Hering. "Next to that, I'd say many graphics you see are either too big or don't render well. Some sites I see appear to have no clear purpose and stray too far from any obvious marketing or business objectives. Being different and unique just for creativity's sake isn't a good objective."

As he cruises the Web checking out current design trends, Hering says he often sees basic design errors, such as backgrounds that make it impossible to read text. "In Web site design, you still need to use good design sense. The tools may be different, but common sense should still apply. Having a black background page with dark navy blue text is only asking your reader to work harder to get to your site content. The same general sense of design skills needs to be applied here just like any place else."

While complete communication packages are the core of his agency's business, Hering also stresses the importance of producing Web sites that accurately reflect a company's existing corporate image. "The design of a site has to be reflective of the company," he says. "You don't want to have a radical design on a Web site if your client and their customers are a conservative, white-collar crowd. The site needs to be in tune with the company's existing identity."

For the AMR site, corporate identity was a strong selling point during the Temerlin McClain presentation. Deviating from a company's identity in many cases will either make or break the selling of a site concept. "I think corporate identity is of paramount importance on the Web," says Hering. "I don't think you should just slap a brochure on the World Wide Web. If you can take the content of the brochure and make it easier, more entertaining, and better to read, then you *should* adapt it to the Web. But, the medium should not drive the message. It should be the other way around. If there is a unique way to communicate it, and use the unique attributes of the World Wide Web, then that's what a Web site designer should be focusing on."

The novelty of site design is also something that can divert a Web designer, says Hering. "I think the worst reason for someone putting up a Web site is just to throw up some wacky content because they think it's cool, neat, shocking, or different. If a company is service oriented, that should be the focus of their Web site."

As for the future of the Web, Hering has his reservations, as do many skeptics of this medium who fear it will eventually reach a saturation point. "I am concerned that one of these days the pipes are going to get clogged, and we're just going to break down because of the sheer volume," he says. "The Web's only

"You don't want to have a radical design on a Web site if your client and their customers are a conservative, white-collar crowd."

limit is the designer's imagination. Eventually, people are going to think of inventive ways to reduce data size, streamline video, or pipe in customized information for individuals. I also think one of the key trends for the future is in personalization. I believe any type of business that's information related should be on the Web. Any company that has a diverse geography and a need to communicate with its employees, sales staff, and its customers, needs to be here."

Moving On

This chapter provided an in-depth case study of the Web site design considerations used by the advertising agency Temerlin McClain. Integrated communications for the AMR Corporation and its existing and potential clients continues to be Temerlin McClain's strategic reason for creating and maintaining the AMR Corporation Web site.

Just ahead in Chapter 11, "Design Case Study: The White House," you'll learn why the White House has a Web site and you'll discover the special considerations that went into designing a Web site for the nation.

11

Design Case Study: The White House

Site:	The White House, http://www.whitehouse.com
Managing Editor:	David Lytel
Design firm:	Internally designed, produced, and maintained by White House personnel

In the process of chronicling the Office of the President, the White House Web site provides the highest (and highest-tech) level of visibility for the United States government. As such, the site supersedes the role of a purely political agenda. In creating the White House site, the Web developer's role was akin to that of an artist commissioned to render a new postage stamp, or to an architect chosen to design a new national monument. Even though the Web adds a high-tech twist, the White House site carries the same lofty air of historical significance. Its successful implementation required both artistic sensibility and a healthy dose of architectural information engineering.

About the Web Site Creators

The White House Web site was developed internally by action of the National Information Infrastructure. As managing editor, David Lytel worked as overseer of the site design and continues to manage the site internally. Lytel says that his office is primarily a policy office. "I work mostly with the President's science advisors. We're the department charged with advising the President in areas related to what used to be called Computing, Media, and Telecom policy. We now call this area the National Information Infrastructure. The real impetus for getting the White House online came from our office. We took the lead because we were looking for a pay back in terms of promoting the administrations policy initiatives set out by the White House, in terms of the commercialization and privatization of the Internet, and the development of more capable networks."

Lytel headed a relatively small Web site planning team that consisted essentially of a site administrator and four full-time White House staff members. During the design and production of the site, Lytel consulted with Web site design experts and had many of the visuals you see at the site today produced on contract by an external advertising agency.

Why Does the White House Have a Web Site?

Unlike most of the business sites on the Web, the White House is not using the site for promotion in the sense of public relations. Instead, the main purpose of the site is geared toward furthering established public policy. "Since the beginning," says Lytel, "it's been the policy of the administration to promote technology policy. Among the technology policies that were thought to be deserving of great attention were policies related to what we call information infrastructure. It's not promotion of the White House in the sense of 'buy this product' or 'vote for me'. It's policy making. We're the first administration to use technology adoption as an active tool for public policy making, which just hadn't been done before. And, it matched our drive to make the civilian side of the U.S. Government and the White House a leading edge technology adopter, which very much reinforced our policy goal."

The welcome page of the White House site (see Figure 11-1) doesn't indicate its depth and breadth. The site features approximately 100 radio addresses, 6,000 press documents, 100 photographs, and 2,000 Web page documents for a total of roughly 10,000 unique items. "It's not a very good measure because a good percentage of the content is generated from other sources," explains Lytel. "I think you'll find with the larger sites that fewer and fewer of them have many static Web pages. More and more will be dynamic Web pages, created on-the-fly depending on what it is the audience is looking for."

Figure 11-1: The welcome page of the site gives the impression of a long-established institution with a sense of history, but does not indicate the depth and breadth of the site.

Creating the Web Site of a Nation

The first legacy of the site was that of the 1992 Clinton campaign site, which resided on a publication server operating out of the Massachusetts Institute of Technology. "By the time we established this Web site," says Lytel, "we already had two Internet services established. One was for presidential electronic mail and the other was an electronic publication service. Unlike a lot of information sites, we already had the basic core of our Web site established."

The approach to the design of this site was quite different—both times it was produced. "Our design process took us eight months both times," says Lytel. "We started working on our site in March 1994 and nobody knew what we were talking about, especially in the government, so we spent from March to September 1994 running around Washington showing this to different internal government organizations, mainly committees, that had something to do with information or computers or communications and with individual agencies." Taking the demo on the road was an important step in the evolution of the project. The interaction with outside parties helped to hone the focus of the Web site.

"We basically sat down and decided that there were three basic functions that the White House serves," says Lytel. "It's the center of the executive branch of government (see Figure 11-2), it's the home of the President and his family (see Figure 11-3), and it's a living museum (see Figure 11-4). So we started out with our home page before we had any graphics or anything, with just three images that linked to three different areas. Our goal wasn't just to get the White House online, but to also establish links to all the cabinet level agencies by the time we opened the service. The site was originally scheduled to open in September 1994, but didn't open until October."

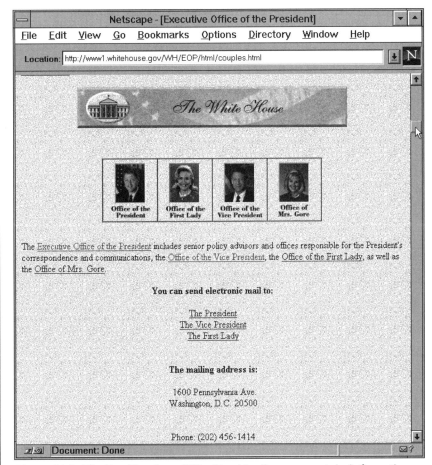

Figure 11-2: The President's and Vice President's pages contain information specific to those offices and the offices held by their respective spouses. There are even Mailto links to send these individuals electronic mail directly.

Figure 11-3: Describing it as a "National treasure," the historical section of the site describes in detail the inner layout and workings of the White House, and includes optional tours for the user to take.

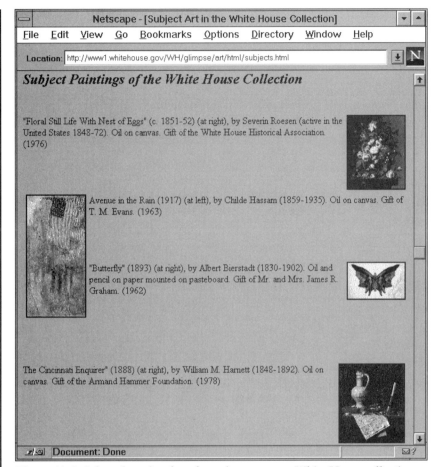

Figure 11-4: Selected works of art from the enormous White House collection can be viewed at the site, complete with information about the artists and how to obtain reprint copies.

Designing & Redesigning

Lytel's internal team was happy with the site after working on their first version. "We'd been working on it for six months at that point," he explains. "Then, we hired a consultant to take a look at it. His opinion was that we'd done a great job, but the site didn't *look* great. It looked like it was designed by government bureaucrats." So, before the site was launched, Lytel's team hired the acclaimed Poppe Tyson advertising agency to make the site look more appealing. The agency first added navigational icons to help users maneuver through the site; next they added graphics that would give the site a unique look and feel. Then, the site was ready to be launched.

Once the site had been launched on the Internet, it was easy for Lytel's team to determine what worked and what didn't. "During our redesign stage," Lytel says, "we were able to do things differently because we didn't have the pressure of a deadline. We actually sat down and did a top level design and then concentrated on the functionality that we wanted to support," says Lytel. The team also considered all the feedback that they received from users, who used a clickable feedback link at the bottom of each page to send Lytel their thoughts. Lytel and his team were able to determine from the feedback what page users were on when they sent comments. This information gave Lytel's group an idea of what areas of the initial design were causing the most problems for users. The group was able to overhaul the site to make it more beneficial for its users.

Catering to All Audiences

According to Lytel's site-tracking statistics, the White House has far-reaching exposure. "Our audience is vast," he states. "It includes basically everybody—and by that I mean not just everybody in the United States, but everybody in the *world*. We have a significant portion of students visiting our site from outside of the United States."

To get these statistics, the White House site uses a Web server trick that some might consider a bit Orwellian. When a browser makes a request to any Web server, that request includes detailed information about the browser being used. Sophisticated scripting can put this browser identification to good use. "Our site actually senses the browser the visitor is using. We have three different versions of the service," Lytel explains. The White House server can then automatically (and invisibly) deliver the appropriate page to the user.

"When the audience links to our site," Lytel explains, "there are basically three streams they can take. These include a Netscape Enhanced version, a non-Netscape version designed especially for America Online browsers and others, and finally a text-only version." In addition, every page with graphics includes a link to a corresponding text-only page. Lytel continues, "If you have a low communications line or slow computer—or if you are blind and are using a Braille reader or a voice-synthesizing device, you'll still be able to use our site. Making sure that our site was accessible to the disabled community is something we had to be sensitive to. We worked very closely with an internal department here that is responsible for making computing accessible to the disabled in the design of specific areas.

"Even before we started our final redesign," continues Lytel, "we had a pretty good idea of what our technical requirements were going to be in terms of our anticipated number of audience hits. I think the big mystery at the beginning of a design is designing for the unknown. You don't know what kind of bandwidth you're going to need, what kind of hardware do you need, or how many people are going to use the site you have designed. This was another advantage we had when we launched our redesign. We had that information at our fingertips." This information made it easier for Lytel and his group to meet the needs of their audience.

Special Features on the Site

The White House Web site includes a number of powerful tools that allow access to government information that heretofore was difficult to extract (at best). In doing so, the site has changed how citizens interact with the federal government. This is a quintessential example of how technology can be used to improve the relationship between a vendor and a customer. Each site feature gives the user a direct link to valuable information about the government. "At our site, there's a new feature that I'm really excited about," says Lytel. "It's an Economic Statistics Briefing Room feature (see Figure 11-5). In just a few pages, we're providing links to 42 of the government's most important economic statistics. I think this really maximizes the technology. With all the statistical departments within the U.S. Government, there's currently no one single place to view what statistics are available. Right now, it's like a giant data warehouse without a showroom. It has no front window, and there's no way to look inside and see what's there. We haven't changed the warehouse, the warehouse still operates the way it did before, but through Web technology we'll be providing a much better overall view."

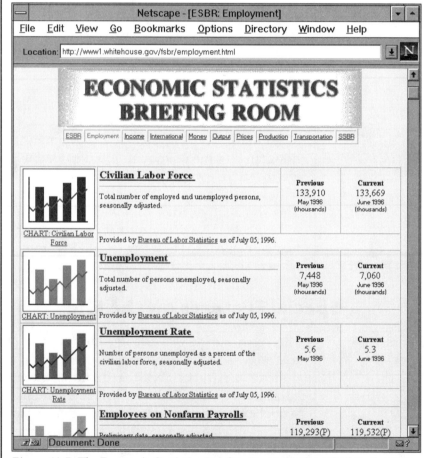

Figure 11-5: The Economic Statistics Briefing Room displays the latest government statistics on nearly any social or economic factor affecting the nation. Charts and graphs show trends and historical data generated automatically.

Another interesting feature at the site is one that you can't necessarily see, but one that you can hear. "Technically speaking, the President's Saturday Radio Address (see Figure 11-6) is one of the most technologically advanced features," says Lytel. "What we did was use a locally designed software tool used for speech recognition in conjunction with software used to index all of the words in the President's addresses."

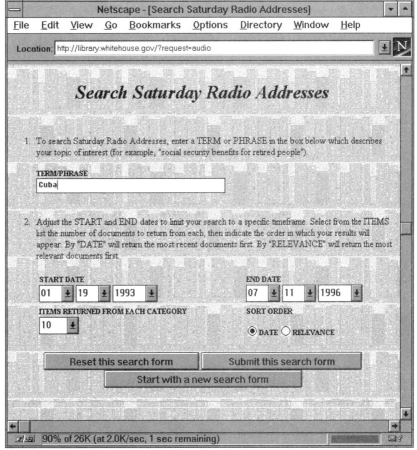

Figure 11-6: A search tool enables the user to search through all of the Presidential radio addresses and pinpoint mentions of a specific topic. The radio address can then be played for the user.

"They are short, three- to five-minute addresses," Lytel says. "We used a software tool called The Aligner. What it does is provide a start and stop time for each word in the address, down to 1/1000 of a second. Users can search the radio addresses for a specific term the President has said and this feature will compile all the relevant terms. Then, users have the option of actually playing back the part of the radio address that mentions the search term. They have the option of either starting from the beginning, or jumping to the point five seconds prior to the mention of the search term. You won't see the ability to search another medium in any other site."

Lytel also cites the Interactive Citizen's Handbook as an innovative feature of the site. The Interactive Citizen's Handbook page provides links for access to nearly every department within the U.S. Government and features comprehensive information about these departments (see Figure 11-7). This link is made possible because of a service built by the University of Massachusetts at Amherst. The service is actually an index to all of the Web pages on all of the Web sites in the government and university domains. This is a multi-terabite-sized database that's updated every few days.

Visitors can use this feature to make a simple English query and will get an absolutely coherent response, complete with relevance ranking and proximity matching. "The huge benefit for users is that they no longer have to know *who* to ask in order to ask a question, which is exactly what the public wants," says Lytel. "They don't want to research how Ford is organized in order to buy a car from them. They aren't really concerned with that. They just want an answer to their question. We're getting quite a bit of attention from the technology community because we're using the technology in an innovative way. We get between 20,000 and 25,000 visitors on a daily basis to this area."

Figure 11-7: The Interactive Citizen's Handbook provides links for access to nearly every department within the U.S. Government.

And for history buffs or parents of school-age children, there are pages at the site that will be of special interest to you. These pages, as shown in Figures 11-8 through 11-10, highlight current events and people in United States Government.

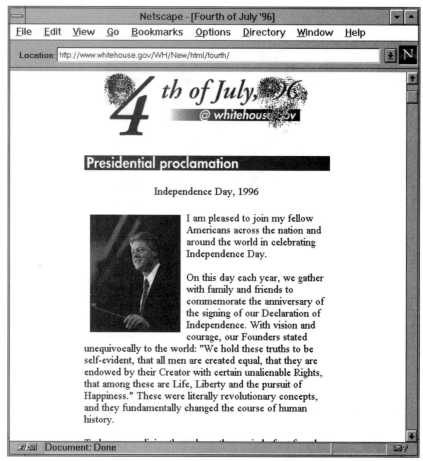

Figure 11-8: The What's New area of the White House site features links to the latest news being released to the public, areas of high user interest, news topics, and Presidential greetings such as that given for Independence Day.

Figure 11-9: An area of the site is devoted to providing biographical and personal information about the President himself, his life, and his rise to the top of government.

Figure 11-10: The White House for Kids area has been designed to appeal directly to younger audiences. A quarterly electronic newsletter informs young Web surfers about issues affecting government and the future of the nation.

Perhaps the most useful tool on the White House Web site is its powerful search engine. The site uses Inquiry, a search engine designed at the University of Massachusetts. This search engine feature allows visitors to quickly find the information they need. "Instead of users having to drill through a long list of links, they can perform a search," says Lytel. "For example, when someone goes to the White House Virtual Library, they specifically narrow a search to examine just the contents of our Web site, or just a White House publication, or just an audio file. This is a feature that enables people to get in and out of the site much faster, if that's what they want to do."

Lytel says that the site's search feature is a quick and convenient way to find specific information. "In fact somebody called me once and asked me if the U.S. Government was involved in regulating international telecommunication links in South America," he recalls. "I didn't have a clue what the answer was, and I didn't think it had very much to do with the United States Government, frankly. But, sure enough, I was able to address his query by punching something into the search engine. It even came up with the name of the exact state department responsible for that area. I was amazed. Here's a tool not just providing details about information I already knew, but it was telling me something that I had no idea about. In fact, I didn't even know there *was* an answer. I think is just a brilliant piece of technology that's doing something really useful."

Site Design Mistakes

"One of the things that I really find annoying," says Lytel, "is that most Web designers unfortunately believe that people come into their sites from the front door, or the home page. The fact is that many people come into a site after doing a search. When they do, they're going to enter the site on a page that's likely not the home page. Web designers should anticipate this in their site designs." Designers can't presume that by the time users get to a certain page they have an understanding of where they are because they started at the beginning. Because users can jump into a site at any point, each page needs to have the proper context to let users know exactly where they are.

Lytel continues that many site designers rely too heavily on graphic images and think that images are the most important part of the site. "We made that mistake when we first started out with our site. I was surprised when we got involved with our advertising agency and they began the design by producing navigational icons that eventually formed the framework of the site. In our first design we weren't worried about navigation because we figured the browser would allow you to go back." Now Lytel understands the importance of helping users navigate through the site.

The Future of the Web

The World Wide Web has altered the consumption patterns and appetite of the information consumer. In the process, it has forced people to reconsider how they spend their precious time. "To me a good Web site provides interactivity and timeliness," says Lytel. "I don't think audiences in general are too far from a time when simple static Web pages will be boring. It reminds me of a time in the early days of television, when networks would just plant a single camera in the middle of a studio and broadcast whatever fell in front of it. I think that's what static Web pages are going to seem like in the future. The audience will see a page of text and view it as incredibly boring.

"In the sense that the World is becoming a global community through the use of the Web, I don't think this is new. To some degree television has already provided this. I think that what the Web offers is the ability for individuals to maximize the time they engage in media consumption. The Web offers individuals a way to locate something that's interesting uniquely to *them*, rather than having a shared experience with tens of millions of other people at the same time. I think people are eventually going to reserve a certain number of hours per day to engage in Web activities."

Moving On

The White House is perhaps the top example of a government Web site that was conceptualized, and is now managed, by an *internal* department and was "dressed up" through the creative support of an *outside* agency. This approach of the White House design team is one that many Web designers will be taking in the future. Penetrating the World Wide Web with minimal investment in labor means a healthy division of the design responsibilities.

This unique approach of developing a government Web site by using an internal team means that the staff can include exactly the things that will be of interest to their visitors, and they know exactly how to use the resources within the maze of systems and information avenues in government. Lytel's team has accomplished something with this site that perhaps no outside agency could have done. To examine a well-done site by an ad agency, see Chapter 12, "Design Case Study: FedEx."

12

Design Case Study: FedEx

Site: FedEx, http://www.fedex.com

Designer: Lynn Brock, president and chief operating officer

Design firm: OnlineFocus

FedEx: The Business of Moving Information

FedEx, or Federal Express as they were originally known, is primarily in the business of moving packages and freight. The company was founded in 1973, and in only two dozen years has become the largest express transportation service in the world. Based in Memphis, Tennessee, FedEx has also headquartered itself in Miami, Brussels, and Hong Kong. Chairman, President, and CEO Frederick W. Smith heads a worldwide work force totaling more than 122,000. The sheer volume of business they do worldwide on a daily basis is incomprehensible.

FedEx is now a multibillion dollar company with estimated earnings of $10.3 billion in fiscal 1996, a phenomenal effort for even a company of their size. FedEx collects an average of two

FedEx's fleet of aircraft alone rivals that of American Airlines and carries more than 40 million pounds of freight per month.

and a half million packages from more than 34,000 U.S. customer drop sites and delivers them to more than 211 countries every single business day. To do this, the company operates a fleet of nearly 560 aircraft through 325 airports, that connect to a ground transportation network of more than 36,000 vehicles servicing 1,800 customer service centers. FedEx's fleet of aircraft alone rivals that of American Airlines and carries more than 40 million pounds of freight per month. The electronic communication network that serves as the crux of their service expediency handles more than 45.5 million transmissions every day, while their customer service network handles nearly 400,000 telephone calls per day.

The volume of business that FedEx handles could not be done in such a timely manner if it weren't for its technological edge. For example, to process packages, each of FedEx's front-line personnel carries a portable electronic device capable of entering and temporarily storing information about a package including its contents and detailed information about its sender and recipient. When this device is returned to a specially designed, home base unit, it automatically downloads its contents. The base unit then transmits the information by cellular, radio, or telephone transmission to a network which eventually connects to the company's central mainframe system. It's one of the most efficient business technology networks in business today.

This process shows that FedEx knows how to utilize technology to its full potential. This is also reflected in the FedEx Web site (see Figure 12-1). The company decided to put its business online to better service its customers, but the evolutionary process of the site was a long one.

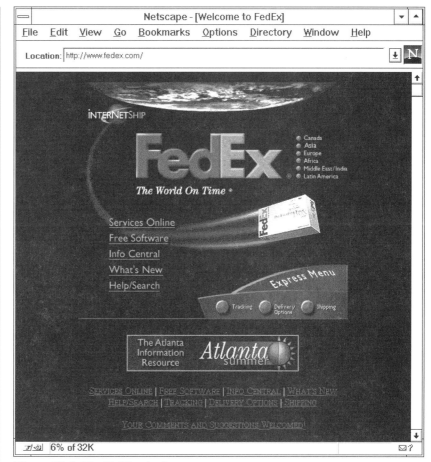

Figure 12-1: The FedEx site home page.

┐ About the Site Designers: OnlineFocus

   Lynn Brock is president and chief executive officer of OnlineFocus, based in Cupertino, California. OnlineFocus has been in business since early 1996. For a very young firm, their list of clients includes high-profile companies, such as Sun Microsystems, Cathay Pacific Airlines, IT Careers, and Apple Computer. Even though at the time of this writing OnlineFocus had been in business a mere six months, they were projecting revenue for their first year at a staggering $5 million.

Brock's experience is based mostly in computer science and management. "You could say I've done everything legal you can do with a computer at least once," says Brock. "I'm not actually into the hacker mentality, but I really enjoy using machines to find solutions to problems. It gives me the benefit of a broad view of the industry, which turns out to be my biggest advantage on the Web."

In terms of personnel, OnlineFocus is a small company. "At this point we have only six full-time people, a couple of whom came to us originally as consultants but have since become part of our team," says Brock. "We have about 20 other contractors that we draw from on an ongoing basis, including programmers, data entry, Web designers, and graphics experts. The nature of this business is kind of interesting, because it requires a set of creative people. As you get bigger you somehow have to leverage that. One of the better ways to do that is by bringing in people from the outside, so you don't necessarily have to have them there all the time. Ours is essentially a project-based business at this point.

"I think the thing that gives us some of our expertise is that, as a group, we're very strong in our respective areas," Brock explains. "We're graphics, programming, and production experts. We also recently had someone join us whose background is in high-tech public relations, which has subsequently led us into another business area, that being writing for the Web.

"When you're working full-time on the Web," Brock says, "you quickly discover that visual images only go so far—you need to have words. The words that you use on the Web are significantly different than the words you'd use in print. For example, we've had a number of experiences where marketing people have written content we can't even use. On the Web it's hard to get your audience to read more than a sentence. That single sentence may be your only chance to capture their attention. It's a whole different style of writing."

> "When you're working full-time on the Web, you quickly discover that visual images only go so far."

However, Brock says that the main problem faced by the company is the absurd rate of growth in their industry. "You're trying to plot out the strategy of a technology that is evolving at an incredible rate. Plus, the competition is fierce and entry costs are low. Needless to say, everybody's trying to get into this area. That means that thinking about the most tactical and strategic site designs is really very important once you're in business. We're already to the point where our design strategies have become a big issue," Brock explains.

The Site Design

Before OnlineFocus became involved with the design of the FedEx Web site, an early version had already been produced by some of the company's own staff. "They didn't even pretend to be site designers, they just kind of put it together," Brock says.

The changes that needed to be made were too extensive to simply rework the existing site. FedEx is a technology company and they needed to be perceived that way. They realized their existing site design looked very primitive, and they needed the site to look sophisticated and professional, Brock says.

"One of the biggest mistakes Web designers can make, is that they fall in love with their designs."

The early designs of the FedEx site had a video game look, says Brock. One of the biggest mistakes Web designers make "is that they fall in love with their designs. Instead of thinking about their client's main priorities, they create what they think is appropriate and often stick with it." This can be a severe blunder. Experience has shown that the most effective Web site designs happen through an evolutionary process. "FedEx wanted a site that reflected their high-tech company culture, but with a subtlety. And, because they do business around the globe, they also wanted it to have international appeal. Plus, the site had to have a strong functionality, which at the time was still very new for the World Wide Web," explained Brock.

For the FedEx site, the entire design process took about two months. It was "unusually long," says Brock. "Partly because we gave them so many choices, and partly because we did some experimenting and refining—much more than we would typically have done." One of Brock's first priorities was to introduce features to the site that reflected the high-tech corporate image of FedEx. FedEx realized they could use their Web site to promote their image by providing free downloadable FedEx software (see Figure 12-2).

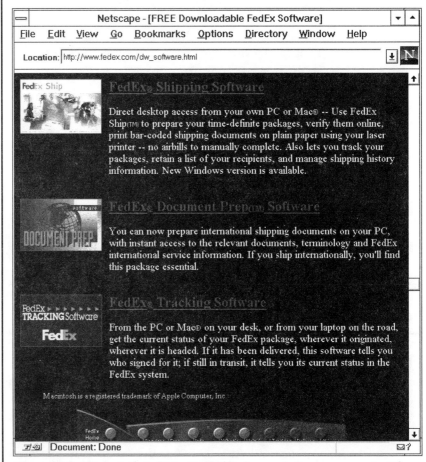

Figure 12-2: Through their Web site, FedEx has made it more convenient for customers to do business with the company. Customers who log onto the site are able to download shipping, preparation, and tracking software to their computers.

Black back-
grounds make it
relatively hard
to read text.
After delivering
an "alpha" site
that had an
actual text page
in it, Brock's
group realized
text would be a
major concern.

Further, the entire look and feel of the site had to match the FedEx image. Although black backgrounds aren't the norm on the Web, FedEx favored this color concept. When OnlineFocus did their initial design presentation, of eight designs proposed, three featured black backgrounds. In fact, initially Brock's designers tried to talk FedEx out of the black background "because of certain readability and human factors reasons," he says, but as it turned out, black is what they wanted. "Like many clients, one of FedEx's goals in creating the site was to be a little bit more dramatic and push the appeal envelope. They wanted to create some 'buzz' about the site so they elected to go with one of the black background designs. In fact, they went with the least traditional version in terms of design."

Black backgrounds can make it difficult to read text. After delivering an "alpha" site that had an actual text page in it, Brock's group realized text would be a major concern. "We realized that simply using normal-sized text wasn't going to work," he says, "and, we determined that all of the text on this site was going to need to be 'plus one' above the default (see Figure 12-3). We also formatted the text color slightly off white because we discovered that the pure white on the black contrast is too difficult to read. After doing quite a bit of experimenting, we chose a slightly orange-beige color to make it as readable as possible."

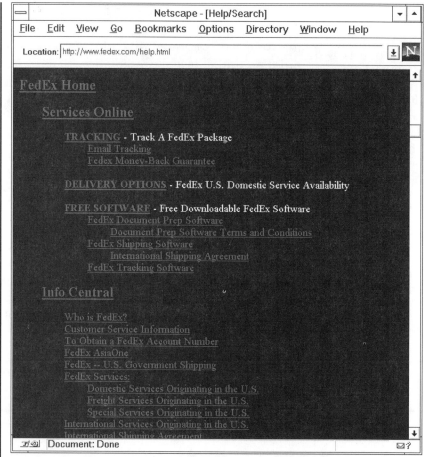

Figure 12-3: To accommodate the black background featured on the site, text sizes were set to display larger-than-normal sizes, while high-contrast text colors such as white were adjusted to an off-white color in an effort to improve readability.

OnlineFocus also discovered a few problems with using black backgrounds in Netscape. Brock says, "Certain form elements such as check boxes disappear on a black background (see Figure 12-4). We needed to make some adjustments to the black background design to accommodate this."

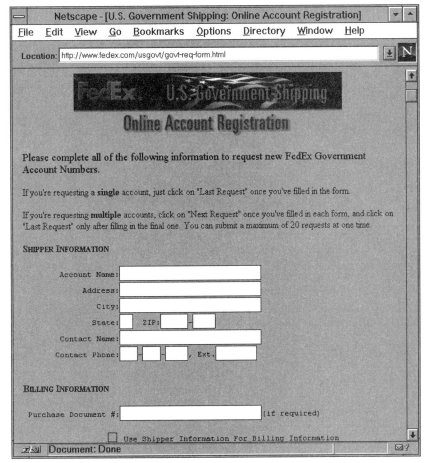

Figure 12-4: Areas of the site such as customer forms for things like account registration for larger customers, have had the black background changed in order to accommodate clear reading of form elements.

The Site Features

As with most larger sites, the home page and its featured links are a mere tip of the iceberg, so to speak—the FedEx site is quite large and features more than 30 different areas, mostly devoted to customer interaction and services. Very little of the site is devoted to corporate "puffery." From the home page, high-energy graphics, color images, and a brief navigation bar (see Figure 12-5) highlight the most commonly used areas of the site including the tracking feature. On the other pages of the site, a more detailed navigation bar (see Figure 12-6) reveals links to: Services Online, Free Software, Info Central, What's New, Help/Search, Tracking, Delivery Options, Shipping, and a link back to the FedEx Home Page.

Figure 12-5: A graphic on the home page provides simplified navigation to the frequently used areas of the site.

Figure 12-6: A smaller and more-detailed navigation toolbar can be found on the other site pages, providing a more complete set of links to different areas.

In terms of services, the site offers FedEx's own prepping software applications for proprietary packaging. The software is compatible with various customer computer platforms. Site visitors may also consult a Search/Help page that specializes in certain types of packaging or shipping arrangements and provides dozens of links to features and information located at the site.

The FedEx site also offers services geared to help its customer's business on the whole. To help businesses identify and communicate to their international customers, Brock's group structured an area to highlight one of the worlds fastest-growing sectors—Asian countries. One of FedEx's newest services, named *AsiaOne,* directly targets customers doing business in various parts of Asia (see Figure 12-7). An interactive route map, as seen in Figure 12-8, provides links to complete contact and package transportation information for local offices in Asian cities. FedEx also features an area of their site called *Learning Lab.* Figure 12-9 shows the Learning Lab page, which is aimed at helping companies to improve their own bottom lines by establishing reliable distribution networks and managing their flow of goods.

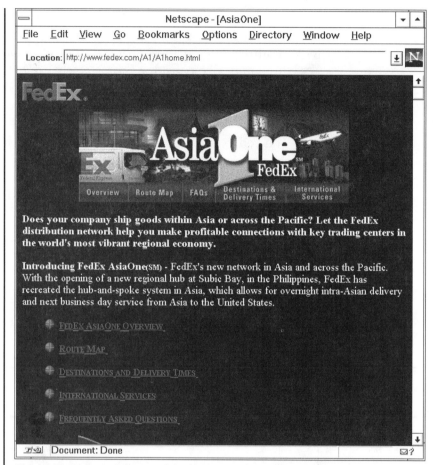

Figure 12-7: A special area of the site, named AsiaOne, has been set to address the needs of customers located in Asian regions of the world, which are growing at a phenomenal rate.

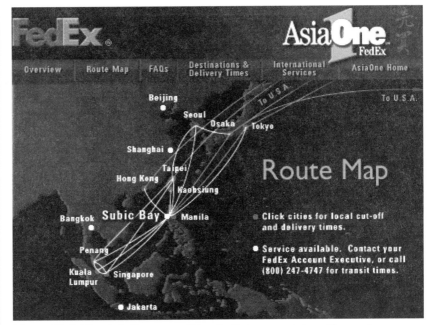

Figure 12-8: The AsiaOne area of the site features an interactive route map that provides specific detailed information and instructions on shipping packages.

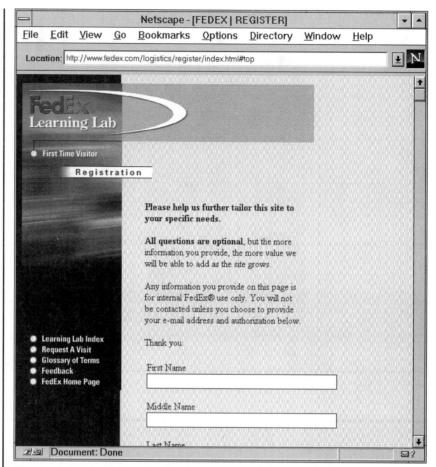

Figure 12-9: The FedEx site also features a special area called Learning Lab, that is designed to assist customers in improving their business strategies through the use of distribution channels such as the ones offered by FedEx.

To the FedEx customers, the single most important feature of this site is its package tracking abilities. From the site the user can access the same database on the FedEx mainframe computer that would be accessed if the user were making an inquiry on the telephone. Having access to the FedEx mainframe computer for package tracking or having access to anyone's mainframe computer is becoming a very common thing. According to Brock,

"You're going to see more and more of it as companies open up certain parts of their internal databases to the World Wide Web. It's usually reasonably straightforward to connect internal databases to the World Wide Web, the main issues are security and potentially performance, since the perceived performance reflects directly on the client's corporate image."

Although the users think the tracking feature is the best site feature, Brock foresees a new favorite. Brock says that "the shipment feature, where you print all the forms including the bar codes online, will rapidly become my favorite. Personally, I don't like filling out forms by hand. It will also make the phone call for you, so it's automating the whole front end of the shipping process. In many ways this offers much more value to the user."

But, while the FedEx site features hundreds of individual areas and customer conveniences, there are no special multimedia effects, plug-ins, or proprietary features. "We deliberately left any special multimedia effects out of this site design," says Brock. "At OnlineFocus, we all have a really strong bias against doing 'cute' stuff for the sake of cuteness. There's been no real reason for us to do 'cute' multimedia things so far."

When customers go to the FedEx site, they're there to quickly find out where their overnight mail is. They're not there to see a cute display of technology.

In designing the site, it was important to Brock to avoid any superfluous features that might clog the pipe—especially since this is one of the busiest business sites on the Web. A conscious effort was made to avoid features that would have negatively impacted the server's response rate. Bandwidth-intensive effects, such as server push, were eschewed. When customers go to the FedEx site, they're there to quickly find out where their overnight mail is. They're not there to see a cute display of technology.

What Makes a Good Web Site?

The true value of a Web site is not determined by the number of hits it receives. While some sites exist primarily to draw a large volume of visitors—essentially for advertising revenue—those sites are few and far between. The blind pursuit of a high hit rate is pure Web folly. A successful and effective Web site is one that brings value to the entity sponsoring the site, by better serving its audience.

For the design team, part of the success of a site can be determined by how it directly impacts a company's bottom line. In the case of the FedEx site, this impact has been significant. "Based on current usage," Brock says, "the tracking page saves FedEx an estimated $5 million in costs annually, for the tracking page alone." These costs equate to the time saved in customer telephone inquiries to the company regarding the status of package delivery. It's a key reason for the site's success, but there are other factors that can affect site success.

Brock takes several factors into consideration in order to measure the success of a site. "I look at site in a broad sense," Brock says. "During our design processes, much of our discussion revolves around human interface, content selection, the layout of content, and graphic design. We do very little in terms of design-related maintenance after our initial delivery. This is because we spend so much time on the initial design and structure of our sites, we often don't have to go back and make any drastic changes after we deliver it to the client. Most of the changes we end up involved in are usually driven by client content changes. We knew the FedEx site was going to continuously expand and most of the maintenance we've done to date has been simply adding more content."

A lot of site designers don't worry as much about return on investments. Brock says that the current trend is that companies are putting up "vanity" sites on the Web. "If you've seen many of the sites out there, that's what's driving them. It's purely a matter of companies wanting to be there, simply for the sake of having a presence of *any* kind. I'm referring to many of the corporate sites you see. But, more and more companies are looking to their Web sites to impact their bottom line. A year ago it was radical to say that the World Wide Web would be the method used by businesses to communicate to people. Now, it's almost a conventional wisdom," explains Brock. "They either want to motivate commerce or sales. I'm seeing companies who are either doing online sales or are having things initiated online that lead to sales.

"But I also think that the Web has been over-hyped enough that the enthusiasm bubble is bound to burst," concludes Brock. "Quite frankly, the vanity sites will soon disappear. The design firms that will survive will be the ones who can provide real value to their clients and the Web sites that will survive will be the ones that provide value to their audience."

The Tools of Choice

The team at OnlineFocus does nearly all of its Web site creation work using the Macintosh platform. "Our software tool set involves the usual suite of Mac tools," he explains, "including Photoshop for images, Adobe Illustrator for developing graphics, and simple editors like BBEdit for producing HTML Web pages. Then, most of our CGI scripting is done in Perl, which is a public domain UNIX application.

"In terms of image tools, much of the work we do is done with Photoshop," says Brock. "In fact, the bulk of it is done in Photoshop. We don't use any Web page creation tools. We essentially hard code pages without using any special editors. We find most of the current applications out there are too limiting. I think ultimately anyone who starts out using one of these page creators will eventually end up doing it by hand.

"For example, none of the applications on the market currently support direct formatting of small caps. To achieve this effect, we end up having to hand tweak everything. That means you're changing font sizes on a character by character basis. The issue is when you are trying to project a certain quality with a company, you have to care about issues like this. That is what gives sites a clean and a crafted look, as opposed to sites that have been quickly thrown together."

Conclusion

Ironically, while the FedEx site enjoys some of the highest hit rates on planet Earth, its main purpose is not to attract Web audience attention, but to service the company's existing customers. And due to the site's overwhelming success at providing an extension to existing services for the convenience of their customers, the FedEx site has provided a conduit for increased business. On top of the added value for their Web surfing customers, FedEx has also used the World Wide Web to open the right doors at the right times, and have tapped into new and expanding growth opportunities for themselves around the globe. By approaching the design of their sites with a more analytical view than many design firms, OnlineFocus has proven that this approach is definitely an ingredient to success on the Web.

Appendix A
About the
Companion CD-ROM

The CD-ROM included with your copy of *Looking Good Online* contains valuable software programs, textures, and icons.

To view the CD-ROM:

✦ Macintosh — Double-click on the LAUNCHME icon after opening the CD-ROM on your desktop. You'll see a menu screen offering several choices. See "Navigating the CD-ROM" below for your options.

✦ Windows3.1/Windows 95/Windows NT — Double-click on the LAUNCHME.EXE file from your Window Explorer or File Manager.

Navigating the CD-ROM

Your choices for navigating the CD-ROM appear on the opening screen. You can quit the CD-ROM, view the software, browse the Hot Picks, or learn more about Ventana.

The software, textures, and icons are listed in the Install folder on the CD-ROM. You can install the items one at a time to your hard drive by dragging them from the folder onto your desktop.

For Macintosh users: If theVentana Viewer does not run properly on your machine, you may install the software using their individual folders.

For Windows users: If you have trouble running the CD-ROM, copy LAUNCHME.EXE to your hard drive and execute it from Windows Explorer or File Manager.

Software on the CD-ROM

Software	Descriptions
Backstage Designer Plus	Macromedia Web page creation tool.
BBEdit Lite 3.5.1	Text editor for the Macintosh.
BBEdit 4.0 Demo	Powerful text editor for the Macintosh.
DeBabelizer Lite LE	Reads and writes BMP, PICT, TIFF, and GIF formats.
DeBabelizer Toolbox Demo	Demo of DeBabelizer's tools.
GifBuilder 0.4	Creates animated GIF files.
HTML Assistant Pro 2.0	Freeware, point and click editor for WWW pages.
Icons	Collection by Kevin Dixon and Extension Computer Technology.
InContext Spider 1.2	Web authoring software.
JPEGView	Image editor.
Lview Pro	Shareware image editor.
Mapedit for Windows	Facilitates the creation of image maps.
Mapthis for Windows	Facilitates the creation of image maps.
PhotoGIF 1.1.4	Plug-in for Adobe Photoshop.
PageSpinner 1.2b2	HTML editor.
PageSpinner 1.1	HTML editor.
Textures folder	Dynamic Web page backgrounds by Gary and Barbara Bouton.
Transparency 1.04b	Freeware that makes images transparent.
HTML Web Weaver Lite 3.0	Macintosh Web page creation tool.

The clip art found on this CD-ROM is from different sources. The first images (icon001.jpg through icon057.jpg) were created by Kevin Dixon of Chapel Hill, NC. The remaining images (icon058.jpg through icon283.jpg) were taken from a collection of clip art on the Web at http://leviathan.tamu.edu:70/. This collection was put together by Extension Computer Technology, a support department in the Texas Agricultural Extension Service (TAEX). The original images came from several different sources: the Department of Agriculture Communications at TAMUS (DAC), the Computer Technology Group at TAEX and TAMUS (CTG), the Illinois Cooperative Extension Service (IL CES), the Epsilon Sigma Phi Extension National Honor Fraternity, (ESP) and the Institute of Food and Agricultural Sciences, University of Florida (IFAS).

The textures found on the CD-ROM were created by the genius of Gary and Barbara Bouton.

LView Pro software is copyright © 1993-1996 by Leonardo Haddad Loureiro.

Technical Support

Technical support is available for installation-related problems only. The technical support office is open from 8:00 A.M. to 6:00 P.M. Monday through Friday, and can be reached via the following methods:

Phone: (919) 544-9404 extension 81
Faxback Answer System: (919) 544-9404 extension 85
E-mail: help@vmedia.com
FAX: (919) 544-9472
World Wide Web: http://www.vmedia.com/support
America Online: keyword Ventana

Limits of Liability & Disclaimer of Warranty

The authors and publisher of this book have used their best efforts in preparing the CD-ROM and the programs contained in it. These efforts include the development, research, and testing of the theories and programs to determine their effectiveness. The authors and publisher make no warranty of any kind expressed or implied, with regard to these programs or the documentation contained in this book.

The authors and publisher shall not be liable in the event of incidental or consequential damages in connection with, or arising out of, the furnishing, performance, or use of the programs, associated instructions, and/or claims of productivity gains.

Some of the software on this CD-ROM is shareware; there may be additional charges (owed to the software authors/makers) incurred for their registration and continued use. See individual program's README or VREADME.TXT files for more information.

Glossary

Address   Allows search engines to look for Web sites. The HTML Address tag used by Web site designers can specify information such as addresses, phone numbers, URLs, and so on. Many browsers, including Netscape, display addresses in italics.

Aliasing   The effect of visibly-jagged edges along angled lines or object edges due to sharp, tonal contrast between colored pixels.

Anchors   A designated link destination in a Web page document.

Animated GIF   A series of multiple images assembled into a single GIF file conforming to the 89a standard. These images display sequentially, creating a basic animation effect

Application Blocks   A collection of data that can be inserted into a GIF file to store private application data.

Aspect Ratio   A value measured as a ratio that represents the relationship between width and height of an object or image.

Background   In the Web page design, the background is the area seen *behind* the contents of a Web page. Backgrounds may be set to appear in certain uniform colors, or may be set to render tiled image files.

Baud   Represents measured hardware transfer rates for exchanging digital data in bits per second over telephone lines.

Bilevel   A type of digital image on a computer containing only black-and-white pixels.

Bit Binary digit. The smallest unit of information in a computer; a 1 or a 0, capable of defining the conditions "on" or "off."

Bitmap A file format containing dot patterns measured in resolution values. Bitmaps may be 1-bit, 2-bit, 4-bit, 8-bit, 24-bit, or 32-bit and contain black-and-white, grayscale, or color information.

Browser A software application that interfaces with data stored on remote servers accessible through the Internet, inherently capable of rendering at least text, hypertext linking information, and images.

Bullet A graphical symbol that attracts attention or adds emphasis to point-form text.

Button In the Web page design, a button may be a graphical image containing a designated link, or a form button that triggers user response or action.

Byte A measurement equivalent to 8 bits of digital information and a standard measure of file sizes.

CGI Script A set of commands that may be preset.

CGI Common Gateway Interface. A programming language that allows communication between a Web browser and a Web server.

Check Box A Web page form design element that can display a condition of "on" or "off" mimicking "yes" or "no" according to user action or response.

CIE Commission Internationale de l'Eclairage. CIE refers to the color standard developed by the commission and is widely used to define the colors contained in digital images.

Color Bleeding The effect caused by error diffusion dithering algorithms. Color bleeding occurs when colors "travel" from left to right as is the nature of error diffusion dithering. Color bleed is noticeable when applied to images containing hard vertical edges. Color bleeding can be reduced using features found in applications such as Paint Shop Pro that lessen the left-to-right color bleed by applying a fractional coefficient to the error value.

Comment Block   An area within a GIF89a file that may contain text describing the image in question, defining its creator or copyright status and so on, without being displayed as part of a GIF file.

Comment   A standard HTML style used for making notations within a HTML document and designated to not appear in the browser screen.

Compression Ratio   The set ratio that exists between the amount of original data representing a digital file and the amount of data needed to represent the same file following a compression process.

Compression   A mathematical process designed to reduce the amount of memory space used to fully describe a collection of data. A compression package is the software program that uses this process to create a native compression file format.

Contone   Continuous-tone. The illusion created by an ultra-high collection of colors and shades formed to describe an image that you see when you look at an original black-and-white or color photograph.

Control Blocks   A designated area within a GIF89a file that defines image transparency and allows for user input. The transparency field of a control block will let you specify that one color in an image or a color used by the text in a plain text block is to be regarded as transparent by a GIF viewer, allowing the underlying image to be visible wherever it occurs.

Dialog Box   A box that contains information and possibly user-definable options generated by any software application.

Digital Halftone   A printed digital image composed of various-sized dots of resolution and arranged in rows to simulate a continuous-tone, photographic, or graphic image. A digital halftone is usually produced from a digital-image manipulation software program.

Digital   A standardized measurement and recording system whereby elements of the physical world, including images, are converted into electrical voltages that correspond to the values of the original. Those electrical values are then converted into groups of binary digits (bits) for interpretation by computers.

Download   To transmit a file from a web server to a client.

Down Sample   The action of reducing the resolution, color mode, and/or size of a digital image.

DPI   Dots per inch. Refers to the resolution of a digital or conventionally printed image.

DTP   Desktop publishing.

Eyedropper   A digital tool used by image editing applications and utilities that enables the user to sample the color, tone, or shades of color contained in a digital image.

File Format   Files that feature a specific data structure and conform to a particular program application or standard.

Font   A comprehensive set of characters that makes up a typestyle adapted for the digital-imaging industry. Individual fonts may also be part of a larger font family and may be designed to emulate a font style within a similar collection such as plain, italic, or bold-italic font styles.

Form   In Web page design, a form is an area composed of user-input devices such as radio buttons, text fields, text areas, pop-up menus, list boxes, and so on.

FTP   File Transfer Protocol. Commonly refers to a set of parameters used in transferring data through telephone lines using predetermined data bit, stop bit, and parity settings for communications.

GIF   Graphical Interchange Format. A proprietary file format developed originally for the CompuServe information service using the LZW compression standard.

Gigabyte   1,024 megabytes or 1,048,576 kilobytes of data.

Global Palette   Supported by the GIF89a file format, global palettes can apply to multiple images to avoid color display anomalies caused by loading image files containing its own individual color palette.

Grayscale   This term comes from the early days of process camera work and hand-developing, where grayscale was the term given to a small printed strip of paper with a row of graduated continuous-tone shades from dark to light. This paper was placed beside the original artwork being photographed and acted as an exposure time control strip during the developing process providing the darkroom operator density values to measure.

Halftone   In the digital world, this refers to an arrangement of pixels of the same size. Shades are indicated by halftone dots combined into cells. Dark areas have a large number of dots per cell, and light areas have a small number of dots per cell.

Header Block   The area that precedes the image information contained in a GIF file defines the size of the screen the GIF files should be displayed on, and an optional global palette.

Header   Information preceding the data representing an image file which features, possibly among other things, a low-resolution representation of the image contained in the file.

Histogram   A chart displaying the tonal ranges present in a digital image as a series of vertical bars. This term also refers to the numerical values produced by calculations performed by image editing software when changing image color modes such as down sampling from 16.7 million to 256 colors.

HTML   Hypertext Markup Language. Essentially a hybrid of SGML (Standard Generalized Markup Language), this is a textual-coding language containing descriptions of text attributes and document-linking information.

Hypertext   Text that is capable of performing a predetermined linking action when triggered by a click, keyboard alternative, or some type of machine or user-initiated action.

Image Map   A collection of predetermined hot spots that have been assigned to either a GIF or JPEG image that, when clicked, causes the browser to seek an associated anchor link in a destination HTML document.

Interactive   The effect created by designating associated actions to take place following a user action.

Interlaced   An effect supported by the GIF standard that displays digital images in such a way as to emulate the opening of Venetian blinds as the images materialize.

Internet Service Provider (ISP)   A service organization that specializes in providing remote access to the Internet for a periodic or time-based user fee.

JPEG   Joint Photographic Experts Group. This refers to a compression standard format for photographic digital images. JPEG format gives you a choice of three levels of file compression depending on the image quality you want to achieve.

Justified   Text that is justified is aligned flush on both the left and right sides. Because of its nature, justified text is not an option available in standard HTML.

Kerning   Spacing between alphanumeric characters.

Line Break   A Shift+Enter keyboard combination (usually) that causes text in a paragraph to begin a new line without beginning a new paragraph.

List-Selection Field   A form element that features a number of choices available within a selection group.

Local Palette   A collection of colors specific to a digital image, for example, colors needed to accurately display visual data found in a GIF file.

Loop Blocks   A specialized area containing information stored within a GIF89a file that controls the continuous and sequential display of multiple-image GIF animation used with Web pages.

Lossy   The effect using a compression standard whereby a digital image loses data in a trade-off between image quality and file size. Lossy compression techniques are user-adjustable and can be set so low as to compromise image quality.

LPI   Lines per inch. A measure of the number of rows of dots which represent a traditional or digital halftone.

LZW Lempel-Ziv-Welch. A technique of data compression that provides the ability to conserve file space without losing significant image quality.

Masking The effect of selecting and isolating a specific area of a digital image as defined by the shape or color of the given area.

Megabyte A term given to quantity of data valued at 1,024 kilobytes or 1,048,576 bytes of data.

Modem Short for modulator/demodulator. A term that refers to a computer hardware peripheral that converts digital computer data into modulated analog data for transfer via non-digital telephone lines.

Moiré A repetitive pattern caused by two or more symmetrical grids of dots or lines having different pitch or angle. A moiré can be either digitally or non-digitally created.

Monochrome The instance where an image contains only a single color scheme such as black and white, or gray and white.

Monospaced A style of font spacing whereby each character occupies the same amount of horizontal space, similar to the spacing found in traditional typewriters.

Native File Format A file format that can only be read by the software application that created it.

Non-Lossy Compression A compression technique that mathematically reduces the amount of data describing an image file without causing a loss of image quality.

Palette In the realm of digital image terms, this is a collection of data that describes all of the color information needed to correctly display a digital image or multiple digital images.

Password Field A form element that requires a predetermined password in order to carry out a specific action, such as linking to a subsequent Web page.

Pixel The smallest digital unit that composes a digital image.

Pop-up Menu A form element that lists multiple choices from which a user may make only one choice. Pop-up describes the interface action seen when the form element is clicked.

Quality Factor   The degree to which image data can be lost in a trade-off against visual quality.

Quotation   A standard HTML style defined as being indented and set below body text, and intended as a format to be used for extended excerpts longer than a line or two of regular text.

Radio Button   A form element that is circular in shape and is activated to either "on" or "off" depending on the choices made.

RAM   Random Access Memory. The type of memory a computer uses to store the information required to perform calculations at any one given moment. RAM is short term so it is cleared or erased when the system is powered down or applications are quit.

Reset Button   A form element that sets the condition of any other form elements that are user-definable to their original or default state when selected.

Resolution   Resolution is the measure of clarity, sharpness, and detail that a digital recording device can record. Input device resolutions are usually measured in dots per inch (dpi) or pixels per inch (ppi) and output resolutions are usually measured in dots per inch or lines per inch (lpi).

RGB   Red, Green, Blue. This is a color model whereby various combinations of these colors projected by a cathode ray tube device can reproduce full-color images. RGB colors are the primary colors of light perceived by the human eye and are conventionally measured in values ranging between 0 and 255.

Sampling   The process of converting analog data into digital data by taking a series of samples or readings at equal distances and time intervals. Sampling often also loosely refers to the digital process of mapping image data from one digital format to another.

Saturation   The extent to which one or two of the three primary RGB (red, green, blue) image display colors becomes the predominant color of an image.

Separator   A design element available to HTML editors that visually and vertically organizes chunks of information in a Web page document. Rows of repeated characters and long and thin image files may also be considered separators in design. Separators are also sometimes referred to simply as "horizontal rules."

Server   A computer that stores Web site data.

Shareware   Applications distributed freely with the understanding that if users like and use the application regularly, they pay the developers a small fee.

Sharpen   A digital effect that, when applied to digital images, causes the image to seem sharper or more focused.

Submit Button   A form button that initiates the transfer of data based on user-definable choices contained in a CGI form to be transmitted back to a server.

Super Sampling   The capture of more gray levels per color than is required for image manipulation or output.

Table   A design format that is capable of visually organizing tabular or columnar information. A table may or may not feature three-dimensional looking vertical and horizontal separator lines.

Text Area   A form design element that allows the user to enter a virtually unlimited amount of text, usually in response to an open-ended query.

Text Field   A form design element that allows the user to enter a limited amount of text, usually in response to a very specific question such as "What Is Your First Name? Last Name?" and so on.

Threshold   The point at which an action begins or changes. The threshold setting in digital images determines which pixels are converted to black and which will become white. Most image editors feature options for converting images to 1-bit black-and-white format and often allow for user-definable threshold limits based on a percentage value of black.

Thumbnail   The nickname given to a small, cruder version of a larger, more detailed—and subsequently cumbersome—image stored in a different location. Thumbnails are often used as teasers or reference images and linked to larger versions.

TIFF   Tagged Image File Format. This is one of the more popular digital image file formats. TIFF is supported by nearly every image-editing, layout, and graphics software package in the digital desktop world.

Toolbar   Name given to a Web page design element based on an image file featuring image mapping and links to other documents. Toolbars are primarily used for organization and navigation within a Web site.

Transparency   A masking effect used by GIF digital image formats where a single color is designated as having "no color value" and subsequently becomes invisible when viewed in a Web page browser.

Transparent color   The color in a GIF file designated as having "no color value" allowing information layered behind to show through such as the background color or pattern designed into a Web page.

URL   Uniform Resource Locator. This is represented as service: //host:port/path.

Web Server   A software application that makes files available to Web browsers.

Webmaster   The contact person administrating an Internet Web site. The Webmaster of a site may be an individual person, or a group of people, depending on the volume of visitors sending mail to a site.

WWW   World Wide Web. Also referred to as W3.

WYSIWYG   What You See Is What You Get. Implies that what you see on your computer screen is an accurate representation of the actual formatting within a document.

Index

H

Y

the online magazine for Netscape™ users

Empower

yourself with up-to-date tools for navigating the Net—in-depth reviews, where to find them and how to use them.

Enhance

your online experience—get to know the latest plug-ins that let you experience animation, video, virtual reality and sound...live, over the Internet.

Enliven

your Web pages—tips from experienced Web designers help you create pages with punch, spiced with multimedia and organized for easy navigation.

Enchant

your Web site visitors—learn to create interactive pages with JavaScript applets, program your own Internet applications and build added functionality into your site.

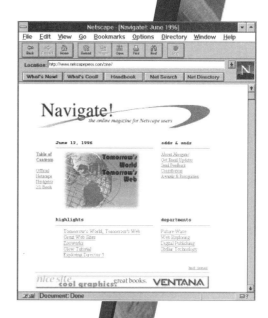

http://www.netscapepress.com/zine

Add Power to Web Pages

Official Netscape JavaScript Book

$29.99, 520 pages, illustrated, part #: 465-0

Add life to Web pages—animated logos, text-in-motion sequences, live updating and calculations—quickly and easily. Sample code and step-by-step instructions show how to put JavaScript to real-world, practical use.

Java Programming for the Internet

$49.95, 806 pages, illustrated, part #: 355-7

Create dynamic, interactive Internet applications. Expand the scope of your online development with this comprehensive, step-by-step guide to creating Java applets. Includes four real-world, start-to-finish tutorials. The CD-ROM has all the programs, samples and applets from the book, plus shareware. Continual updates on Ventana's *Online Companion* will keep this information on the cutting edge.

The Comprehensive Guide to VBScript

$34.99, 408 pages, illustrated, part #: 470-7

The only encyclopedic reference to VBScript and HTML commands and features. Complete with practical examples for plugging directly into programs. The companion CD-ROM features a hypertext version of the book, along with shareware, templates, utilities and more.

 Books marked with this logo include a free Internet *Online Companion*™, featuring archives of free utilities plus a software archive and links to other Internet resources.

Make it Multimedia

Macromedia Director 5 Power Toolkit

$49.95, 800 pages, illustrated, part #: 289-5

Macromedia Director 5 Power Toolkit views the industry's hottest multimedia authoring environment from the inside out. Features tools, tips and professional tricks for producing power-packed projects for CD-ROM and Internet distribution. Dozens of exercises detail the principles behind successful multimedia presentations and the steps to achieve professional results. The companion CD-ROM includes utilities, sample presentations, animations, scripts and files.

Shockwave!

$49.95, 400 pages, illustrated, part #: 441-3

Breathe new life into your web pages with Macromedia Shockwave. Ventana's *Shockwave!* teaches you how to enliven and animate your Web sites with online movies. Beginning with step-by-step exercises and examples, and ending with in-depth excursions into the use of Shockwave Lingo extensions, *Shockwave!* is a must-buy for both novices and experienced Director developers. Plus, tap into current Macromedia resources on the Internet with Ventana's *Online Companion*. The companion CD-ROM includes the Shockwave player plug-in, sample Director movies and tutorials, and much more!

The Comprehensive Guide to Lingo

$49.99, 700 pages, illustrated, part #: 463-4

Master the Lingo of Macromedia Director's scripting language for adding interactivity to presentations. Covers beginning scripts to advanced techniques, including creating movies for the Web and problem solving. The companion CD-ROM features demo movies of all scripts in the book, plus numerous examples, a searchable database of problems and solutions, and much more!

Official Online
Marketing With
Netscape Book
$34.99
453-7
544 pages

Official HTML
Publishing for
Netscape
$39.95

Windows 288-7
Macintosh 417-0
600 pages

Official Netscape
Power User's Toolkit
$49.95
386-7
696 pages

Official Netscape
Plug-in Book
$39.99
468-5
408 pages

Official Multimedia
Publishing for Netscape
$49.95
381-6
512 pages

Official Netscape
Guide to Online
Investments
$24.99
452-9
400 pages

Official Netscape
Beginner's Guide
to the Internet
$24.99
522-3
350 pages

SAVE
15%
Order online!

http://www.netscapepress.com
Netscape Press is an imprint of **VENTANA**.

Follow the leader!

250,000+ in its first edition!

Hot on the heels of the runaway international bestseller comes the complete Netscape Press line—easy-to-follow tutorials; savvy, results-oriented guidelines; and targeted titles that zero in on your special interests. All with the official Netscape seal of approval!

"Destined to become the bible to the world's most popular browser."
—PC Magazine

OFFICIAL

Netscape Navigator 3.0 BOOK

The definitive guide to the world's most popular Internet navigator

BY PHIL JAMES
FOREWORD BY MARC ANDREESSEN

International Bestseller! More than 250,000 in print!

Web Favorites

Voodoo Windows 95

$24.95, 504 pages, illustrated, part #: 145-7

Users will need voodoo to make the move to Windows 95!
Nelson is back with more secrets, shortcuts and spells than
ever. Scores of tips—many never before published—on
installing, customizing, editing, printing, virtual memory,
Internet connections and much more. Organized by task
for easy reference. The companion disk contains
shareware utilities, fonts and magic!

The Windows 95 Book

$39.95, 1232 pages, illustrated, part #: 154-6

The anxiously awaited revamp of Windows means new
working styles for PC users. This new handbook offers an
insider's look at the all-new interface–arming users with
tips and techniques for file management, desktop design,
optimizing and more. A must-have for a prosperous '95!
The companion CD-ROM features tutorials, demos,
previous and online help plus utilities, screensavers,
wallpaper and sounds.

Windows 95 Power Toolkit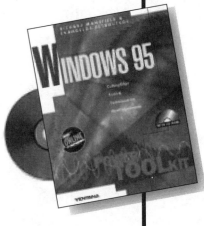

$49.95, 744 pages, illustrated, part #: 319-0

If Windows 95 includes everything but the kitchen sink, get
ready to get your hands wet! Maximize the customizing
capabilities of Windows 95 with ready-to-use tools,
applications and tutorials, including a guide to VBA. CD-
ROM: the complete toolkit, plus additional graphics, sounds
and applications.Online Companion: updated versions of
software, hyper-linked listings and links to helpful resources
on the Internet.

TO ORDER ANY VENTANA TITLE, COMPLETE THIS ORDER FORM AND MAIL OR FAX IT TO US, WITH PAYMENT, FOR QUICK SHIPMENT.

TITLE	PART #	QTY	PRICE	TOTAL

SHIPPING

For all standard orders, please ADD $4.50/first book, $1.35/each additional.
For software kit orders, ADD $6.50/first kit, $2.00/each additional.
For "two-day air," ADD $8.25/first book, $2.25/each additional.
For "two-day air" on the kits, ADD $10.50/first kit, $4.00/each additional.
For orders to Canada, ADD $6.50/book.
For orders sent C.O.D., ADD $4.50 to your shipping rate.
North Carolina residents must ADD 6% sales tax.
International orders require additional shipping charges.

SUBTOTAL = $ _____
SHIPPING = $ _____
TAX = $ _____
TOTAL = $ _____

**Or, save 15%–order online.
http://www.vmedia.com**

Mail to: Ventana • PO Box 13964 • Research Triangle Park, NC 27709-3964 ☎ 800/743-5369 • Fax 919/544-9472

Name _____

E-mail _____ Daytime phone _____

Company _____

Address (No PO Box) _____

City_____ State_____ Zip_____

Payment enclosed ____VISA ____MC ____ Acc't # _____ Exp. date_____

Signature _____ Exact name on card _____

Check your local bookstore or software retailer for these and other bestselling titles, or call toll free: **800/743-5369**

All technical support for this product is available from Ventana.
The technical support office is open from 8:00 A.M. to 6:00 P.M. (EST) Monday through
Friday and can be reached via the following methods:

World Wide Web: http://www.netscapepress.com/support

E–mail: help@vmedia.com

Phone: (919) 544-9404 extension 81

FAX: (919) 544-9472

America Online: keyword **Ventana**

MACROMEDIA End-User License Agreement PLEASE READ THIS DOCUMENT CAREFULLY
BEFORE BREAKING THE SEAL ON THE MEDIA PACKAGE. THIS AGREEMENT LICENSES THE
ENCLOSED SOFTWARE TO YOU AND CONTAINS WARRANTY AND LIABILITY DISCLAIMERS.
BY BREAKING THE SEAL ON THE MEDIA ENVELOPE, YOU ARE CONFIRMING YOUR ACCEP-
TANCE OF THE SOFTWARE AND AGREEING TO BECOME BOUND BY THE TERMS OF THIS
AGREEMENT. IF YOU DO NOT WISH TO DO SO, DO NOT BREAK THE SEAL. INSTEAD,
PROMPTLY RETURN THE ENTIRE PACKAGE, INCLUDING THE UNOPENED MEDIA PACKAGE,
TO THE PLACE WHERE YOU OBTAINED IT, FOR A FULL REFUND.

1. Definitions

    (a) "Macromedia« Software" means the software program included in the enclosed package, and all
related updates supplied by Macromedia.

    (b) "Macromedia Product" means the Macromedia Software and the related documentation and
models and multimedia content (such as animation, sound and graphics), and all related updates
supplied by Macromedia.

2. License. This Agreement allows you to:

    (a) Use the Macromedia Software on a single computer.

    (b) Make one copy of the Macromedia Software in machine-readable form solely for backup
purposes. You must reproduce on any such copy all copyright notices and any other proprietary
legends on the original copy of the Macromedia Software.

    (c) Certain Macromedia Software is licensed with additional rights as set forth in the Supplementary
Rights Addendum that may be included in the package for this Macromedia Product.

3. Supplementary Licenses

Certain rights are not granted under this Agreement, but may be available under a separate agreement.
If you would like to enter into a Site or Network License, please contact Macromedia.

4. Restrictions

You may not make or distribute copies of the Macromedia Product, or electronically transfer the
Macromedia Software from one computer to another or over a network. You may not decompile,
reverse engineer, disassemble, or otherwise reduce the Macromedia Software to a human-perceivable
form. You may not modify, rent, resell for profit, distribute or create derivative works based upon the
Macromedia Software or any part thereof. You will not export or reexport, directly or indirectly, the
Macromedia Product into any country prohibited by the United States Export Administration Act and
the regulations thereunder.

5. Ownership

The foregoing license gives you limited rights to use the Macromedia Software. Although you own the
disk on which the Macromedia Software is recorded, you do not become the owner of, and Macromedia
retains title to, the Macromedia Product, and all copies thereof. All rights not specifically granted in this
Agreement, including Federal and International Copyrights, are reserved by Macromedia.

6. Limited Warranties

    (a) Macromedia warrants that, for a period of ninety (90) days from the date of delivery (as evi-
denced by a copy of your receipt): (i) when used with a recommended hardware configuration,
the Macromedia Software will perform in substantial conformance with the documentation
supplied as part of the Macromedia Product; and (ii) that the media on which the Macromedia
Software is furnished will be free from defects in materials and workmanship under normal use.
EXCEPT AS SET FORTH IN THE FOREGOING LIMITED WARRANTY, MACROMEDIA
DISCLAIMS ALL OTHER WARRANTIES, EITHER EXPRESS OR IMPLIED, INCLUDING THE
WARRANTIES OF MERCHANTABILITY, FITNESS FOR A PARTICULAR PURPOSE AND
NON-INFRINGEMENT. IF APPLICABLE LAW IMPLIES ANY WARRANTIES WITH RESPECT
TO THE MACROMEDIA PRODUCT, ALL SUCH WARRANTIES ARE LIMITED IN DURATION
TO NINETY (90) DAYS FROM THE DATE OF DELIVERY. No oral or written information or
advice given by Macromedia, its dealers, distributors, agents or employees shall create a
warranty or in any way increase the scope of this warranty.

(b) SOME STATES DO NOT ALLOW THE EXCLUSION OF IMPLIED WARRANTIES, SO THE ABOVE EXCLUSION MAY NOT APPLY TO YOU. THIS WARRANTY GIVES YOU SPECIFIC LEGAL RIGHTS AND YOU MAY ALSO HAVE OTHER LEGAL RIGHTS WHICH VARY FROM STATE TO STATE.

7. Exclusive Remedy

Your exclusive remedy under Section 6 is to return the Macromedia Software to the place you acquired it, with a copy of your receipt and a description of the problem. Macromedia will use reasonable commercial efforts to supply you with a replacement copy of the Macromedia Software that substantially conforms to the documentation, provide a replacement for the defective media, or refund to you your purchase price for the Macromedia Software, at its option. Macromedia shall have no responsibility with respect to Macromedia Software that has been altered in any way, if the media has been damaged by accident, abuse or misapplication, or if the non conformance arises out of use of the Macromedia Software in conjunction with software not supplied by Macromedia.

8. Limitations of Damages

(a) MACROMEDIA SHALL NOT BE LIABLE FOR ANY INDIRECT, SPECIAL, INCIDENTAL OR CONSEQUENTIAL DAMAGES (INCLUDING DAMAGES FOR LOSS OF BUSINESS, LOSS OF PROFITS, OR THE LIKE), WHETHER BASED ON BREACH OF CONTRACT, TORT (INCLUDING NEGLIGENCE), PRODUCT LIABILITY OR OTHERWISE, EVEN IF MACROMEDIA OR ITS REPRESENTATIVES HAVE BEEN ADVISED OF THE POSSIBILITY OF SUCH DAMAGES AND EVEN IF A REMEDY SET FORTH HEREIN IS FOUND TO HAVE FAILED OF ITS ESSENTIAL PURPOSE.

(b) Macromedia's total liability to you for actual damages for any cause whatsoever will be limited to the greater of $500 or the amount paid by you for the Macromedia Software that caused such damages.

(c) SOME STATES DO NOT ALLOW THE LIMITATION OR EXCLUSION OF LIABILITY FOR INCIDENTAL OF CONSEQUENTIAL DAMAGES, SO THE ABOVE LIMITATION OR EXCLUSION MAY NOT APPLY TO YOU.

9. Basis of Bargain

The limited warranty, exclusive remedies and limited liability set forth above are fundamental elements of the basis of the bargain between Macromedia and you. Macromedia would not be able to provide the Macromedia Software on an economic basis without such limitations.

10. Government End Users

The Macromedia Product is "Restricted Computer Software."

RESTRICTED RIGHTS LEGEND

Use, duplication, or disclosure by the Government is subject to restrictions as set forth in subparagraph (c)(1)(ii) of the Rights in Technical Data and Computer Software clause at DFARS 252.227-7013. Manufacturer: Macromedia, Inc., 600 Townsend, San Francisco, CA 94103

11. General

This Agreement shall be governed by the internal laws of the State of California. This Agreement contains the complete agreement between the parties with respect to the subject matter hereof, and supersedes all prior or contemporaneous agreements or understandings, whether oral or written. All questions concerning this Agreement shall be directed to: Macromedia, Inc., 600 Townsend Street, San Francisco, CA 94103, Attention: Chief Financial Officer.

Macromedia is a registered trademark of Macromedia, Inc.

Suzanne Porta
Publisher Programs Associate
Macromedia, Inc. 600
Townsend Street, Suite 310
San Francisco, CA, 94103 USA
email: sporta@macromedia.com